Maths
in Practice
Year 8 Pupil's Book

Author team:
David Bowles, Sophie Goldie,
Andrew Manning, David Pritchard,
Shaun Procter-Green, Alan Smith

DYNAMIC LEARNING
Innovate • Motivate • Personalise

HODDER EDUCATION
PART OF HACHETTE LIVRE UK

The Publishers would like to thank the following for permission to reproduce copyright material:
Photo credits: p1 (twice): Musée de la Tapisserie, Bayeux, France/The Bridgeman Art Library; **p24:** © Stefano Bianchetti/Corbis; **p60:** PurestockX; **p89:** The Print Collector/Alamy; **p103:** © Stephen Finn – Fotolia.com; **p204(twice):** The Bridgeman Art Library/Getty Images; **p220:** © CORBIS

Acknowledgements p38: population pyramids taken from U.S. Census Bureau, International Data Base; **p42:** table on consumption of canned drinks adapted from CensusAtSchool, www.censusatschool.ntu.ac.uk, reproduced by permission of the Royal Statistical Society Centre for Statistical Education based at The Nottingham Trent University.

Every effort has been made to trace all copyright holders, but if any have been inadvertently overlooked the Publishers will be pleased to make the necessary arrangements at the first opportunity.

Although every effort has been made to ensure that website addresses are correct at time of going to press, Hodder Education cannot be held responsible for the content of any website mentioned in this book. It is sometimes possible to find a relocated web page by typing in the address of the home page for a website in the URL window of your browser.

Hachette UK's policy is to use papers that are natural, renewable and recyclable products and made from wood grown in sustainable forests. The logging and manufacturing processes are expected to conform to the environmental regulations of the country of origin.

Orders: please contact Bookpoint Ltd, 130 Milton Park, Abingdon, Oxon OX14 4SB. Telephone: (44) 01235 827720. Fax: (44) 01235 400454. Lines are open from 9 a.m. to 5 p.m., Monday to Saturday, with a 24-hour message-answering service. Visit our website at www.hoddereducation.co.uk.

© Sophie Goldie, Andrew Manning, David Pritchard, Shaun Procter-Green, 2008
First published in 2008 by
Hodder Education,
Part of Hachette UK
338 Euston Road
London NW1 3BH

Impression number   10 9 8 7 6 5 4 3 2 1
Year   2013 2012 2011 2010 2009 2008

Cover photo © Georgette Douwma/Getty
Illustrations by Oxford Designers and Illustrators
Typeset in 10.5/13.5 VAG Rounded Light by Pantek Arts Ltd, Maidstone, Kent
Printed in Italy

A catalogue record for this title is available from the British Library.

ISBN: 978 0 340 94859 0

Contents

1 Collecting data

Coming up ...

- collecting data
- constructing frequency tables for continuous data
- designing and using two-way tables

Do you remember?
- how to use tally marks
- how to use inequality symbols
- how to interpret bar charts

Chapter starter

This is a famous scene from the Bayeux Tapestry showing the death of King Harold.

It gives an idea of what happened at the Battle of Hastings in the year 1066.

It is a **source** of data and information.

1. Make a tally chart of the number of people, horses and dogs represented in this section.

2. Assume the section shown is 2 m long. The whole Bayeux Tapestry is 70 m long.

   Use your answer to question 1 to estimate how many horses, dogs and people are shown on the whole tapestry.

   Why might your estimate be wrong?

Key words

data	secondary data
survey	source
experiment	frequency table
data logging	tally
observation	frequency
sample	discrete data
sample size	continuous data
population	two-way table
primary data	

1.1 Methods of collecting data

In Year 7 you learnt that data can be collected by a **survey**.

There are other ways of collecting data.

An **experiment** is a way of collecting data often used in science.

Much care must be taken to set up the experiment so that the results are reliable.

You need to try to keep all the conditions the same except the one you are interested in.

It should be possible to repeat an experiment under the same conditions and get similar results.

Another way of collecting data is **data logging**.

Data logging is when the collection is made automatically by a machine.

FOR EXAMPLE   Machines can count the numbers of cars entering and leaving a car park.

The data collected can be used to activate signs when the car park is full.

Data can also be collected by **observation**.

This really means just by watching something.

It is important that the people doing the watching are well trained.

They need to know exactly what they are looking for.

The number of people or items involved in an experiment or observation is called the **sample size**.

A census involves *everybody* or the whole **population**.

A **sample** involves only some people or items from the population.

The sample is used to give an approximation of the results for the population.

Collecting results from 5% to 10% of the population will give a good picture of the whole population.

However, in reality, the size of the sample will depend upon how easy the data is to collect. Often the sample size will be smaller than 5% of the population.

Continued ...

Data you have collected yourself, using any of the methods mentioned, is called **primary data**.

You can also use the internet, books or other things such as the Bayeux tapestry to find data.

These are **sources** of data.

It is important to realise, however, that these sources *may* not be accurate.

Data that has been collected already is called **secondary data**.

Example

(a) Choose the best method of collecting data to answer these questions.
   (i) How long do children at age 5 sit on their chairs in class?
   (ii) How quickly does a metal rod get to 100°C when heated?
   (iii) How quickly can the fastest man run 100 metres?
(b) How big should the sample be to answer the question in part (a) (i)?
(c) Suggest another question similar to part (iii).

Solution

(a) (i) Data should be collected by observing a class.
   (ii) Data should be collected by an experiment.
   (iii) This data should be easily found on the internet.
(b) Clearly it is impossible to observe 5% to 10% of all 5-year-olds.
   A sample of about 20 pupils would be practical.
   Observing a greater number would be very time-consuming and costly.
   It would be important to observe 20 pupils from different schools.
   The behaviour of children in the same class may be similar.
(c) Examples of similar questions are: How quickly can the fastest woman run 100 metres?
   How quickly can the fastest man run 200 metres?

Now try these 1.1

1 Choose the best method of collecting data to answer these questions.
   (a) What was the weather like in New York yesterday?
   (b) How far can a Year 8 girl throw a tennis ball?
   (c) Do sheep always stay together when they are in a field?

2 In question **1 (b)**, how big should the sample be?

3 For each of the choices made in question **1**,
   (i) list any problems that may arise when collecting the data
   (ii) suggest an alternative source of data.

4 For each part in question **1** suggest another similar question.

5 How can you collect data to find out whether
   (a) there are more boys than girls in school wearing glasses
   (b) more number 1 singles have been sung by groups than by individuals
   (c) cats prefer 'moggymunch' food to 'cattycrunch' food?

6 For each part of question **5**, how big should the sample be?

1.2 Frequency tables

Kate has collected this data about the number of apple trees pupils in her class have in their gardens.

She has recorded the data in a frequency table.

Number of apple trees	Tally	Frequency
0	ⵍⵍⵍⵍ ⵍⵍⵍⵍ IIII	14
1	ⵍⵍⵍⵍ III	8
2	III	3
3	I	1
4 or more	II	2

This data is **discrete** data.

Discrete data is counted.

Pupils can have no apple trees or one or two but they can't have one and a half trees.

Continuous data is measured rather than counted.

Measuring lengths, masses and times all result in continuous data.

Continuous data can take any value.

Example

Kate weighs 30 apples.

These are the masses in grams to 1 decimal place.

62.4	55.9	38.0	45.1	64.4	59.7	62.8	39.7	45.6	53.4
57.8	53.8	66.8	63.2	58.3	60.0	47.0	55.8	68.3	54.8
52.6	44.4	48.8	42.1	47.9	51.9	50.5	59.6	52.6	47.6

Organise the data into this frequency table.

Mass (grams)	Tally	Frequency
30 up to 40		
40 up to 50		
50 up to 60		
60 up to 70		

Solution

Put a tally mark for each value in the correct row.

> 62.4 is in the 60 up to 70 group so you put a tally mark in that row.

Continued ...

The completed frequency table will look like this.

30 up to 40 means a mass of 30 g is included but a mass of 40 g is not included.

Mass (grams)	Tally	Frequency
30 up to 40	II	2
40 up to 50	HHT III	8
50 up to 60	HHT HHT III	13
60 up to 70	HHT II	7
Total		30

Add up the frequencies to check your tallying.

Now try these 1.2

① Here is another table that can be used to organise the data in the example in the section above.

Mass m (grams)	Tally	Frequency
$30 \leqslant m < 40$		
$40 \leqslant m < 50$		
$50 \leqslant m < 60$		
$60 \leqslant m < 70$		

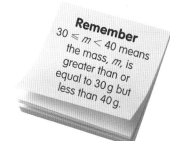

Remember
$30 \leqslant m < 40$ means the mass, m, is greater than or equal to 30 g but less than 40 g.

Copy and complete the table.

② A school head teacher is worried about the speed of cars outside his school.
He records the speed, in miles per hour, of 30 cars as children come to school.

27.5	31.2	37.5	33.4	42.3	29.7	34.7	38.5	45.8	30.4
32.9	37.6	31.8	42.5	39.6	40.0	32.2	25.6	34.9	22.8
27.6	22.8	37.8	23.2	29.9	31.3	30.7	28.6	26.5	27.0

(a) Copy and complete this frequency table for the data.

Speed (mph)	Tally	Frequency
20 up to 25		
25 up to 30		
30 up to 35		
35 up to 40		
40 up to 45		
45 up to 50		

(b) The speed limit is 30 miles per hour.
Do you think the head teacher is right to be worried?
Explain your answer.

Continued...

③ There are 20 pupils trying to get into the school running team.
These are their times to run 100 metres.

| 14.3 | 15.8 | 17.3 | 14.3 | 15.2 | 16.9 | 15.0 | 15.7 | 14.8 | 13.8 |
| 14.9 | 15.4 | 16.3 | 16.9 | 14.7 | 18.3 | 14.7 | 13.9 | 16.8 | 14.6 |

(a) Copy and complete this frequency table for the data.

Times (t seconds)	Tally	Frequency
$12 \leqslant t < 14$		
$14 \leqslant t < 16$		
$16 \leqslant t < 18$		
$18 \leqslant t < 20$		

(b) Pupils who run 100 metres in under 16 seconds can join the team.
How many pupils get into the team?

④ There are 25 pupils trying to get into the long jump team.
These are the lengths, in metres, of their best jumps.

3.78	4.03	3.88	4.23	4.51	3.29	4.87	4.02	3.68	3.99
4.12	4.35	4.65	4.99	5.02	3.75	4.04	4.75	3.96	4.00
3.75	3.86	4.44	4.29	4.78

Display this data in a grouped frequency table.

Remember
You want to divide the data into four to six groups.

1.3 Two-way tables

A **two-way table** is a table showing information about two aspects of the data at the same time.

For example this table shows information about the children in one class.

It tells you about the gender of the children (that is, whether the child is a girl or a boy) *and* whether they are left- or right-handed.

	Boys	Girls
Left-handed	2	4
Right-handed	13	11

There are lots of things you can tell from the table.

FOR EXAMPLE   There are 2 left-handed boys.
There are 24 right-handed children.
There are 15 girls.
There are 30 children in the class in total.

Continued …

With a friend

1 The list on the previous page is not complete.

Write five more statements using the table.

2 Collect the same data for your class.

3 Use your table to write nine statements about your class.

Research

Collect examples of two-way tables from newspapers or magazines.

Make a poster to display the tables.

Example

Display this information as a two-way table.

80 people went to a meeting in a village hall.

36 walked, the rest came by car.

One quarter of those who walked were men.

Half of those who came by car were women.

Solution

Before completion the table looks like this.

The table will have information about how the people travelled to the meeting …

… and the gender of the people.

	Men	Women
Walked		
Came by car		

36 walked and one quarter of these were men.

36 ÷ 4 = 9, so nine men walked.

36 − 9 = 27 so 27 women walked.

The number who came by car is 80 − 36 = 44.

Half of these were women and therefore half were men.

44 ÷ 2 = 22 so 22 women and 22 men came by car.

Check that the total of the four frequencies is 80.

9 + 27 + 22 + 22 = 80 ✓

Use the numbers you have worked out to complete the table.

	Men	Women
Walked	9	27
Came by car	22	22

1. The two-way table shows whether the children in a year group live in a house or a flat and whether they have a dog or cat.

	Have a dog	Have a cat
Live in a house	13	5
Live in a flat	2	11

(a) How many children
   (i) live in a house and have a dog
   (ii) live in a flat and have a cat
   (iii) have a dog?
(b) Explain why you cannot tell how many children there are in the year group.

2. Rhys wants to know whether families in villages own more cars then those in towns.
This two-way table shows the results of his survey.

	Do not own a car	Own one car	Own two cars	Own three or more cars
Live in a town	3	13	38	2
Live in a village	1	9	42	12

(a) How many families
   (i) live in a village and own two cars
   (ii) live in a town
   (iii) own three or more cars?
(b) How many families took part in the survey?
(c) Does the data show that families in villages own more cars then those in towns?
Give a reason for your answer.

3. Display this information as a two-way table.

50 households were asked about holidays.
30 of these households had children.
All except 3 of the households with children had been on a holiday in the last year.
Three-quarters of the households without children had been on a holiday in the last year.

4. This bar chart shows access to computers for 100 primary school children and 100 secondary school children.
(a) Use the chart to complete this two-way table.

	Own computer	Share with brother or sister	Use parents'	No access
Primary				
Secondary				

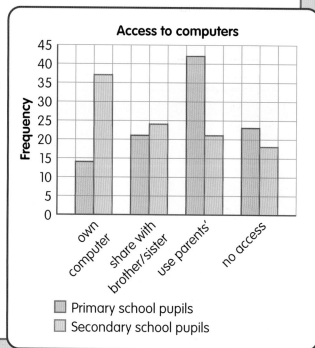

Access to computers

☐ Primary school pupils
☐ Secondary school pupils

(b) Compare the access to computers for primary and secondary school pupils.

2 Rules of arithmetic

Coming up ...

● squares and square roots
cubes and cube roots
what indices are and how to use them
reading and writing positive integer powers of ten
working with powers and roots on a calculator
the order of operations

Chapter starter

An eccentric (and rich!) maths professor places this advert in the local paper.

Wanted:	Maths Games Tester
Needed for:	28 days
Pay:	£1000 per day
	or 1p for day 1
	2p for day 2
	4p for day 3
	8p for day 4 and so on

Investigate both methods of payment.

How would you like to be paid?

Do you remember?
● what square and cube numbers are
● about the order of operations
● about inverse operations
● how to round to 1 decimal place
● how to use algebraic notation

Key words

square
square root
cube
cube root
power
index (plural: indices)
to the power of
index notation

You met square numbers in Year 7.

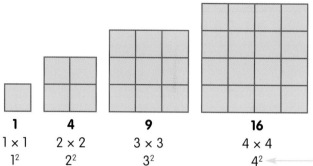

Square numbers

1	4	9	16
1×1	2×2	3×3	4×4
1^2	2^2	3^2	4^2

4^2 is a short way of writing 4×4.

The **square root** of a number can be squared to make that number.

So 4 is the square root of 16 because 4×4 is 16.

$^-4$ is also a square root of 16 because $^-4 \times {}^-4$ is also 16.

Squaring and square rooting are inverse operations.

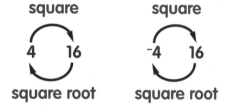

Multiplying a negative number by a negative number gives a positive result.
You will meet this in more detail in Chapter 9.
When finding square roots, remember to watch for negative square roots as well as positive square roots.

If you see $\sqrt{16}$ it is asking you for the positive square root.

$\sqrt{16} = 4$

If you are asked for the square root of 16 or $\pm\sqrt{16}$ you should give both the positive and the negative square root as your answer.

$\pm\sqrt{16} = 4$ and $^-4$

You can write this as $\pm\sqrt{16} = \pm4$.

You met cube numbers in Year 7.

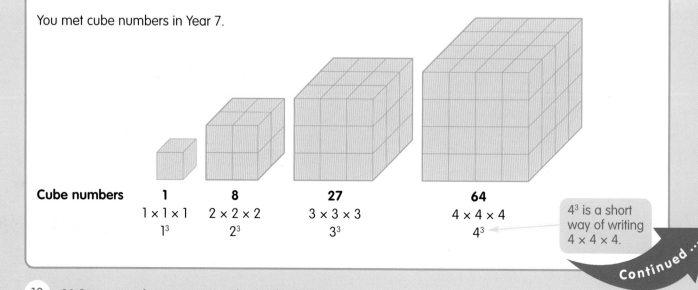

Cube numbers

1	8	27	64
$1 \times 1 \times 1$	$2 \times 2 \times 2$	$3 \times 3 \times 3$	$4 \times 4 \times 4$
1^3	2^3	3^3	4^3

4^3 is a short way of writing $4 \times 4 \times 4$.

Continued ...

The **cube root** of a number can be cubed to make that number.

So 2 is the cube root of 8 because 2 × 2 × 2 is 8.

You can write that the cube root of 8 is 2 as $\sqrt[3]{8} = 2$.

You do not have to watch for negative cube roots because ⁻2 cubed is ⁻8, not 8.

Cubing and cube rooting are inverse operations.

cube

2   8

cube root

When you cannot use a calculator, you use your knowledge of square and cube numbers to find the square roots and cube roots.

Example

Find these.

(a) The square root of 81.

(b) $\sqrt{6400}$

(c) The cube root of 64.

Solution

(a) 81 = 9 × 9 so 9 is a square root of 81.
Also, 81 = ⁻9 × ⁻9 so ⁻9 is another square root of 81.

(b) 6400 = 80 × 80 so $\sqrt{6400} = 80$.

(c) 64 = 4 × 4 × 4 so the cube root of 64 is 4.

Now try these 2.1

Note
You should learn the square numbers to at least 12^2 and cube numbers to at least 5^3. You should also learn 10^3.

1 Find the square roots of these numbers.
Remember to include the negative square roots as well.

(a) 49   (b) 64   (c) 9   (d) 81   (e) 4   (f) 1

2 Find the cube roots of these numbers.

(a) 27   (b) 1000   (c) 64   (d) 1   (e) 125   (f) 8

3 (a) Given that $16^2 = 256$, write down $\sqrt{256}$.

(b) Given that $2.4^2 = 5.76$, write down $\sqrt{5.76}$.

4 (a) Given that $9^3 = 729$, write down $\sqrt[3]{729}$.

(b) Given that $2.8^3 = 21.952$, write down $\sqrt[3]{21.952}$.

(c) Given that $0.6^3 = 0.216$, write down $\sqrt[3]{0.216}$.

6 Brain strain

Katie is estimating square roots.

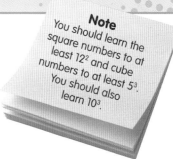

$\sqrt{9} = 3$ and $\sqrt{16} = 4$

12 is between 9 and 16 so $\sqrt{12}$ must be between $\sqrt{9}$ and $\sqrt{16}$.

$\sqrt{12}$ must be between 3 and 4.

Use Katie's method to estimate these.

(a) $\sqrt{30}$ (b) $\sqrt{61}$ (c) $\sqrt{85}$

5 Puzzle

Amy thinks of a whole number between 2 and 10 and squares it.

Rhian thinks of a number between 2 and 10 and cubes it.

Amy and Rhian both end up with the same result.

What numbers did they think of?

Note
The plural of index is indices.

In the previous section you saw that you can write the square number 5×5 as 5^2.

When you do this you are using **index notation**.

5^2 ← The 2 is called the **index** or **power**.

You say this as 'five squared' or 'five **to the power of** two'.

You also saw that you can write cube numbers using index notation.

For example, you can write $5 \times 5 \times 5$ as 5^3.

You say this as 'five cubed' or 'five to the power of three'.

You can continue the pattern.

$5 \times 5 \times 5 \times 5$ can be written as 5^4.

You say this as 'five to the power of four'.

You can also use indices in algebra.

In the same way as $5 \times 5 \times 5 \times 5$ can be written as 5^4,

4 5s multiplied together is written as 5^4.

$n \times n \times n \times n$ can be written as n^4.

4 n's multiplied together is written as n^4.

You say this as 'n to the power of four'.

n can represent any number, it could be 5 or it could be $^-7$, $\frac{3}{4}$, 10.34 or 1247.

ICT task

You can use your calculator to work out any power. The powers key is different on different calculators.

It can be [^] or [x^y], but it might be something different.

Here [^] is used.

The order you press the keys will be the same whatever the power key looks like.

To work out 5^4 you press these keys.

[5] [^] [4] [=]

The answer should be 625.

1 Find the powers key on your calculator.
   Check that you can use it correctly by calculating the value of 5^4.

2 Copy this table.

	Power	Value	In words
(a)	10^2	100	One hundred
(b)	10^3		
(c)	10^4		
(d)	10^5		
(e)	10^6		
(f)	10^9		

Use your calculator to help you complete the table. The first one has been done for you.

Note
n^1 is just written as n.

Continued...

Example

(a) Write $7 \times 7 \times 7 \times 7 \times 7$ as a single power of 7.
(b) Write $a \times a \times a \times a \times a \times a$ as a single power of a.
(c) Simplify $b^3 \times b^2$.

Solution

(a) $7 \times 7 \times 7 \times 7 \times 7 = 7^5$
(b) $a \times a \times a \times a \times a \times a = a^6$
(c) $b^3 \times b^2 = b \times b \times b \times b \times b$
$= b^5$

Example

(a) Without using a calculator, work out 11^3.
(b) Evaluate y^4 when $y = 6$.

Note
Evaluate means 'find the value of'.

Solution

(a) $11^3 = 11 \times 11 \times 11$
$= 121 \times 11$ ← $= 121 \times 10 + 121$
$= 1331$

(b) $y^4 = y \times y \times y \times y$
So when $y = 6$,
$y^4 = 6 \times 6 \times 6 \times 6$
$= 36 \times 36$
$= 1296$

```
      3 6
  ×   3 6
    2 1 6
  1 0 8 0
  1 2 9 6
```

Now try these 2.2

Hint
This is another way of saying write these using index notation.

① Write these as single powers. The first one has been done for you.
(a) $6 \times 6 \times 6 \times 6 \times 6 = 6^5$
(b) $5 \times 5 \times 5 \times 5 \times 5 \times 5$
(c) 4×4
(d) $3 \times 3 \times 3$
(e) $8 \times 8 \times 8 \times 8$
(f) $10 \times 10 \times 10 \times 10 \times 10 \times 10$
(g) $2 \times 2 \times 2 \times 2 \times 2$
(h) 9 cubed
(i) 5.3 squared

② Write these as single powers. The first one has been done for you.
(a) $a \times a = a^2$
(b) $b \times b \times b \times b$
(c) $c \times c \times c \times c \times c$
(d) $d \times d \times d$
(e) e squared
(f) $f \times f \times f \times f \times f \times f$
(g) $g \times g \times g \times g \times g \times g$

③ Use your calculator to work out these.
(a) 5^6
(b) 6^5
(c) 8^3
(d) 3^8
(e) 4^7
(f) 9^4
(g) 16.7 squared
(h) 3.2 cubed

④ Evaluate x^2 when
(a) $x = 3$
(b) $x = 10$

⑤ **(a)** Write these numbers using figures and as 10 multiplied by itself a number of times.
For example, a hundred is $100 = 10 \times 10$.
(i) A thousand **(ii)** A million **(iii)** A billion
(b) Write your answers to part **(a)** in index form.
(c) 10^{100} is called a googol.
How many zeros are there in 10^{100}?

⑥ Brain strain
Write these as single powers.
(a) $3^2 \times 3^4$ **(b)** $4^3 \times 4^2$ **(c)** 7×7^3
Check your answers on your calculator.

⑦ Brain strain
Write these as single powers.
(a) $x^2 \times x^2$ **(b)** $y^3 \times y$ **(c)** $z^2 \times z^3$

Research
Powers of two are used to help write binary numbers.
Find out about binary numbers.
What are they used for?
How would you write these numbers as binary numbers?
(a) 8 **(b)** 20 **(c)** 100

In Year 7 you met the idea that operations in arithmetic and brackets need to be done in a certain order.

Brackets   first.

Multiplication
Division   } next, with equal priority.

Addition
Subtraction   } last, again with equal priority.

Note
An index is another name for a power; the plural of index is indices.

You now need to include **indices**, such as squares, cubes, square roots, into the order.

Brackets   must always be worked out first.
Indices   are done next.

Division
Multiplication   } are done next, with equal priority.

Addition
Subtraction   } are done last, again with equal priority.

Hint
You may find the word **BIDMAS** helps you to remember the correct order of operations.

Example

Work out the value of $3^2 + 5 \times 4$.

Solution

$3^2 + 5 \times 4 = 9 + 5 \times 4$ Work out the index first …

$= 9 + 20$ … then the multiplication …

$= 29$ … and finally the addition.

Example

Work out the value of $(2 + 5)^2 + 12 \div 2$.

Solution

$(2 + 5)^2 + 12 \div 2 = 7^2 + 12 \div 2$ Work out the bracket first …

$= 49 + 12 \div 2$ … then the index …

$= 49 + 6$ … then the division …

$= 55$ … and finally the addition.

ICT task

Scientific calculators are programmed to do multistep calculations using the correct order of operations. You simply enter the calculation as it appears, making sure to press the [=] key only at the end.

FOR EXAMPLE   These are the keys you press to work out $215 - (56 + 19) \div 5^2$.

$$\boxed{2}\ \boxed{1}\ \boxed{5}\ \boxed{-}\ \boxed{(}\ \boxed{5}\ \boxed{6}\ \boxed{+}\ \boxed{1}\ \boxed{9}\ \boxed{)}\ \boxed{\div}\ \boxed{5}\ \boxed{x^2}\ \boxed{=}$$

1   Enter the calculation on your calculator and check you get the answer 212.

2   Use your calculator to work out these.

    (a) $108 - (115 - 71) + 4^3$ **(b)** $(27 \times 16) - 17^2 + 38$ **(c)** $6 \times 8^3 - 9 \times 12^2$ **(d)** $763 \times (26 + 67)^2 \div 465$

Now try these 2.3

1 Work out these.
(a) $4 + 8 \times 3$ (b) $6 + 10 \div 2$
(c) $3 + 7 - 4$ (d) $12 - 2 - 5$
(e) $60 \div 5 \times 2$ (f) $10 - 3 + 1$
(g) $8 + 11 \times 12$ (h) $121 \div 11 + 9$

2 Work out these.
(a) $3 + 4 \times 7$ (b) $(3 + 4) \times 7$
(c) $20 \div 5 - 3$ (d) $20 \div (5 - 3)$
(e) $9 + 3 \times 9 - 3$ (f) $(9 + 3) \times (9 - 3)$

3 Work out these.
(a) $(10 - 3) \times (4 + 6)$ (b) $6 \times (2 + 5)$
(c) $(5 + 7) \times (3 + 8)$ (d) $12 + 9 \times 8 - 7$
(e) $64 - (32 - 16)$ (f) $12 \div 6 \div 2$

4 Work out these.
(a) $6 + 3^2$ (b) $2^3 \div 4$
(c) 2×6^2 (d) $10^2 \div 5$
(e) 7×2^2 (f) $54 \div 3^3$
(g) $(3 + 2)^2$ (h) $(4 \times 2)^2$
(i) 4×2^2 (j) $4^2 \times 2$

5 Work out these.
(a) $3^2 + 2^2$ (b) $5 + (14 - 8) \times 3^2$
(c) $6 \times 2^3 - (25 - 14)$ (d) $200 + 10^2 \div (32 - 12)$

6 Puzzle

Where should the brackets go to make this calculation correct?

$20 \div 2 + 3 \times 7 = 28$

3 Lines and angles

Subject links
- design and technology
- geography

Coming up ...

- recognising interior and exterior angles
- recognising corresponding and alternate angles
- understanding proofs of angle facts

Do you remember?

- how to recognise parallel lines
- how to recognise acute, right, obtuse and reflex angles
- how to label lines and angles
- how to measure and draw angles
- how to solve equations
- that the angles on a straight line add up to 180°
- that the angles at a point add up to 360°
- how to draw parallel lines
- how to recognise vertically opposite angles
- that vertically opposite angles are equal
- that the angles in a triangle add up to 180°

Chapter starter

1. Are the bricks in this wall horizontal?

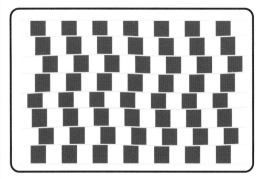

2. Are the diagonal lines in this picture parallel?

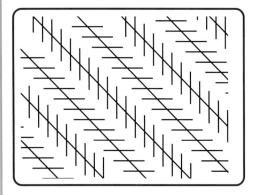

3. The pictures in parts **1** and **2** are well-known optical illusions which confuse your brain.

   Can you find other examples of optical illusions?

Key words

horizontal

vertical

parallel

interior angle

exterior angle

supplementary angles

complementary angles

corresponding angles

alternate angles

vertically opposite angles

proof

interior opposite angles

Angles inside a polygon are called **interior angles**.

The angle ABC is labelled x in the diagram.

It is an **interior** angle.

Angles BAC and ACB are also interior angles.

Angle DCA (labelled y) is an **exterior** angle.

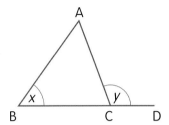

The exterior angle is *not* the reflex angle ACB.
Imagine a fly walking along the line BC. When it gets to C, it turns anticlockwise to face A.
The angle it turns through is the exterior angle DCA.

The exterior angle ACD and the interior angle ACB lie on a straight line, so they add up to 180°.

Angles that add up to 180° are called **supplementary** angles.

In this diagram, angles CDE and EDF add up to 90°.

Angles that add up to 90° are called **complementary** angles.

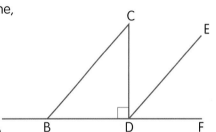

Now try these 3.1

① **(a)** Name the exterior angle in this diagram.
  (b) Which two angles are supplementary?
  (c) Measure angle BCD.

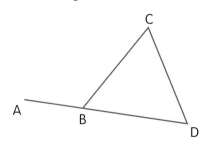

② **Puzzle**

Put the angles below into two pairs of complementary angles and three pairs of supplementary angles.

58°	28°	54°	32°	64°
78°	26°	102°	152°	126°

③ Angle CBD = 67°.
Angles ABC and CBD are complementary.
Angles CBD and DBE are supplementary.

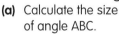

  (a) Calculate the size of angle ABC.
  (b) Calculate the size of angle DBE.

④ A triangle has three equal angles.
  (a) What is the size of each interior angle of the triangle?
  (b) What is the size of each exterior angle of the triangle?

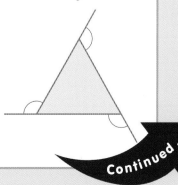

Continued ...

5 A triangle has two angles of 70° each.
  (a) What is the size of the third angle?
  (b) What is the size of each exterior angle?

Hint
Draw a sketch and mark on the information you know.

Investigation

1 Is it possible to draw a triangle with an acute exterior angle?

2 Is it possible to draw a triangle with two acute exterior angles?

3 What is the maximum number of acute exterior angles in a triangle?

Give a reason for your answer.

4 What is the maximum number of acute exterior angles in a quadrilateral?

5 Investigate further.

3.2 Angles and parallel lines

Draw a pair of parallel lines on a piece of paper.

Fold another piece of paper to make an acute angle.

Put one edge of the paper along the top parallel line.

Put a ruler along the other edge of the paper.

Draw a line using the ruler (shown in blue in the diagram).

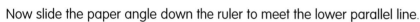

Now slide the paper angle down the ruler to meet the lower parallel line.

This shows that the two angles (*a* and *b* in the diagram) are equal.

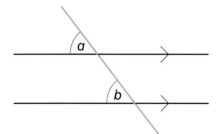

Angles on parallel lines which can slide in this way are always equal.

They are called **corresponding** angles because they are in matching positions.

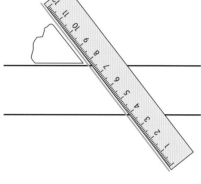

Hint
Corresponding angles always make an F-shape – although the F might be upside down or back to front!

Continued …

Now put your paper angle above the lower parallel line.

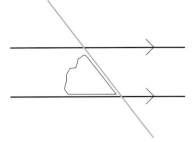

Move your paper angle to show that it fits below the top line in the position shown.

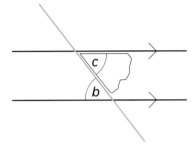

This shows that angles *b* and *c* are equal.

They lie on opposite sides of the diagonal line so they are called **alternate** angles.

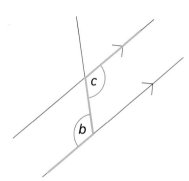

Hint
Alternate angles always make a Z-shape – although the Z might be back to front!

When a line crosses a pair of parallel lines and you are given one of the angles, you can work out any of the others.

Example

Calculate the angles marked with letters in this diagram.

Give reasons for your answers.

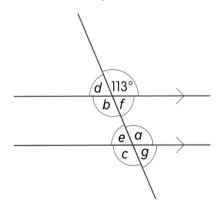

Continued ...

Solution

angle $a = 113°$ The angle of 113° and angle a are corresponding angles.

angle $b = 113°$ The angle of 113° and angle b are vertically opposite.

angle $c = 113°$ Angles b and c are corresponding angles.

angle $d = 67°$ Angle d and the angle of 113° make a straight line.
$180° - 113° = 67°$

angle $e = 67°$ Angles d and e are corresponding angles.

angle $f = 67°$ Angles e and f are alternate angles.

angle $g = 67°$ Angles f and g are corresponding angles.

> **Hint**
> It is usually best to work out the angles in alphabetical order. There is often more than one way to work out an angle in a set of parallel lines.
> It doesn't matter which method you use but you must give your reason if you are asked to.

> You may have to use other angle facts you know such as the sum of angles on a straight line or the sum of angles in a triangle.

Now try these 3.2

> **Remember**
> Make sure you use the correct names.

① Look at this diagram.

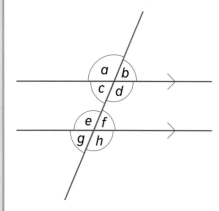

② Calculate the angles marked with letters in these diagrams.
Explain how you worked them out.

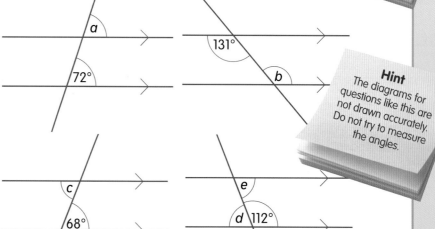

> **Hint**
> The diagrams for questions like this are not drawn accurately. Do not try to measure the angles.

(a) Below is a list of pairs of equal angles.
Say whether they are corresponding angles, alternate angles or vertically opposite angles.
  (i) a and e
  (ii) a and d
  (iii) d and e
  (iv) c and g
  (v) d and h
  (vi) e and h

(b) How many pairs of these types of angles are there?
  (i) Vertically opposite angles
  (ii) Corresponding angles
  (iii) Alternate angles

③ **Puzzle**

Copy these letters.

E F H N W Z

Find three pairs of corresponding angles and six pairs of alternate angles.

Continued ...

4 Calculate the angles marked with letters in these diagrams.
Explain how you worked them out.

Remember
It is usually easiest to work out the angles in alphabetical order.

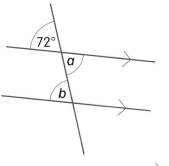

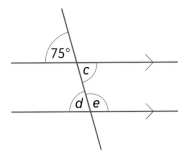

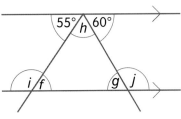

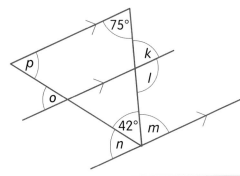

5 **Brain strain**

This design is based on the flag of Scotland.

(a) How many pairs of these types of angles does it have?
   (i) Vertically opposite angles
   (ii) Corresponding angles
   (iii) Alternate angles
(b) Create your own flag design and identify all the vertically opposite, corresponding and alternate angles.

3.3 Understanding proof

Draw a large triangle.
Cut it out.
Tear off the corners as shown.

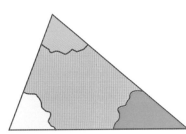

The three pieces can be arranged to make a straight line.

This is a **demonstration** that the angles in a triangle always add up to 180°.
But how can you be sure that it is always true?
A **proof** often uses algebra, so you are not dealing with a particular example.

Continued ...

A proof that the angles in triangle ABC add up to 180°

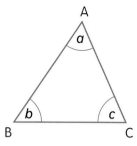

First, extend the line BC to D.

Then, draw a line CE, parallel to BA.

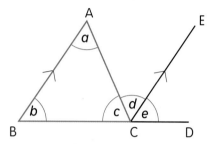

Angle a = angle d as they are alternate angles on parallel lines.

Angle b = angle e as they are corresponding angles on parallel lines.

So the sum of the angles in a triangle, $a + b + c = d + e + c$.

Angles c, d and e make a straight line which is 180°,
so $a + b + c = 180°$.

Proofs can be difficult to follow, as you must start as if you did not know that the angles in a triangle add up to 180°.

The aim of a proof is to produce a convincing argument that cannot be contradicted.

Now try these 3.3

1. Does the proof above work for an obtuse-angled triangle?
   Try it and see.

2. **(a)** Draw a large triangle and one of its exterior angles.
   Measure the exterior angle d.

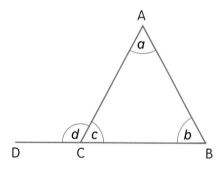

   (b) Angles a and b are called the **interior opposite** angles.
   They are interior angles, and opposite angle d.
   Measure the two interior opposite angles.
   Then add them together.
   The sum should equal the exterior angle d.

Continued...

(c) Copy and complete these statements to prove that this is *always* true, for any triangle.

> Angles $d + c$ = ... because ....
>
> Angles $a + b + c$ = ... because ....
>
> So angles ... + ... = angles ... + ... + ... because ....
>
> So angle d = angles ... + ...
>
>
> You can write this as
>
> **the exterior angle of a triangle equals the sum of the interior opposite angles**.

③ Puzzle

Paul thinks he has proved that the angles in a triangle do not always add up to 180°.

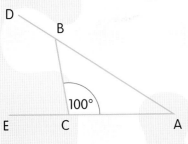

Find his error.

> ABC is a triangle, angle BCA = 100°.
>
> Angle DBC = angle BCA = 100° because they are alternate angles.
>
> So angle ABC = 80° because angles on a straight line add up to 180°.
>
> Angle BCA + angle ABC = 180°, so angle BCA + angle ABC + angle BAC must be greater than 180°.

④ CD and EF are parallel lines.

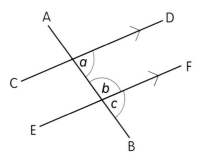

(a) What type of angles are *a* and *c*?
(b) What do angles *b* and *c* add up to?
(c) So what do angles *a* and *b* add up to?

You have just proved that the **interior angles in parallel lines are supplementary**.

⑤ Use this diagram to prove that the angles of a quadrilateral add up to 360°.

Hint
$a + b + c = $ ....?

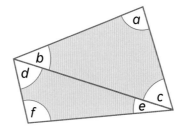

⑥ Brain strain

The opposite sides of a rhombus are parallel.

(a) How do you know that angles BAC and BCA are equal?
(b) How do you know that angles BCA and CAD are equal?
(c) Explain how you know that the diagonals of a rhombus bisect the angles.

Subject links
● science
● geography

Coming up ...

● generating sequences
● finding the rule for a sequence

Chapter starter

Peter downloads some pop and hip-hop tracks on to his MP3 player.

Peter likes pop music much more than he likes hip hop.

He decides

● he doesn't want two hip-hop tracks next to each other

● he is happy to have several pop tracks in a row.

Peter lists some of the ways of arranging five tracks on his MP3 player.

Pop	Pop	Hip-hop	Pop	Hip-hop	✓
Hip-hop	Pop	Pop	Pop	Hip-hop	✓
But not	Hip-hop	Hip-hop	Pop	Hip-hop	Pop	✗

1 Has Peter worked systematically? Explain your answer carefully.

2 How can Peter record his results more quickly?

3 Find how many different arrangements Peter can have of

(a) 1 track
(b) 2 tracks
(c) 3 tracks.

Think carefully about how you set out your work.

4 Investigate further. What patterns do you notice? What is the rule?

Research

Leonardo Pisano or Leonardo of Pisa was born in Pisa, Italy in 1170 and died in 1250. He is often called by his nickname Fibonacci, which means son of Bonacci. There is a special number sequence called the Fibonacci sequence.

Find out about the Fibonacci sequence. Make a poster about it.

Do you remember?

● how to use algebraic notation
● how to substitute numbers into expressions
● about special number sequences such as odd and even numbers, square numbers and triangular numbers

Key words

sequence

term

generate

rule

general term

nth term

difference

arithmetic sequence

linear sequence

A number **sequence** is a set of numbers which follows a rule.

Each number in the sequence is called a **term**.

You can **generate** the terms in a sequence using the **rule**.

> The dots '...' show that the sequence carries on like this forever. It is an **infinite sequence**.

Example

This is the rule for a sequence.

> The first term is 1.
> To find the next term, multiply by 3.

Write down the first five terms of the sequence.

Solution

Term number

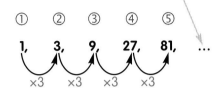

You can use T(1) as an abbreviation for 'first term', T(2) for 'second term' and so on.

A rule can be given to find any term directly.

You call any term in the sequence the ***n*th term** or T(*n*).

This is also known as the **general term**.

Example

The rule for the *n*th term of a sequence is 180 − 10*n* or T(*n*) = 180 − 10*n*.

Find the first four terms in the sequence.

Solution

Use the rule

The 1st term is when $n = 1$.

The 2nd term is when $n = 2$.

The 3rd term is when $n = 3$.

The 4th term is when $n = 4$.

$T(n) = 180 - 10n$.

$T(1) = 180 - 10 \times 1 = 170$

$T(2) = 180 - 10 \times 2 = 160$

$T(3) = 180 - 10 \times 3 = 150$

$T(4) = 180 - 10 \times 4 = 140$

This is the sequence from the example.

Term number

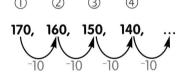

Each term is 10 less than the one before.

You say that the **difference** is ⁻10.

When all the differences are the same you say that the sequence is an **arithmetic sequence** or a **linear sequence**.

1 Write down the first five terms of each of these sequences.

	The first term is ...	To find the next term you ...
(a)	3	add 2
(b)	20	subtract 3
(c)	1	multiply by 4
(d)	625	divide by 5

2 Write down the first five terms of each of these sequences.

	The first term is ...	To find the next term you ...
(a)	5	add 1.6
(b)	6	subtract 4
(c)	1	multiply by 10
(d)	1	divide by 2

3 Find the first five terms of each of these sequences.
   (a) The rule for the nth term is $2n$.
   (b) The rule for the nth term is $n + 3$.
   (c) The rule for the nth term is $n - 1$.
   (d) The rule for the nth term is $3n - 2$.

4 Find the first five terms of these sequences.
   (a) $T(n) = 1 + 2n$ **(b)** $T(n) = 99 - 9n$
   (c) $T(n) = 110 - 10n$ **(d)** $T(n) = n + \frac{1}{2}$

5 Puzzle

This is the rule for a sequence.

> The first term is $\diamond$.
>
> To find the next term add $\square$.

Find the numbers to go in the $\diamond$ and the $\square$ so the sequence consists of only

(a) even numbers
(b) odd numbers
(c) multiples of 5
(d) numbers which have a 7 as the final digit.

6 Look at these patterns.

Pattern 1   Pattern 2   Pattern 3

(a) Draw the next two patterns.
(b) Copy and complete this table.

Pattern number	1	2	3	4	5	6
Number of red triangles						
Number of blue triangles						
Total number of triangles						

(c) What is the special name for the sequences found in part **(b)**?
(d) For each sequence, write down any patterns in the differences.
(e) Work out how many of each colour triangle there will be in pattern 10.
   How many triangles are there altogether in pattern 10?

7 Brain strain

Tiles are used to make a sequence of patterns.

This is the rule to find the number of tiles, t, needed for pattern n.

$$t = 6n - 5$$

(a) How many tiles are needed to make pattern number 10?
(b) Which pattern number needs 67 tiles?
(c) Rebecca has 120 tiles.
   She wants to use them to make just one pattern.
   (i) Which is the highest pattern number she can make?
   (ii) How many tiles does she have left over?
(d) Alfie also has 120 tiles.
   He wants to make as many different patterns as he can.
   (i) What pattern number can he make up to?
   (ii) How many tiles does he have left over?

Continued ...

⑧ Puzzle

(a) (i) Find the next term in this sequence.

1,   11,   21,   1211,   111221,   ...

(ii) Will the digit 4 ever appear in this look-and-say sequence?

(b) A similar sequence starts with 2 instead of 1.
After the second term, how will each term end?

(c) Can you find a look-and-say sequence where every term is the same?

> **Hint**
> This is called a 'look-and-say' sequence!

4.2 Finding the rule for a sequence

ICT task

The difference between one term and the next in a sequence gives a clue to the rule.
This investigation shows how to find the rule by looking at the **differences**.

① (a) Open a new spreadsheet and type in the headings as shown below.

(b) In cell C1 enter this formula.

> Every formula must start with '='.

=B1+1

	A	B	C	D	E	F
1	Term number	1	=B1+1			
2	Term					

> **Remember**
> When you enter the formula you will see the answer not the formula.

> Highlight cell C1. Click on the square at the bottom right of the cell and drag to highlight other cells in that row.

(c) Copy the formula across the row.

(d) What has happened?

② (a) In cell B2 enter this formula.

=6*B1+4

> '*' means 'x' in a spreadsheet

(b) Copy the formula across the row.

③ (a) In cell A3 enter this heading.

Difference

Leave cell B3 blank.
In cell C3 enter this formula.

=C2-B2

(b) Copy the formula across the row.

(c) What do you notice?

④ (a) In cell A4 enter this heading.

Times table

(b) In cell B4 enter this formula.

=B1*B3

And copy it across row 4 to give the times table of the difference.

(c) Compare row 2 and row 4.
What do you notice?

⑤ Change the rule in cell B2 and **copy** the new rule across row 2.
Here are some rules to try.

=3*B1-1   =5*B1   =20-2*B1

Compare row 2 and row 4.
Investigate further.

⑥ How can the differences help you find the rule for a sequence?

Continued ...

When you are working with sequences derived from patterns, you can use the shape of the pattern to explain the rule for the sequence.

Example

Look at these patterns.

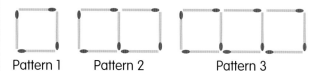

Pattern 1   Pattern 2   Pattern 3

(a) Draw the next two patterns in the sequence.
(b) Copy and complete this table.

Pattern number, n	1	2	3	4	5
Number of matchsticks	4				

(c) Find a rule for the sequence.
(d) Explain your rule.

Solution

(a)

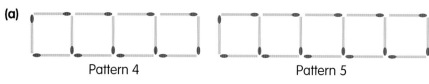

Pattern 4   Pattern 5

(b)

Pattern number, n	1	2	3	4	5
Number of matchsticks	4	7	10	13	16

(c) **Sequence:**

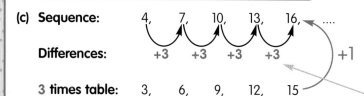

Sequence: 4,   7,   10,   13,   16, ...

Differences: +3   +3   +3   +3   +1

3 times table: 3,   6,   9,   12,   15

> The difference is 3 so the rule is based on the 3 times table.

The rule for the 3 times table is $3n$.
Each term in the sequence is 1 more than the 3 times table.
So the rule for the nth pattern is
  $1 + 3n$ or $3n + 1$.

> **Check**
> Pattern 1: $3 \times 1 + 1 = 4$ ✓
> Pattern 2: $3 \times 2 + 1 = 7$ ✓
> Pattern 3: $3 \times 3 + 1 = 10$ ✓

(d) Each pattern can be broken into:

  1 + 1 lot of 3   1 + 2 lots of 3   1 + 3 lots of 3

and so on.
So the number of matches in pattern 10 is: $1 + 10$ lots of $3 = 31$
So the number of matches in pattern n is: $1 + n$ lots of 3

> This is the same as $1 + 3n$ or $3n + 1$.

1 Write down the rule for each of these sequences.

(a) 2, 4, 6, 8, 10, ...   (b) 5, 10, 15, 20, 25, ...

(c) 7, 14, 21, 28, 35, ...   (d) 9, 18, 27, 36, 45, ...

2 (a) Write down the rule for this sequence.

   4, 8, 12, 16, 20, ...

(b) Use your answer to part (a) to help you find a rule for these sequences.

   (i) 5, 9, 13, 17, 21, ...

   (ii) 7, 11, 15, 19, 23, ...

   (iii) 2, 6, 10, 14, 18, ...

   (iv) 0, 4, 8, 16, 20, ...

3 Find a rule for these sequences.

(a) 1, 5, 9, 13, 17, ...

(b) 3, 5, 7, 9, 11, ...

(c) 5, 8, 11, 14, 17, ...

(d) 9, 14, 19, 24, 29, ...

(e) 5, 12, 19, 26, 33, ...

(f) 3, 11, 19, 27, 35, ...

4 Look at these patterns.

   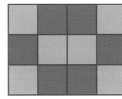   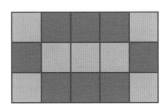

   Pattern 1   Pattern 2   Pattern 3

(a) Copy and complete this table.

Pattern number, n	1	2	3	4	5
Number of purple squares, P					
Number of green squares, G					
Total number of squares, T					

(b) Draw pattern 5 to check your predictions.

(c) Find numbers to go in the boxes to complete these rules.

$P = n + \boxed{}$

$G = \boxed{} n + \boxed{}$

$T = \boxed{} n + \boxed{}$

(d) Add together the rules for the number of purple squares and green squares.
What do you notice?

Continued ...

⑤ Brain strain

Look at how Olivia works out the rule for this sequence.

Use Olivia's method to work out the rule for each of these sequences.

(a) 22, 20, 18, 16, 14, ...
(b) 50, 45, 40, 35, 30, ...
(c) 50, 40, 30, 20, 10, ...
(d) 18, 15, 12, 9, 6, ...
(e) 22, 16, 10, 4, -2, ...
(f) 10, 9, 8, 7, 6, ...

20, 17, 14, 11, 8, ... +23

Differences: -3   -3   -3   -3

'-3' times table: -3,   -6,   -9,   -12,   -15

The rule for the '-3' times table is -3n.

Each term in the sequence is 23 more than the '-3' times table.

So the nth term is   23 − 3n

⑥ For each of these patterns
  (i)   draw the next pattern in the sequence
  (ii) copy and complete the table
  (iii) find a rule for the sequence
  (iv) explain why your rule works.

Pattern number, n	1	2	3	4	5	6
Number of matchsticks						

(a)

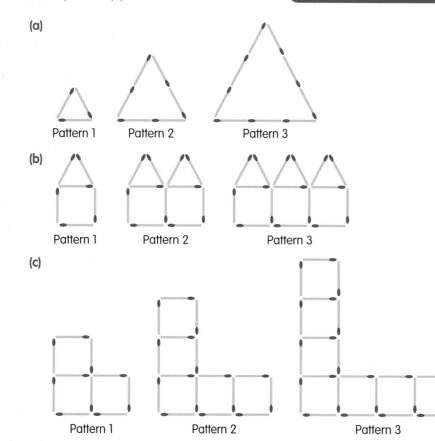

Pattern 1   Pattern 2   Pattern 3

(b)

Pattern 1   Pattern 2   Pattern 3

(c)

Pattern 1   Pattern 2   Pattern 3

Subject links
- science
- geography
- PHSE

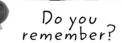

Coming up …

- the mode, modal class, mean and median
- the range
- calculating the mean from a frequency table
- comparing sets of data

Do you remember?

- how to find the mode, the modal class, the mean and the median
- how to find the range
- how to do mental and written calculations
- how to interpret tables and diagrams

Chapter starter

In sales and manufacturing it is often important to know an average value.

1 Sarah is the buyer for a chain of shoe shops. She has this data about men's shoe sizes. Which of these figures will she find the most useful?

Men's shoe sizes	
Mean:	9.7
Median:	10
Mode:	9

2 What other situations can you think of where knowing the most common outcome is helpful?
Can you think of any situations where knowing the mean outcome is more important than knowing the most common outcome?

3 On the label of a jar or can of food the ingredients should be listed, in order with the ingredient making up the greatest part of the contents first.
You will also find nutritional information about the contents.
Look at this label.

(a) Why do you think the figures in the third column of the table about nutritional information are given for 210 g?

(b) Do you think the percentages of the ingredients are a mode, a median or a mean?

(c) What about the typical values given in the table about nutritional information?

Baked beans
420 g

Ingredients: Beans (52%), Tomatoes (36%), Water, Sugar, Modified Maize Starch, Salt, Paprika, Ground White Pepper, Flavouring, Spices

Nutritional information

Typical values	Per 100 g	Per 210 g
Energy (KJ)	370	777
Energy (Kcal)	87	183
Protein (g)	4.8	10.1
Carbohydrate (g)	16.1	33.8
of which sugars	5.9	12.4
Fat (g)	0.4	0.8
of which saturates	0.1	0.2
Fibre (g)	5.5	11.6
Sodium (g)	0.3	0.7
Salt equivalent (g)	0.9	1.8

Key words

average

mode

modal class

mean

median

range

frequency table

distribution

You met the three types of average and the range in Year 7.

> The **mode** is the item that occurs the most often.
> It is the *most common* item.
>
> The **modal class** is the class or group of items which occurs the most often.
> It is the class or group with the highest frequency.
>
> The **mean** is $\dfrac{\text{the sum of all the values}}{\text{the number of values}}$
>
> The **median** is the *middle* number when all the numbers have been put *in order*.
>
> The **range** is the difference between the largest and the smallest numbers in the data.

Use the questions that follow to make sure you can work these out.

Now try these 5.1

1 Find the mode or modes for each data set.
If there is no mode explain why.
- (a) 3   5   2   8   12   5
       7   3   5
- (b) 12   14   16   18   20   22
- (c) rain   sun   wind   rain   snow   fog
       wind   mist   cloud   sun
- (d) # $ @   @ $ *
       Σ   €   ©   Ω

2 The table shows the time taken by a group of pupils to run one lap of a track.

Time taken to run one lap (t seconds)	Frequency
$60 \leqslant t < 70$	4
$70 \leqslant t < 80$	22
$80 \leqslant t < 90$	16
$90 \leqslant t < 100$	18
$100 \leqslant t < 110$	6

Find the modal class.

3 Find the mean of each set of data.
- (a) 3   5   6   8   13
- (b) 12   13   16   23
- (c) 0.3   0.5   0.7   0.8   0.9
- (d) 20   50   100   230   310   490

4 Find the median of each set of data.
- (a) 5   7   2   6   8
- (b) 12   8   21   19   13   11   7
- (c) 34   21   36   43
- (d) 9   16   4   21   15   22

5 Find the range for each set of data in question **4**.

6 A group of Year 8 pupils each estimated the length of a minute by saying 'start' at the beginning of the test and 'stop' when they thought a minute was up. These are the actual times, rounded to the nearest 0.1 second.

47.7 56.6 61.2 54.9 42.0 57.1 68.3 55.5
60.6 56.9 35.7 37.0 52.3 68.9 50.4 52.7

- (a) Is there a mode for this data? Explain your answer.
- (b) Work out the median for this data.
- (c) Work out the mean for this data.
- (d) Find the range of this data.

7 This grouped frequency table shows the heights of Year 6 pupils.

Find the modal class and estimate the range.

Height (cm)	Frequency
130–134	8
135–139	14
140–144	17
145–149	12
150–154	4

Continued ...

ⓐ Brain strain

(a) Write down or find out the number of days in each month in an ordinary year and in a leap year.
(b) Predict which of the mean, mode, median and range of the number of days in a month will be different for the two years.
(c) Calculate the mean, mode, median and range for the two sets of data. How good was your prediction?

5.2 Calculating the mean of a discrete frequency distribution

A set of data is called a **distribution**.

The table in the example shows a discrete frequency distribution.

Example

Alex did a survey of the number of people sitting at the tables in his restaurant one evening.

These are his results.

Calculate the mean number of people sitting at a table in the restaurant.

Number of people	Frequency
1	2
2	15
3	4
4	8
5	0
6	1

Solution

Mean number of people sitting at a table = $\dfrac{\text{total number of people}}{\text{number of tables}}$

Add a column to the table to help you find the total number of people.

Number of people	Frequency	Total number of people
1	2	$2 \times 1 = 2$
2	15	$15 \times 2 = 30$
3	4	$4 \times 3 = 12$
4	8	$8 \times 4 = 32$
5	0	$0 \times 5 = 0$
6	1	$1 \times 6 = 6$
Total	30	82

There are two tables with one person on them.

There are 15 tables with two people on them.

Add the numbers in this column to find the total number of people.

Add the numbers in this column to find the total number of tables.

Remember
Check that you answer is sensible. The mean should be a number around the centre of the data.

Mean number of people sitting at a table = $\dfrac{\text{total number of people}}{\text{number of tables}}$

$= 82 \div 30$

$= 2.73$

① Leon plays a round of golf.
The table shows his score for each of the 18 holes.

Score	Frequency
2	1
3	3
4	7
5	5
6	1
7	1

Calculate the mean score per hole.

② The table shows the number of tracks on each of the CDs in the top twenty in March 2008.

Number of tracks	Frequency
7	1
8	0
9	3
10	6
11	2
12	3
13	0
14	3
15	1
16	0
17	1

Calculate the mean number of tracks on a CD in the top twenty in March 2008.

③ **Brain strain**

The till in Edna's corner shop has these coins and notes in it.

Value of coin or note	Frequency
1p	23
2p	14
5p	6
10p	18
20p	25
50p	11
£1	31
£5	7
£10	9
£20	3

(a) Calculate the mean value of a coin in Edna's till.
(b) Calculate the mean value of a note in Edna's till.
(c) Explain why the mean value of an item in Edna's till (note or coin) is not the mean of your answers to parts (a) and (b).
(d) Find the mean value of an item in Edna's till.

Investigation

① (a) Collect data about the number of tracks on each of the CDs in the current top 20.

Make a frequency table similar to the one in Now try these 5.2 question **2**.

(b) Calculate the mean number of tracks on a CD in the current top 20.

(c) Compare your answer to part **(b)** with your answer to Now try these 5.2 question **2**.

② (a) Now collect data about the number of tracks on the CDs at numbers 21 to 40 in the charts.

(b) Calculate the mean number of tracks for this set of CDs.

(c) Compare the mean number of tracks on a CD in the top twenty with the mean number of tracks on a CD at numbers 21 to 40.

Is there any evidence that the best selling CDs have more tracks on average?

To compare two or more sets of data, or distributions, you use one, or more, of the mode, mean or median to comment on the difference between the average of the different sets of data.

You then use the range to comment on the difference between the spread of the different sets of data.

Example

There are 13 members of the Maths club in Year 8 at a school.
There are seven girls and six boys.
The club met 35 times.
The tables shows the number of times each pupil attended.

Girls	Attendance
Abby	22
Bethany	34
Carla	12
Indira	21
Jolene	35
Kathy	32
Meena	30

Boys	Attendance
Dipak	24
Enrico	20
Felix	26
Niles	28
Peter	18
Robert	28

Compare the attendance of boys and girls at the club.

Solution

To compare the attendance you need a measure of average and a measure of spread.
The mode, mean and median are available as measures of average.

The mode is not suitable as there is no mode for the girls.
Either the mean or the median would be acceptable.

> You can choose either the median or the mean. The median is easier find in this case so it is used here.

Attendances are, in order, 12, 21, 22, 30, 32, 34, 35.
The median is 30.

For the boys the attendances are, in order, 18, 20, 24, 26, 28, 28.
The median is 25.

Use the range as the measure of spread.

For the girls the range is 35 – 12 = 23
For the boys the range is 28 – 18 = 10

> Don't forget to write a conclusion.

So, the girls have a higher average attendance at the club but their attendances are more spread out.

Continued...

Example

The tables show the number of portions of fruit and vegetables eaten in a day by two groups of children.

The parents of the children in the first group both work.

At least one of the parents of the children in the second group stays at home.

Children whose parents both work

Number of portions of fruit and vegetables eaten	Frequency
0	2
1	11
2	23
3	19
4	31
5	16
6	2

Children with at least one parent staying at home

Number of portions of fruit and vegetables eaten	Frequency
0	0
1	16
2	24
3	28
4	29
5	9
6	1

Compare the number of portions of fruit and vegetables eaten by the two groups.

Solution

To compare the average number it is probably easiest to use the modal value.

For children whose parents both work the mode is 4.

For children with at least one parent staying at home the mode is also 4.

To compare the spread of the numbers use the range.

For children whose parents both work the range is 6 – 0 = 6.

For children with at least one parent staying at home the range is 6 – 1 = 5.

On average, the same number of portions of fruit and vegetables are eaten by children whose parents both work and by children with at least one parent staying at home.

There is, however, a greater variation (spread) for the results for children with at least one parent staying at home.

Note
Because the modal number of portions of fruit and vegetables eaten are the same, it might be worth calculating the mean for each group to get more information.

1. Year 7 and Year 11 at Hodder High School did a sponsored walk to raise money for a local charity.
   The table shows some information about the money raised.

Year	Largest amount raised by a pupil	Smallest amount raised by a pupil	Mean amount raised by a pupil
7	£45	£2.00	£12.45
11	£80	£0.50	£11.98

   Compare the amounts raised by pupils in the different year groups.

2. There are two hotels in a small town.
   At the Palace Hotel rooms cost from £29.99 to £49.99 with most costing £44.99.
   At the Imperial rooms cost from £45 to £60 with most costing £52.50.
   Compare the cost of rooms at the two hotels.

3. Franz and Karel are both keen skiers.
   Over the course of the winter they keep a record of how many times they fall over during each skiing session.
   The tables show the data for the two skiers.

Number of times Franz falls	Frequency
1	0
2	12
3	24
4	16
5	3

Number of times Karel falls	Frequency
1	7
2	10
3	11
4	12
5	4
6	2
7	1

   Use the mean and the range to compare the number of falls for the two skiers.

4. Megan did some research into the temperature in the UK in 2007.
   She concludes

   It was warmer on average in June than May but the temperature varied more in May.

Month 1:	Mean temperature 17.7°C
Month 2:	Mean temperature 18.9°C
Month A:	Highest temperature 28.3°C
	Lowest temperature 5.1°C
Month B:	Highest temperature 27.9°C
	Lowest temperature 9.7°C

   Which of these sets of figures represent May and which represent June.
   Explain your choice.

Continued …

5 The population pyramids show the age distribution for men and women in the United Kingdom in 2000 and the expected age distribution in 2050.

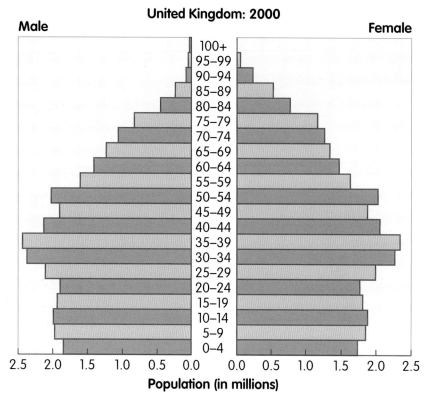

United Kingdom: 2000

Male | Female

Population (in millions)

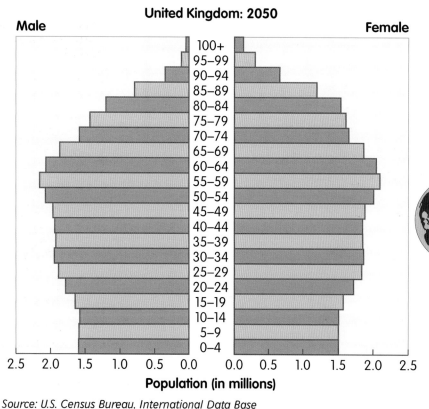

United Kingdom: 2050

Male | Female

Population (in millions)

Source: U.S. Census Bureau, International Data Base

(a) In the year 2000 in the 5 to 9 age group were there more males or more females?

(b) Is it predicted that there will be more or fewer children under 5 in 2050 than in 2000?

(c) (i) Estimate the number of people altogether in the over 100 age group in 2050.

(ii) How does this compare with the number of people over 100 years of age in 2000?

(d) Look for one other difference
(i) between males and females
(ii) between 2000 and 2050.

Research

Find data for temperatures in your nearest big town for the months of March and November.
Find out which of these months has the higher average temperature. Which has the more variable temperatures?

6 Statistical diagrams

Subject links
- geography
- science
- design and technology
- PHSE

Coming up ...

- drawing and interpreting line graphs, bar charts and pie charts
- drawing and interpreting stem-and-leaf diagrams
- drawing and interpreting frequency diagrams for continuous data

Chapter starter

Charlotte's class had a recycling day.

Each pupil was asked to bring in some items that could be recycled.

Many of the pupils brought in glass bottles.

The table shows the number of glass bottles brought in by pupils.

Number of bottles brought	Number of pupils
0	3
1	12
2	10
3	4
4	1

1. How many pupils brought in some glass bottles?

2. What fraction of the class did not bring in glass bottles?

The pupils were asked to produce a diagram using ICT to show this data.

Some of the pupils produced diagrams that were suitable, others produced unsuitable diagrams.

Here are three of the diagrams produced.

Connor produced a line graph.

Line graph showing number of bottles brought in

(y-axis: Frequency, 0 to 14; x-axis: Number of bottles, 0 to 4)

Do you remember?
- how to draw and interpret line graphs, bar charts and pie charts
- how to partition numbers
- how to find the mean, median, mode and modal class
- how to find the range
- how to use inequality symbols

Key words

frequency

stem-and-leaf diagram

discrete data

continuous data

frequency diagram

Continued ...

Charlotte produced this bar chart.

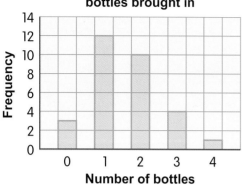

Grace produced this pie chart.

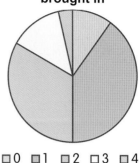

3 Discuss how each diagram was produced.

4 Which diagram is definitely unsuitable?
Why?

5 Which diagram is definitely suitable and gives clear information about the situation?

6 The pie chart is not unsuitable but nor is it the best diagram to illustrate the data.
Discuss the good and bad points of the pie chart drawn by Grace.

Research

1 Find some examples of these types of charts in newspapers and on the internet.
2 Are any of the examples unsuitable for the data they illustrate?
3 Could any of the data have been illustrated more clearly using another type of diagram?

6.1 Line graphs and bar charts

This section will allow you to practise drawing and interpreting some of the graphs and diagrams you have met before.

You will need to know about line graphs, including time series and bar charts.

Note
The graph of a time series has time (in minutes, weeks, as times, or months, for example) on the horizontal axis.

1   This line graph shows a time series.
    It shows the wind speed measured
    every 5 minutes during and after a
    thunderstorm one evening.
    (a)   At what time was the strongest
          wind recorded?
    (b)   What was the strongest wind
          speed recorded?
    (c)   As the thunderstorm finished the
          wind suddenly became much
          less strong.
          Estimate the time the
          thunderstorm finished.
    (d)   Calculate the mean wind speed
          throughout the time period
          shown.

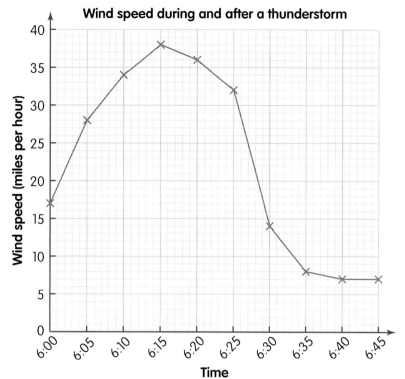

2   The table shows information about the temperature in an office on a summer's day.

Time	9 a.m.	11 a.m.	1 p.m.	3 p.m.	5 p.m.	7 p.m.	9 p.m.
Temperature (°C)	18	19	21	23	28	29	26

   (a)   Draw a fully labelled line graph to show the data.
   (b)   Estimate the two times that the temperature was 27°C.
   (c)   Explain how the data might support the fact that the office faces West.

3   The bar chart shows information about the number of wickets taken by
    Shane on the last 20 occasions he bowled in a game of cricket.

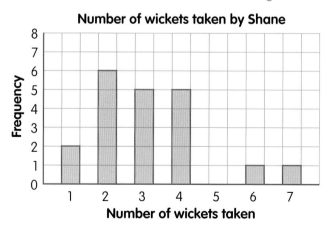

   (a)   What was the greatest number of wickets taken by Shane in one game?
   (b)   What is the modal number of wickets taken by Shane?
   (c)   In what fraction of these games did he take more than five wickets?
   (d)   Use the diagram to comment on Shane's performance in these games.

Continued …

④ The table shows information about the consumption of canned drinks by male and female pupils in England.

	Percentage of male pupils	Percentage of female pupils
0 cans	35.12	49.96
1 can	16.81	19.73
2 cans	18.92	15.93
3 cans	10.55	6.58
4 cans	7.15	3.52
5 or more cans	11.45	4.21

Adapted from CensusAtSchool www.censusatschool.ntu.ac.uk

(a) Draw a suitable bar chart to show the data for boys and girls in the same diagram.
(b) Use the data to make three statements highlighting the differences between the numbers of cans of drink consumed by boys and girls.

⑤ Every two weeks the local council collects unwanted newspapers from Tom's house for recycling.
The table shows the **frequency distribution** of the number of newspapers collected over a year.

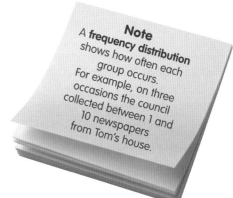

Note
A **frequency distribution** shows how often each group occurs.
For example, on three occasions the council collected between 1 and 10 newspapers from Tom's house.

Number collected	Frequency
1–10	3
11–20	7
21–30	8
31–40	6
41–50	2

(a) Explain why the total frequency adds up to 26.
(b) Explain why the data is discrete.
(c) Why do you think the data has been grouped?
(d) Draw a frequency diagram for this data.

6.2 Pie charts

This section will allow you to practise drawing and interpreting pie charts.

1. The pie chart shows the classification of films shown at a cinema during 2007.

Film classification

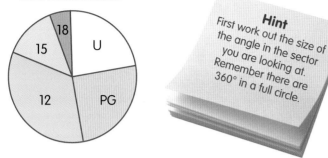

> **Hint**
> First work out the size of the angle in the sector you are looking at. Remember there are 360° in a full circle.

(a) Which category of film was shown most often at this cinema?

(b) Approximately what fraction of films were rated PG?

Altogether 90 different films were shown at the cinema in 2007.

(c) How many U certificate films were shown?

(d) Josh is 12 years old.
    How many of the cinema's films was he able to see in 2007?

(e) Josh's sister Shannon is 16 years old.
    How many more films than Josh could Shannon see at this cinema in 2007?

2. 60 pupils were asked which method of transport they thought produced the most pollution per mile of travel.
The table shows the results of the survey.

Method of transport	Number of pupils
Aeroplane	33
Bus	14
Car	6
Minibus	5
Train	2

Draw a pie chart to show this information.

ICT task

(a) Collect data about the amount of pollution produced by different methods of transport.

(b) Put the data into a spreadsheet. Construct a suitable diagram to show your results.

(c) What advice would you give to people about how they can reduce pollution when they travel
    (i) to work or school
    (ii) on holiday?

A good way of displaying numerical data that is in a list is a **stem-and-leaf diagram**.

The finished stem-and-leaf diagram gives an idea of the way the data is spread out as well as keeping the actual values of the individual pieces of data available.

Example

The number of telephone calls received by a company each morning was recorded over a 4-week period.

27	32	19	33	28
42	28	34	30	41
18	22	37	15	47
34	31	36	27	25

Draw a stem-and-leaf diagram to illustrate the data.

Solution

Step 1

Find the lowest and highest values in the data.
This allows you to draw the outline of the diagram.

Here the lowest value is 15 and the highest value is 47.
The **stem** of the diagram needs to go from 1 to 4.

> 1 represents numbers in the tens;
> 4 represents numbers in the forties.

You draw a line after the stem.

```
1 |
2 |
3 |
4 |
```

Step 2

Go through the data and write a number for each data value according to the size of the second digit.

```
1 |
2 | 7
3 | 2
4 |
```

> The first data value is 27.
> To show this you write a 7 (the second digit of 27) alongside the 2 (the first digit of 27) in the stem.

> The next data value is 32.
> To show this you write a 2 alongside the 3 in the stem.
> Make sure you line the numbers up vertically.

Continued...

The complete but **unordered** stem-and-leaf diagram will look like this.

```
1 | 9  8  5          ←     These are the leaves.
2 | 7  8  8  2  7  5
3 | 2  3  4  0  7  4  1  6
4 | 2  1  7
```

Step 3

Redraw the diagram with the leaves in order, smallest first.

The diagram is now an **ordered** stem-and-leaf diagram.

```
1 | 5  8  9
2 | 2  5  7  7  8  8
3 | 0  1  2  3  4  4  6  7
4 | 1  2  7
```

Step 4

Finally, give a key to explain the diagram.

1 | 5 represents 15 calls.   ←   It is usual to explain the first value in the diagram.

```
1 | 5  8  9
2 | 2  5  7  7  8  8
3 | 0  1  2  3  4  4  6  7
4 | 1  2  7
```

A stem-and-leaf diagram

- keeps the original values of the data visible
- shows the spread of the values
- is helpful in finding the range
- is helpful in finding the mean, median and mode.

Sometimes there are two sets of data that can be shown on the same diagram.

The stem then runs down the middle and the leaves go either side according to which set of data they are from.

The diagram is called a **back-to-back stem-and-leaf diagram**.

Continued ...

Example

The stem-and-leaf diagram shows the number of children absent from an infant school each day for three weeks and the number of children absent from the neighbouring junior school over the same three weeks.

	Infant school							Junior school						
							0	9						represents 9 pupils absent.
9	9	8	8	7	7	0	9						
	8	6	4	3	2	1	2	2	3	4	6	7	
			5	3	0	2	0	1	5	6	8	9	
					6	3	1						
						4	2						

(a) For the junior school, find
  (i)   the range of the number of pupils absent
  (ii) the modal number of pupils absent
  (iii) the median of the number of pupils absent
  (iv) the mean of the number of pupils absent.
(b) On one of the days most of one class in the junior school were off with a sickness bug.
    How many were absent from school that day?
(c) Use the mean and the range to compare absences in the two schools.

Solution

(a) (i)   Range = highest value – lowest value
          = 42 – 9
          = 33

> Make sure you look at the correct side of the diagram. Look at the first and last leaves to find the values you need to calculate the range.

  (ii) The modal number of pupils absent is the number that occurs most often.
        There is just one value for the junior school that occurs twice (12), all the others occur just once.
        Therefore the modal value is 12.

> Look at the leaves to identify repeated numbers in one particular row.

  (iii) To find the median all the numbers need to be in order, you then choose the middle one.
        There are 15 values, so the middle one is the eighth.
        Therefore the median is 20.

> In an ordered stem-and-leaf diagram the numbers are in order.
> Count the leaves until you reach the eighth.

  (iv) The mean is found by adding up all the numbers then dividing by the number of pieces of data.

        9 + 12 + 12 + 13 + … + 42 = 315

        Mean = 315 ÷ 15
             = 21
        So the mean is 21.

(b) Having so many of one class off almost certainly means that the total absent is the highest for the three weeks.
    The best estimate of that day's total is therefore 42.

> It is an estimate because you cannot be sure that the day of the sickness bug was the day on which the greatest number of children were absent.

(c) The range for the infant school is 36 – 7 = 29.
    So the data for the junior school is more spread out and less consistent.
    The mean for the infant school is 225 ÷ 15 = 15.
    So the mean number of absences is fewer for the infant school.

1 Abigail recorded the number of eggs laid by her pet chicken each month for two years.

```
35  56  44  22  23  31
40  38  35  46  52  45
48  32  33  42  26  27
18  50  35  27  41  36
```

Illustrate this data in a stem-and-leaf diagram.

2 A market garden sets tomato plants in rows of 100. The manager makes this stem-and-leaf diagram to show how many plants in each of 20 rows survive and grow into fruit-bearing plants.

7 | 9 represents 79 plants surviving.

```
 7 | 9  9
 8 | 2  3  5  5  5  6  7  7  8
 9 | 0  0  0  1  5  7  8  9
10 | 0
```

(a) Find the range of the number of plants surviving.
(b) Find the mean of the number of plants surviving.
(c) Find the median of the number of plants surviving.
(d) Find the two modes for the number of plants surviving.
(e) Find the mean number of plants in a row that did *not* survive.

> **3 Brain strain**
>
> A surviving tomato plant produces an average profit of £32 for the market garden in question **2**.
>
> Use the data in question **2** to calculate the total profit from all the tomato plants which survived.

4 To reduce congestion a town council introduces a lane on a main road which can only be used by cars with more than one person in them.
The council counts the number of cars out of every set of 50 that have more than one person in them on 20 occasions before the lane is introduced and on 20 occasions after the lane is introduced.

The data is shown in this back-to-back stem-and-leaf diagram.

Before lane is introduced		After lane is introduced
9 8 8 7 7 6 6 4 3 2 1	1	6 7 8 8 9 9 9
8 7 7 5 5 4 2 2	2	0 0 1 2 3 3 4 5 7 7 9
4	3	5 9

(a) Write a suitable key for the diagram.
(b) Calculate the mean number of cars which have more than one person in them for both before and after the lane is introduced.
(c) Calculate the range of the number of cars which have more than one person in them for both before and after the lane is introduced.
(d) What effect has the introduction of the lane had on the number of cars with more than one person in them?
Use your answers to parts **(b)** and **(c)** to explain your answer.

Continued …

⑤ Brain strain

⑤ Brain strain

(a) Copy this table.
Use the data in question **4** to complete the table.

Number of cars with only one person in	Frequency before lane introduced	Frequency after lane introduced
1 to 10		
11 to 20		
21 to 30		
31 to 40		
41 to 50		

(b) Use the data in your table to draw a different type of diagram for the data.
(c) What are the advantages and disadvantages of your diagram over the stem-and-leaf diagram?

6.4 Grouped continuous data

You have already met bar charts.

These are frequency diagrams for **discrete data**, including grouped discrete data.

Discrete data is countable.

Bar charts have bars with gaps between them.

Frequency diagrams for **continuous data** have bars without gaps.

Continuous data must be measured.

All numerical values are possible.

Continuous data does not have spaces in between values.

Example

A group of Year 8 students run one lap of an athletics track.

The table shows their times.

Time taken to run one lap (t seconds)	Frequency
$60 \leqslant t < 70$	4
$70 \leqslant t < 80$	16
$80 \leqslant t < 90$	22
$90 \leqslant t < 100$	18
$100 \leqslant t < 110$	6

Draw a frequency diagram for this data.

Continued...

Solution

First, look at the groups in the table.

The first group is $60 \leqslant t < 70$.

This means a time of 60 seconds is included in the group but a time of 70 seconds is not included.

A time of 70 seconds would go into the second group, $70 \leqslant t < 80$.

Do not label the horizontal axis with the group labels

Draw axes like those for a graph.

The vertical axis, axxs usual, has the frequency scale on it.

The horizontal axis also has a continuous scale.

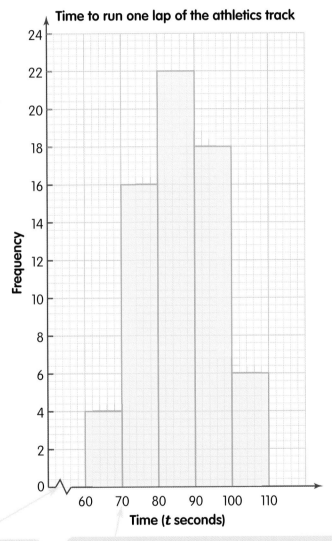

Time to run one lap of the athletics track

As the data does not start near zero you use this sign to show that there is a break in the scale.

You draw the line for the end of the first bar and the beginning of the second bar at 70.
70 is not included in the first group but you can get as close as you like to it; values of 69.9, 69.99, 69.999, ... would all be included in the first group.

1 Carbon dioxide is emitted whenever a car is driven.
The emissions are measured in grams per kilometre.
The emissions are harmful to the environment.
The table shows the emissions of 40 of the most popular models of small car.

Emissions (e grams per kilometre)	Frequency
$80 \leqslant e < 100$	3
$100 \leqslant e < 120$	4
$120 \leqslant e < 140$	16
$140 \leqslant e < 160$	11
$160 \leqslant e < 180$	5
$180 \leqslant e < 200$	1

Draw a frequency diagram to show the data.

2 The frequency diagram shows the age of the first 400 visitors to the London Eye
one Monday morning in June.

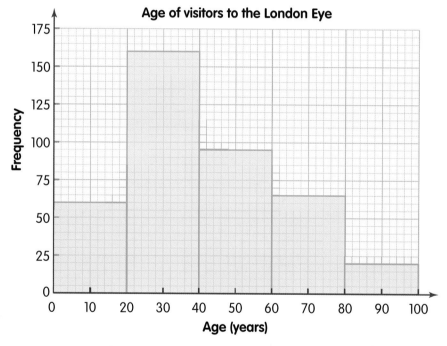

Age of visitors to the London Eye

(a) What is the modal age group?
(b) Jack says

Most of the first 400
visitors were under 40.

Explain why Jack is right.
(c) What fraction of the visitors were 80 years or older?

Continued …

This table shows the ages of the first 400 visitors one Monday morning in August.

(d) Using the same scales as the diagram on the previous page, draw a frequency diagram to show the data for this Monday in August.

(e) Use both diagrams to comment on the differences between the two sets of data.

(f) Suggest explanations of the differences you found in part (e).

Age (A years)	Number of visitors
$0 < A \leqslant 20$	140
$20 < A \leqslant 40$	160
$40 < A \leqslant 60$	60
$60 < A \leqslant 80$	35
$80 < A \leqslant 100$	10

③ Applicants for a job as a newsreader take a test where they have to read a long piece of writing as quickly as possible without making a mistake.
The times for the 57 applicants who did not make a mistake are given in the table.

(a) Copy and complete this sentence.
All the applicants who made no mistakes completed in between … and … minutes.

(b) Draw a frequency diagram for the data.

(c) The applicants who made no mistakes and completed in less than 4 minutes were then invited for an interview.
On your diagram, indicate the bars representing these people.

(d) Tanya finished in 155 seconds but made 1 mistake. Comment on the selection procedure.

Time (t seconds)	Frequency
$180 \leqslant t < 200$	2
$200 \leqslant t < 220$	4
$220 \leqslant t < 240$	3
$240 \leqslant t < 260$	11
$260 \leqslant t < 280$	14
$280 \leqslant t < 300$	9
$300 \leqslant t < 320$	7
$320 \leqslant t < 340$	6
$340 \leqslant t < 360$	1

Research

① Collect data about the emissions of larger cars.
Put the data into a grouped frequency table like the one in Now try these 6.3 question **1**.
You will need groups with higher values.

② Draw a frequency diagram for the data.

③ What conclusions can you draw about helping the environment when buying and using a car?

Investigation

You will need
Sensitive weighing scales
A bag of dried apricots or similar

① Weigh each apricot separately and record the value to 1 decimal place.

② Add up all the weights.
Does the total exceed the weight of the contents given on the bag?

③ Produce a grouped frequency table with four to six groups.

④ Draw a frequency diagram to show the data.

⑤ Divide the claimed weight of contents given on the bag by the number of apricots in the bag.
This will give you the claimed mean weight of one apricot.

⑥ Draw a vertical line on your frequency diagram at the point where this average falls.
You will now have a visual idea of how the weights are distributed around the claimed mean.

⑦ Comment on your findings in part **6**.

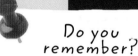
7 Multiples and factors

Divisible
by 2

Divisible
by 3

6

7

25

Divisible
by 5

Coming up ...

● finding the prime factors of a number
● finding the highest common factor of a set of numbers
● finding the lowest common multiple of a set of numbers

Chapter starter

1 Look at this diagram.

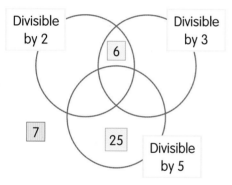

Put these numbers in the correct places in the diagram.

The first three have been done for you as examples.

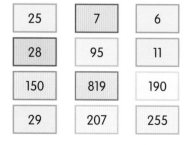

2 A **perfect number** is a number which equals the sum of all the numbers it is exactly divisible by except itself.
For example, 6 is a perfect number.
It is divisible by 1, 2, 3 and 6 and 1 + 2 + 3 = 6.
(a) Find the next perfect number.
(b) Alex says that the third perfect number is 496.
Check that 496 is a perfect number.

In Year 7 you learnt that a prime number has exactly two different factors, itself and 1.

Here is a reminder of the first few prime numbers.

2,   3,   5,   7,   11,   13,   17,   19,   23,   29,   ...

Other numbers can be written as a product of two or more prime numbers.

These prime numbers are called the **prime factors**.

FOR EXAMPLE $6 = 2 \times 3$

$20 = 2 \times 2 \times 5$

One way of writing a large number as a **product of its prime factors** is a factor tree.

Example

Write 90 as a product of its prime factors.

Note
You can also call this process **prime factor decomposition**.

Solution

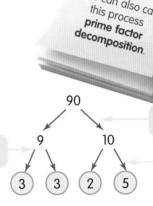

9 is 3 times 3 and these are both prime. Circle the prime numbers.

90 decomposes into 9 times 10.

10 is 2 times 5. Again these are both prime so you circle them.

So 90 = 3 × 3 × 2 × 5
$\quad\ \ = 2 \times 3 \times 3 \times 5$
$\quad\ \ = 2 \times 3^2 \times 5$

The process stops when all the factors are circled to indicate that they are prime.

The neatest way to write a number as a product of its prime factors is using index notation, which you learnt about in Chapter 2.

There are other ways of setting out the steps, but the end result will be the same.

For example, if you split 90 into 2 times 45 at the first stage then the factor tree might look like this.

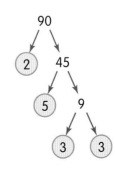

1. Write these numbers as products of their prime factors.
   (a) 24   **(b)** 80   **(c)** 32   **(d)** 36
   (e) 60   **(f)** 68   **(g)** 75   **(h)** 88

2. Copy and complete these factor trees.
   Then write 140 and 300 as products of their prime factors.
   (a)

   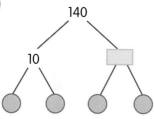

   (b)

   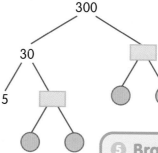

3. You can use prime factorisation to cancel fractions.
   This is Charlie's working to simplify $\frac{42}{63}$.

   $$42 = 2 \times 3 \times 7$$
   $$63 = 3 \times 3 \times 7$$
   $$\frac{42}{63} = \frac{2 \times 3 \times 7}{3 \times 3 \times 7}$$
   $$= \frac{2}{3}$$

   Use Charlie's method to write these fractions in their simplest form.

   (a) $\frac{42}{70}$ **(b)** $\frac{30}{105}$ **(c)** $\frac{63}{84}$

4. Express 1001 as a product of its prime factors.

   Hint
   Try 11 as a factor.

5. **Brain strain**
   Copy and complete this factor tree.
   Then write 1800 as a product of its prime factors.

   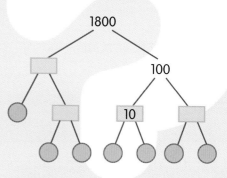

6. **Brain strain**
   120 written as a product of its prime factors is $2^3 \times 3 \times 5$.
   (a) Express 360 as a product of its prime factors.
   (b) Express 1200 as a product of its prime factors.

7.2 Highest common factor

The factors of 6 are 1, 2, 3 and 6.
The factors of 15 are 1, 3, 5 and 15.

Some numbers (1 and 3) appear in both lists.
They are called **common factors** of 6 and 15.
The **highest common factor (HCF)** of 6 and 15 is 3.

Continued ...

The highest common factor of a set of numbers is the largest factor that divides exactly into all the numbers in the set.

You can find the highest common factor of a set of numbers by listing all the factors of each of the numbers and comparing the lists, as was done with 6 and 15 above.

You can also use prime factorisation to find the highest common factor of a set of numbers.

This is particularly useful for larger numbers but the examples use simpler numbers to help you see the process.

Example

Use prime factorisation to find the highest common factor of 10 and 14.

Solution

$10 = 2 \times 5$ $14 = 2 \times 7$

The diagram shows the prime factors of 10 inside one circle and the prime factors of 14 inside the other.

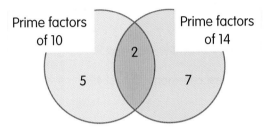

The overlap indicates the highest common factor, which in this case is just 2.

So the highest common factor of 10 and 14 is 2.

Example

Find the highest common factor of 24 and 30.

Solution

$24 = 2 \times 2 \times 2 \times 3$ $30 = 2 \times 3 \times 5$

Use factor trees to find the prime factor decomposition of the numbers.

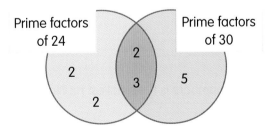

The overlap indicates the *factors* of the highest common factor, 2 and 3.

$2 \times 3 = 6$

To find the highest common factor, multiply together the numbers in the overlap.

So the highest common factor of 24 and 30 is 6.

Now try these 7.2

1 Find the highest common factor of 12 and 18.

2 You are given that 40 = 2 × 2 × 2 × 5 and 48 = 2 × 2 × 2 × 2 × 3.

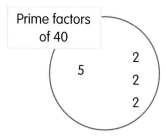

Prime factors of 40

5   2   2   2

(a) Copy and complete the diagram to show this information.
(b) Use your diagram to find the highest common factor of 40 and 48.

3 Find the highest common factor of 36 and 40.

4 You are given that 42 = 2 × 3 × 7 and 180 = 2 × 2 × 3 × 3 × 5.
(a) Draw a diagram like the ones in the examples to show this information.
(b) Use your diagram to find the highest common factor of 42 and 180.

5 Find the highest common factor of 50 and 60.

6 Brain strain

A coach company has a fleet of small buses.

All the buses can carry the same number of passengers.

On Monday morning a certain number of buses were in service and could carry a total of 161 passengers.

On Monday afternoon a different number of buses were in service and could carry a total of 253 passengers.

How many passengers can one bus carry?

7.3 Lowest common multiple

The first few multiples of 2 are 2, 4, 6, 8, 10 and 12.

The first few multiples of 3 are 3, 6, 9, 12 and 15.

Some numbers (6 and 12) appear in both lists.

They are called **common multiples** of 2 and 3.

There will be more if you add to the lists.

The **lowest common multiple (LCM)** of 2 and 3 is 6.

The lowest common multiple of a set of numbers is the smallest multiple that all the original numbers will divide into exactly.

You can find the lowest common multiple of a set of numbers by listing the multiples of the numbers and comparing the lists, as was done with 2 and 3 above.

As for finding the highest common factor, you can also use prime factorisation to find the lowest common multiple of a set of numbers.

Continued ...

Example

Use prime factorisation to find the lowest common multiple of 10 and 14.

Solution

$10 = 2 \times 5$ $14 = 2 \times 7$

The diagram shows the prime factors of 10 inside one circle and the prime factors of 14 inside the other.

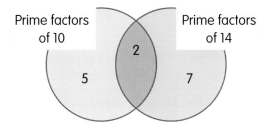

Note
You use the numbers in the diagram once only.

To find the lowest common multiple, you multiply together the numbers in all three regions.

So the lowest common multiple of 10 and 14 is $5 \times 2 \times 7 = 70$.

Example

Find the lowest common multiple of 24 and 30.

Solution

$24 = 2 \times 2 \times 2 \times 3$ $30 = 2 \times 3 \times 5$

Use factor trees to find the prime factor decomposition of the numbers.

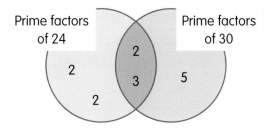

The lowest common multiple is $2 \times 2 \times 2 \times 3 \times 5 = 120$.

So the lowest common multiple of 24 and 30 is 120.

1. Find the lowest common multiple of 12 and 18.

2. You are given that $40 = 2 \times 2 \times 2 \times 5$ and $48 = 2 \times 2 \times 2 \times 2 \times 3$.
   Look back at the diagram you drew for Now try these 7.2, question **2**.
   Use your diagram to find the lowest common multiple of 40 and 48.

3. Find the lowest common multiple of 36 and 40.

4. You are given that $18 = 2 \times 3 \times 3$ and $21 = 3 \times 7$.
   (a) Draw a diagram like the ones in the examples to show this information.
   (b) Use your diagram to find the lowest common multiple of 18 and 21.

5. Find the lowest common multiple of 50 and 60.

6. **(a)** Write 20 as a product of its prime factors.
   (b) Write 32 as a product of its prime factors.
   (c) Hence find the highest common factor and the lowest common multiple of 20 and 32.

Don't confuse highest common factor and lowest common multiple.
The highest common factor is always less than or equal to the smallest number.
The lowest common multiple is always greater than or equal to the largest number.

7. **Puzzle**

   The highest common factor of two numbers is 25.

   The lowest common multiple of the same two numbers is 150.

   What are the two numbers?

8. **Brain strain**

   In the harbour there is a lighthouse and two buoys.

   The lighthouse flashes once every 60 seconds.

   One buoy flashes once every 80 seconds.

   The other buoy flashes once every 90 seconds.

   All three lights flash together at 07:30.

   What time will they next all flash together?

Subject links
- PHSE
- science
- design and technology

Coming up ...

- rounding numbers
- adding and subtracting decimals
- using division to convert a fraction into a decimal
- terminating and recurring decimals
- multiplying and dividing integers and decimals by 0.1 and 0.01
- multiplying and dividing by other decimals

Do you remember?
- about the place value of digits in a number
- how to read and write powers of 10
- how to add, subtract, multiply and divide integers
- how to order decimals
- how to write a number as a product of its prime factors
- how to multiply and divide by 10 and 100
- how to find equivalent fractions

Chapter starter

Play this game.

You have to try to make the target number.
You can use any of the six numbers and any of the four operations, +, − , ×, and ÷.
You may only use each number once.

You score 10 points for hitting the target number.
Or the player nearest the target scores

- 7 points for being within 5 of the target number
- 5 points for being within 10 of the target number.

Round 1

100	1	9
4	7	6

Target number 720

Round 2

75	8	10
3	2	8

Target number 839

Round 3

25	100	10
3	7	9

Target number 381

Round 4

50	8	1
5	7	2

Target number 331

Key words

round
ten thousand (10 000)
hundred thousand (100 000)
million (1 000 000)
tenth ($\frac{1}{10}$)
hundredth ($\frac{1}{100}$)
decimal
integer
place value
add
subtract
multiply
divide
fraction
equivalent fraction
denominator
terminating decimal
recurring decimal

The Breast Cancer Site is a charity.

It raises sponsorship money based on the number of hits on its website, www.thebreastcancersite.com.

It uses the money to pay for tests to find breast cancer.

These are the number of hits received in the first five months in 2008.

January 8 339 874
February 9 136 274
March 9 311 829
April 8 633 127
May 8 766 111

You learnt how to round to the nearest 10, 100 or 1000 in Year 7.

You can use a similar technique to round to the nearest 10 000, 100 000, 1 000 000, … .

Do you remember?
10 000 is ten thousand.
100 000 is a hundred thousand.
1 000 000 is a million.

Megan says

In January there were about 8 million hits.

Megan has rounded to the nearest million.

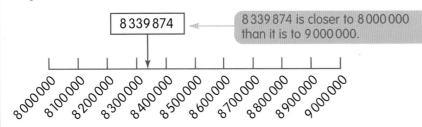

8 339 874

8 339 874 is closer to 8 000 000 than it is to 9 000 000.

You don't have to draw a number line.

Think of the multiple of 1 000 000 above and below the number you are rounding.

Then decide which it is closer to.

Example

In May 2008, the Breast Cancer Site received 8 766 111 hits.

Round this number to the nearest hundred thousand.

Solution

8 766 111 lies between 8 700 000 and 8 800 000.

Look at the multiples of one hundred thousand above and below the number you are rounding.

It is closer to 8 800 000.
8 766 111 is 8 800 000 to the nearest hundred thousand.

Continued …

Rounding can be applied to decimals too.

You can round a decimal to a whole number or to 1, 2 or any number of decimal places.

This is especially useful at the end of a task involving a calculator.

Example

A rock has a mass of 12.2 kilograms.

Give this figure to the nearest kilogram.

Solution

The mass lies between 12 and 13 kilograms.

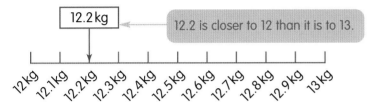

12.2 is closer to 12 than it is to 13.

You don't have to draw a number line.

Look at the first digit after the cut-off point.

In this case look at the digit in the first decimal place.

If it is less than 5, round down.

If it is 5 or more, round up.

12.2 lies between 12 and 13.

The first digit after the cut-off point is 2, so round down. You just write the integer part of the number.

12.2 kg rounded to the nearest kilogram is 12 kg.

Example

Ravi works out 24 ÷ 7 on his calculator.

This is what the calculator display shows.

| 3.428 571 429 |

Round this answer to 2 decimal places.

Solution

3.428 571 429 lies between 3.42 and 3.43.

The first digit after the cut-off point is 8, so round up. You add one to the digit in the second decimal place.

3.428 571 429 is 3.43 to 2 decimal places.

Continued...

You have to take care with answers that have a zero at the end of the decimal.

Example

Round 2.96 to 1 decimal place.

Solution

2.96 lies between 2.9 and 3.0.

2.96 is 3.0 to 1 decimal place.

The first digit after the cut-off point is 6, so round up.
You add one to the digit in the first decimal place.
9 + 1 = 10
Write the 0 in the first decimal place and add one to the digit in the units place.

⚠ You must include the zero at the end of the number.
If you write just 3 you are rounding to the nearest integer, not 1 decimal place.

Now try these 8.1

① Here are the number of hits received at The Breast Cancer Site in the first five months in 2008 again.

January   8 339 874
February 9 136 274
March   9 311 829
April   8 633 127
May   8 766 111

(a) Round the numbers for February, March April and May to the nearest million.
(b) Round the numbers for January, February, March and April to the nearest hundred thousand.
(c) Round all the numbers to the nearest thousand.

② Round these numbers to the stated accuracy.
(a) 8.233 to 1 decimal place
(b) 16.5474 to 2 decimal places
(c) 0.086 to 1 decimal place
(d) 22.5151 to 2 decimal places
(e) 16.39 to the nearest whole number
(f) 3.96 to 1 decimal place
(g) 1.447 to 2 decimal places
(h) 11.9 to the nearest whole number
(i) 12.099 to 2 decimal places
(j) 15.5 to the nearest whole number

③ The length of a running track is 1.16 km.
Write this length correct to 1 decimal place.

④ A doctor's patient has a temperature of 37.63 degrees Celsius.
Write this temperature
(a) to the nearest 0.1 degree.
(b) to the nearest degree.

⑤ Ben works out the area of a circle in square centimetres.
This is what his calculator shows.

| 78.539 816 34 |

Write this answer
(a) correct to 2 decimal places
(b) correct to the nearest whole number of square centimetres.

⑥ A humming bird has a mass of 1.827 grams.
Write this figure
(a) correct to 2 decimal places
(b) correct to the nearest whole number of grams.

⑦ A car is 5.368 metres long.
Write this length correct to the nearest centimetre.

⑧ When Mike works out $\frac{2}{3}$ as a decimal his calculator says
0.666 666 666 7.
Give this answer correct to 2 decimal places.

Note
1 cm = 0.01 m so this question is asking you to round to 2 decimal places.

⑨ **Brain strain**

A turkey weighs 11 kg to the nearest kilogram.

What is the smallest value its weight could actually be?

When you are adding and subtracting decimals, write the numbers so
that the decimal points and the digits with the same place value line up.

Example

Work out 3.94 + 5.37.

Solution

```
  3 . 9 4
+ 5 . 3 7
  9 . 3 1
  1   1
```

Example

Work out 37.7 + 0.652 + 4.73.

Solution

```
  3 7 . 7 0 0
  0 0 . 6 5 2
+ 0 4 . 7 3 0
  4 3 . 0 8 2
  1   2
```

Put zeros in the empty places to help you keep the digits lined up.

Example

Work out 7.4 − 3.58.

Solution

```
  ⁶7 . ¹³4 ¹0
−   3 . 5 8
    3 . 8 2
```

Now try these 8.2

Hint
Remember you can add and subtract in any order.
Remember to keep the sign with the number that follows it.

① Work out these.
- (a) 3.72 + 5.24
- (b) 1.65 + 7.23
- (c) 5.34 + 0.87
- (d) 5.83 + 3.29

② Work out these.
- (a) 39.9 + 2.68
- (b) 0.834 + 3.55
- (c) 34.9 + 8.943
- (d) 17.49 + 4.76

③ Work out these.
- (a) 456.8 + 67.8 + 12.94
- (b) 3.7 + 0.054 + 1.5

④ Work out these.
- (a) 5.8 − 4.3
- (b) 4.73 − 1.32
- (c) 57.18 − 31.09
- (d) 84.37 − 52.54

⑤ Work out these.
- (a) 6.83 − 2.367
- (b) 10.6 − 1.74
- (c) 248.53 − 28.777
- (d) 0.036 − 0.0036

⑥ Work out these.
- (a) 23.5 + 29.64 − 15.72
- (b) 6.37 − 7.31 + 4.6
- (c) 15.7 − 17.38 + 9.96
- (d) 3.5 − 4.322 + 5.03

⑦ These are the results of a 100-metre running race.

1st S. Gonzalez   10.3 seconds
2nd B. Whizz   10.48 seconds
3rd T. Railing   11.1 seconds

- (a) How many seconds before Railing did Gonzalez finish?
- (b) How many seconds before Railing did Whizz finish?
- (c) The world record for the 100-metres is 9.72 seconds.
  How many seconds slower is Gonzalez than this?

In Year 7 you learnt how to convert simple fractions into decimals.

You may know facts like $\frac{1}{2} = 0.5$ and $\frac{3}{4} = 0.75$.

Some fractions can be converted into decimals by changing them to an equivalent fraction with a denominator of 100.

FOR EXAMPLE

$$\overset{\times 4}{\underset{\times 4}{\frac{7}{25} = \frac{28}{100}}} = 0.28$$

Another method is to divide the numerator by the denominator.

Note
Here short division is used but you can use whichever method you prefer.

$$8 \overline{)5.^50^20^40}$$ 0. 6 2 5

Example

Convert $\frac{5}{8}$ into a decimal.

Solution

Work out $5 \div 8$.

5 is the same as 5.000.

$\frac{5}{8} = 0.625$

You can add as many zeros as you need.
5 is the same as 5.000.

You can convert fractions into decimals to help you order them.

This method is particularly useful if you can use a calculator.

Example

Write these numbers in ascending order.

0.89 $\frac{7}{8}$ $\frac{9}{11}$ $\frac{15}{17}$

Note
Ascending order means start with the smallest.

Solution

Convert the fractions into decimals.

$\frac{7}{8} = 7 \div 8 \qquad = 0.875$

$\frac{9}{11} = 9 \div 11 \qquad = 0.818\ 181\ 818\ \ldots$

$\frac{15}{17} = 15 \div 17 \quad = 0.882\ 352\ 941\ \ldots$

0.89

Write the numbers with the digits with the same place value lined up.
All the numbers have 0 units.

They all have 8 tenths.

The hundredths are different.

The numbers in ascending order are $\frac{9}{11}$ $\frac{7}{8}$ $\frac{15}{17}$ 0.89.

You saw in the example above that using division allows you to convert any fraction into a decimal.

Fractions such as $\frac{1}{2} = 0.5$, $\frac{9}{100} = 0.09$ or $\frac{7}{8} = 0.875$ result in **terminating decimals**.

Continued …

After a certain number of decimal places the number terminates or ends.

Other fractions such as $\frac{1}{3}$ = 0.333 333 333..., $\frac{9}{11}$ = 0.818 181 818...

or $\frac{5}{6}$ = 0.833 333 333... result in decimals which carry on forever.

These are called **recurring decimals** because the same numbers keep recurring or repeating.

The dots at the end of the number show that the number carries on in the same way.

There is a short way of writing recurring decimals.

$\frac{1}{3}$ = 0.333 333 333... can be written as 0.$\dot{3}$.

> The dot over the 3 shows that the digit 3 repeats forever.

$\frac{9}{11}$ = 0.818 181 818... can be written as 0.$\dot{8}\dot{1}$.

> The dots over the 8 and the 1 show that the digits 81 repeat forever.

$\frac{5}{6}$ = 0.833 333 333... can be written as 0.8$\dot{3}$.

> Only the 3 repeats in this number. There is no dot over the 8.

Now try these 8.3

① Convert these fractions into decimals.

(a) $\frac{3}{8}$ (b) $\frac{7}{20}$ (c) $\frac{13}{25}$ (d) $\frac{17}{40}$ (e) $\frac{3}{200}$

② Convert these fractions into decimals.

(a) $\frac{1}{3}$ (b) $\frac{2}{3}$ (c) $\frac{1}{6}$ (d) $\frac{7}{9}$ (e) $\frac{4}{11}$

③ Convert these fractions into decimals.
Say whether each decimal is a terminating decimal or a recurring decimal.

(a) $\frac{7}{11}$ (b) $\frac{21}{25}$ (c) $\frac{15}{16}$

(d) $\frac{17}{32}$ (e) $\frac{19}{30}$ (f) $\frac{1}{24}$

④ Write these numbers in ascending order.

$\frac{11}{15}$ 0.8   0.795 $\frac{36}{41}$

⑤ Write these numbers in descending order.

$\frac{14}{25}$ 0.58 $\frac{27}{40}$ $\frac{67}{102}$

Note
Ascending order means starting with the smallest.
Descending order means starting with the largest.

Investigation

Use your calculator to convert these fractions into decimals.

Write down all the numbers shown in your calculator display.

$\frac{1}{9}$ $\frac{2}{9}$ $\frac{3}{9}$ $\frac{4}{9}$ $\frac{5}{9}$ $\frac{6}{9}$ $\frac{7}{9}$ $\frac{8}{9}$

What do you notice?

Investigation

① Investigate to see which fractions are terminating decimals and which are recurring decimals.

Copy the table.

Continue the pattern with $\frac{1}{4}$, $\frac{1}{5}$, ...

You could also look at $\frac{2}{3}$, $\frac{3}{4}$, ...

What patterns do you notice?

Fraction	Decimal	Terminating or recurring?
$\frac{1}{2}$	0.5	T
$\frac{1}{3}$	0.333...	R

② Write down the denominators of the fractions which terminate.

Write the denominators as products of their prime factors.

What do you notice?

In Year 7 you learnt how to multiply and divide by 10 and 100.

When you multiply a number by 10 you move the digits one place to the left.

When you multiply a number by 100 you move the digits two places to the left.

When you divide a number by 10 you move the digits one place to the right.

When you divide a number by 100 you move the digits two places to the right.

Example

Work out these.

(a) 3.2 × 100

(b) 8.4 ÷ 10

Solution

(a) 3.2 × 100 = 320

H	T	U	.	t
		3	.	2
3	2	0	.	

(b) 8.4 ÷ 10 = 0.84

U	.	t	h
8	.	4	
0	.	8	4

Now, look at this place value table.

U	.	t
1	.	
0	.	1

It shows this calculation.

1 ÷ 10 = 0.1

It also tells you that multiplying by 0.1 is the same as dividing by 10.

The digits move one place to the right.

Example

Work out 45 × 0.1.

Solution

45 × 0.1 = 45 × 1 ÷ 10 ◄── Write 0.1 as 1 ÷ 10.

= 45 ÷ 10 ◄── 45 × 1 = 45

= 4.5

T	U	.	t
4	5	.	
	4	.	5

Similarly multiplying by 0.01 is the same as dividing by 100.

The digits move two places to the right.

Continued ...

Example

Work out 270 × 0.01.

Solution

270 × 0.01 = 270 ÷ 100

= 2.7

H	T	U	.	t	h
2	7	0	.		
		2	.	7	0

Note
2.70 is the same as 2.7.

Division is the inverse of multiplication.

So dividing by 0.1 is the same as multiplying by 10

and dividing by 0.01 is the same as multiplying by 100.

0.1 is the same as $\frac{1}{10}$.

So you can think of dividing by 0.1 as asking how many tenths there are in 1.

The answer is 10.

To find the answer to how many tenths there are in 2, you multiply 2 by 10 to get 20.

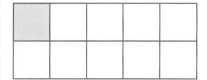 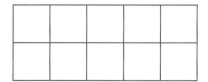

Example

Work out these.

(a) 83 ÷ 0.1

(b) 6.32 ÷ 0.01

Solution

(a) 83 ÷ 0.1 = 83 × 10
= 830

H	T	U	.	t
	8	3	.	0
8	3	0	.	

(b) 6.32 ÷ 0.01 = 6.32 × 100
= 632

H	T	U	.	t	h
		6	.	3	2
6	3	2	.		

Note
You don't need to draw the place value tables.
You can move the digits in your head.

 Now try these 8.4

① Work out these.
(a) 850 × 0.1
(b) 2500 × 0.1
(c) 165 × 0.1
(d) 9.23 × 0.1
(e) 2.1 × 0.1
(f) 3.7 × 0.1

② Work out these.
(a) 3800 × 0.01
(b) 640 × 0.01
(c) 100 × 0.01
(d) 6 × 0.01
(e) 4.32 × 0.01
(f) 6.9 × 0.01

③ Work out these.
(a) 1600 × 0.1
(b) 203 × 0.1
(c) 8.02 × 0.01
(d) 1350 × 0.01
(e) 3.11 × 0.1
(f) 500 000 × 0.01

④ Work out these.
(a) 16 ÷ 0.1
(b) 320 ÷ 0.1
(c) 3040 ÷ 0.1
(d) 35 000 ÷ 0.1
(e) 1000 ÷ 0.1
(f) 3.85 ÷ 0.1

Continued …

(5) Work out these.
(a) 25 ÷ 0.01   (b) 450 ÷ 0.01
(c) 705 ÷ 0.01   (d) 10 500 ÷ 0.01
(e) 360 ÷ 0.01   (f) 3.91 ÷ 0.01

(6) Work out these.
(a) 33 ÷ 0.1   (b) 76 ÷ 0.01
(c) 862 ÷ 0.01   (d) 23.19 ÷ 0.1
(e) 37.6 ÷ 0.01 (f) 49.83 ÷ 0.1

(7) (a) How many tenths are there in 72.6?
(b) How many hundredths are there in 5.9?
(c) How many tenths are there in 35?
(d) How many hundredths are there in 832?
(e) Multiply 2.6 by one tenth.
(f) Multiply 3286 by one hundredth.

---

(8) **Puzzle**

Copy and complete these calculations.

(a) 2.8 × ☐ = 0.28

(b) ☐ ÷ 0.1 = 46.8

(c) 52 ÷ ☐ = 5200

(d) ☐ × 0.01 = 0.657

(e) ☐ × 0.1 = 3

(f) 590 ÷ ☐ = 5900

(g) ☐ × 0.01 = 35.91

(h) ☐ ÷ 0.1 = 4

---

(9) **Brain strain**

Mohammed says

When you multiply 6 by another positive number you always get an answer that is greater than 6.

Give two examples to show that he is not correct.

(10) **Brain strain**

Alisha is dividing 30 by different numbers.

30 ÷ 10 = 3
30 ÷ 2 = 15
30 ÷ 6 = 5
30 ÷ 1 = 30

Mrs Crawford says

Can you get an answer that is more than 30?

Write down two examples that Alisha could use.

8.5 Multiplying by other decimals

The methods used in the previous section can help you to multiply by other decimals.

Example

Work out these.

(a) 6 × 0.03
(b) 3.2 × 0.8
(c) 0.7 × 0.06

Continued ...

Solution

(a) $6 \times 0.03 = 6 \times 3 \div 100$

> Write 0.03 as $3 \div 100$.
> Now you only have to deal with integers.

$\qquad = 18 \div 100$

$\qquad = 0.18$

(b) $3.2 \times 0.8 = 32 \div 10 \times 8 \div 10$

> It doesn't matter which order you multiply and divide in.

$\qquad = 32 \times 8 \div 10 \div 10$

> Dividing by 10 twice is the same as dividing by 100.

$\qquad = 256 \div 100$

> You may need to use the methods you know for multiplying integers too.
>
> $\quad\;\; 3\;\; 2$
> $\times \quad\;\; 8$
> $\overline{2\;\; 5\;\; 6}$
> $\quad\;\;\; 1$

$\qquad = 2.56$

(c) $0.7 \times 0.06 = 7 \div 10 \times 6 \div 100$

$\qquad = 7 \times 6 \div 10 \div 100$

$\qquad = 42 \div 1000$

> Dividing by 10 and then by 100 is the same as dividing by 1000.

$\qquad = 0.042$

Notice that the number of decimal places in the answer is the same
as the *total* number of decimal places in the question.

Now try these 8.5

① Work out these.
   (a) 19×0.3 **(b)** 68×0.2 **(c)** 37×0.9 **(d)** 138×0.4

② Work out these.
   (a) 64×0.02 **(b)** 82×0.08 **(c)** 156×0.06 **(d)** 2195×0.07

③ Work out these.
   (a) 0.2×0.4 **(b)** 0.7×0.6 **(c)** 0.8×0.9 **(d)** 0.4×0.7

④ Work out these.
   (a) 0.4×0.04 **(b)** 0.7×0.05 **(c)** 0.06×0.7 **(d)** 0.03×0.9

⑤ Work out these.
   (a) 6.3×0.4 **(b)** 4.6×0.9 **(c)** 5.2×0.05 **(d)** 8.3×0.02

⑥ Work out these.
   (a) 3.1×1.4 **(b)** 2.7×2.3 **(c)** 0.39×1.7 **(d)** 0.65×0.17

⑦ Work out these.
   (a) 4.36×0.18 **(b)** 4.47×6.9 **(c)** 32.8×0.37 **(d)** 2.1×1.62

Continued ...

8 Bananas cost £1.68 per kilogram.

Holly buys 2.4 kilograms.

How much does she pay?

9 Nathan buys 6.8 metres of material.

It costs £7.35 per metre.

How much does he pay?

10 Joe's weekly school bus pass costs £3.65.

Joe goes to school 39 weeks a year.

How much does he spend on travel to school each year?

11 A group of friends are going on holiday to Spain.

> Exchange Rate
>
> £1 = 1.24 euros

Work out how many euros each person takes.

(a) John changes £55 into euros.

(b) Connor changes £130 into euros.

(c) Molly changes £95 into euros.

12 Brain strain

Sarah spends £1.45 a day on her school lunch.

Sarah goes to school 39 weeks a year.

How much does she spend on school lunches each year?

8.6 Dividing by other decimals

When you need to divide by a decimal you use your knowledge of equivalent fractions.

A division can always be written as a fraction.

FOR EXAMPLE $3 \div 4 = \frac{3}{4}$

You know that $\frac{3}{4} = \frac{30}{40}$

$\times 10$

$\times 10$

This tells you that $3 \div 4$ is equivalent to $30 \div 40$.

This allows you to change a division involving decimals to one involving integers.

Example

Work out these.

(a) $6 \div 0.2$

(b) $1.2 \div 0.03$

(c) $5.6 \div 0.4$

Solution

(a) $6 \div 0.2$ can be written as $\frac{6}{0.2}$.

×10
$$\frac{6}{0.2} = \frac{60}{2}$$
×10

$= 60 \div 2$
$= 30$

(b) $1.2 \div 0.03$ can be written as $\frac{1.2}{0.03}$.

×100
$$\frac{1.2}{0.03} = \frac{120}{3}$$
×100

$= 120 \div 3$
$= 40$

(c) $5.6 \div 0.4$ can be written as $\frac{5.6}{0.4}$.

×10
$$\frac{5.6}{0.4} = \frac{56}{4}$$
×10

$= 56 \div 4$
$= 14$

$$\begin{array}{r} 1\,4 \\ 4\overline{)5^16} \end{array}$$

Now try these 8.6

1 Work out these.
- **(a)** $0.8 \div 0.2$
- **(b)** $4.5 \div 0.9$
- **(c)** $4.8 \div 0.6$
- **(d)** $2.8 \div 0.4$

2 Work out these.
- **(a)** $0.6 \div 0.03$
- **(b)** $0.8 \div 0.04$
- **(c)** $2.7 \div 0.03$
- **(d)** $0.54 \div 0.06$

3 Work out these.
- **(a)** $7.2 \div 0.6$
- **(b)** $16.6 \div 0.2$
- **(c)** $6.5 \div 0.5$
- **(d)** $10.5 \div 0.7$

4 Work out these.
- **(a)** $4.06 \div 0.07$
- **(b)** $1.84 \div 0.02$
- **(c)** $2.28 \div 0.03$
- **(d)** $9.54 \div 0.09$

5 Brain strain

Use the fact that $34 \times 17 = 578$ to match together these questions and answers.

$578 \div 17$	340
$57.8 \div 1.7$	
	34
$5.78 \div 1.7$	
$5.78 \div 0.17$	
	3.4
$578 \div 1.7$	
$57.8 \div 0.17$	0.34

Coming up ...

● multiplying using negative numbers
● dividing using negative numbers

Chapter starter

You will need:
2 dice
2 coins
9 counters
9 more counters of a different colour

Copy the grid on to squared paper, making the squares big enough to fit your counters.

12	0	5	⁻4	1	6
9	11	⁻1	⁻3	5	10
8	⁻3	7	3	⁻2	⁻5
⁻5	⁻12	⁻6	⁻4	0	⁻7
⁻11	1	4	⁻1	⁻8	2
4	3	⁻2	⁻9	2	⁻10

Play this game with a friend.

● Take it in turns to roll the dice and toss the coins.
   If the coin shows heads the number on the dice is positive.
   If the coin shows tails the number on the dice is negative.
● You can either add or subtract the numbers.

FOR EXAMPLE

This is ⁻3.

This is ⁺5.

So the score could be:

	⁻3 + ⁺5 = 2
or	⁺5 + ⁻3 = 2
or	⁻3 − ⁺5 = ⁻8
or	⁺5 − ⁻3 = 8

You can place a counter on either '2', '⁻8' or '8'.

● If you can't place your counter then you miss your turn.
● The winner is the first player to place four counters in a line.
   The line can be horizontal, vertical or diagonal.

Key words

positive number   product
negative number   divide
multiply   inverse operation

With a friend

Discuss these situations with a friend.

The discussions will help you with some of the ideas in the next section.

❶ The temperature of the purple liquid can be changed by either
  - adding or removing hot water in the red container
  - or adding or removing ice in the green container.

| Container for hot water | | | Container for ice |

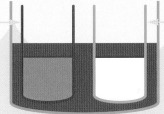

Copy and complete this table to show whether the temperature of the purple liquid will increase or decrease.

	... hot water	... ice
Add some ...		
Remove some ...		

❷ When you owe money it is called a **debt**.

When someone pays (or owes) you money it is called a **credit**.

Copy and complete this table to show whether the amount of money in Toby's bank account increases or decreases.

	... credit	... debt
Add ...		
Subtract ...		

❸ What patterns do you notice in the tables?

In this section you will learn how to multiply by negative numbers.

You know that 3 × 4 = 4 + 4 + 4 = 12. ◄─── Multiplication is repeated addition.

So when you multiply a positive number by a positive number the answer is also positive.

Toby owes three friends £2 each.

So Toby owes £6 altogether.

This can be written as $3 \times {}^-2 = {}^-2 + {}^-2 + {}^-2 = {}^-6$.

Continued ...

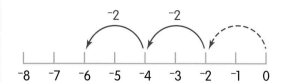

When you multiply a positive number by a negative number the answer is negative.

$^-4 \times 2$ is the same as $2 \times {}^-4$.

So $^-4 \times 2 = 2 \times {}^-4 = {}^-4 + {}^-4 = {}^-8$.

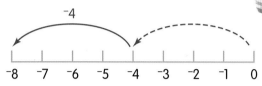

> **Remember**
> It doesn't matter which order you multiply in.

When you multiply a negative number by a positive number the answer is negative.

Now think about multiplying two negative numbers.

Look at this pattern.

$$3 \times {}^-4 = {}^-12$$
$$2 \times {}^-4 = {}^-8$$
$$1 \times {}^-4 = {}^-4$$
$$0 \times {}^-4 = 0$$

The answers increase by 4 each time.

The next line in the pattern will be $\quad {}^-1 \times {}^-4 = 4$
And then $\quad\quad\quad\quad\quad\quad\quad\quad {}^-2 \times {}^-4 = 8$

So when you multiply a negative number by a negative number the answer is positive.

The results can be put into a table like the ones in the With a friend activity.

×	Positive	Negative
Positive	Positive	Negative
Negative	Negative	Positive

Example

Work out these.

(a) $6 \times {}^-2$
(b) $^-4 \times {}^-5$

Solution

(a) $6 \times {}^-2 = {}^-12$

First ignore the signs and work out $6 \times 2 = 12$.
Then use the rules above to work out the sign of the answer.

(b) $^-4 \times {}^-5 = 20$

First ignore the signs and work out $4 \times 5 = 20$.
Then use the rules above to work out the sign of the answer.

1 Work out these.
(a) 5×3 (b) $5 \times {}^-3$
(c) ${}^-5 \times 3$ (d) ${}^-5 \times {}^-3$
(e) ${}^-1 \times 6$ (f) ${}^-4 \times {}^-2$
(g) ${}^-3 \times {}^-1$ (h) ${}^-2 \times {}^-9$
(i) ${}^-4 \times 3$ (j) $7 \times {}^-5$

Hint
When you multiply two numbers with
• the **same** signs the answer is positive.
• **different** signs the answer is negative.

2 Work out these.
The first one has been done for you.
(a) ${}^-2 \times 4 \times {}^-5 = {}^-8 \times {}^-5 = 40$
(b) $4 \times 2 \times {}^-3$
(c) $6 \times 5 \times {}^-2$
(d) ${}^-3 \times 4 \times {}^-2$
(e) $5 \times {}^-2 \times {}^-1$
(f) ${}^-6 \times {}^-3 \times {}^-10$

Remember
There is a key on your calculator $[{}_-]$ that allows you to input negative numbers.

3 Work out these.
(a) ${}^-56 \times {}^-19$
(b) $456 \times {}^-0.74$
(c) ${}^-23.5 \times 6.3$
(d) ${}^-11 \times 14 \times {}^-12$
(e) $42 \times {}^-22 \times 5$
(f) ${}^-1.2 \times {}^-3.5 \times {}^-2.2$

4 Use the fact that $26 \times 65 = 1690$
to write down the answers to these.
(a) ${}^-26 \times {}^-65$ (b) ${}^-26 \times 65$
(c) $26 \times {}^-65$ (d) ${}^-65 \times {}^-26$

5 Puzzle

In these number walls the number in each brick is the *product* of the two bricks underneath it.

Copy and complete the puzzles.

(a)

| ${}^-1$ | 4 | 2 | ${}^-5$ |

(b)

| ${}^-3$ | ${}^-3$ | 2 | ${}^-1$ |

(c)

| 2 | ${}^-3$ | 1 | 2 | ${}^-2$ |

6 Write down six different pairs of integers that multiply to make ${}^-12$.

Remember
An integer is a whole number.

7 Brain strain

Write down ten different pairs of integers that multiply to make ${}^-48$.

8 (a) Work out these.
    (i) $({}^-1)^2$ (ii) $({}^-2)^2$ (iii) $({}^-3)^2$
(b) Su Ling says

${}^-36$ is a square number because ${}^-6 \times {}^-6 = {}^-36$.

Is Su Ling right?
Is it possible for a square number to be negative?
Give a reason for your answer.

(c) Dan says

The square roots of 36 are 6 and ${}^-6$ because $6 \times 6 = 36$ and ${}^-6 \times {}^-6 = 36$.

Is Dan right?
Write down the square roots of these numbers.
(i) 49   (ii) 81   (iii) 100

Dividing by ⁻7 is the inverse operation of multiplying by ⁻7.

$$^-3 \times ^-7 = 21$$

multiply by ⁻7

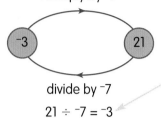

divide by ⁻7

$$21 \div ^-7 = ^-3$$

> When you divide a positive number by a negative number the answer is negative.

Dividing by 4 is the inverse operation of multiplying by 4.

$$^-5 \times 4 = ^-20$$

multiply by 4

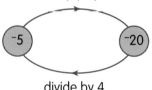

divide by 4

$$^-20 \div 4 = ^-5$$

> When you divide a negative number by a positive number the answer is negative.

Dividing by ⁻2 is the inverse operation of multiplying by ⁻2.

$$8 \times ^-2 = ^-16$$

multiply by ⁻2

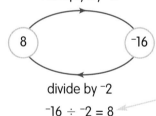

divide by ⁻2

$$^-16 \div ^-2 = 8$$

> When you divide a negative number by a negative number the answer is positive.

Example

Work out these.

(a) $14 \div ^-2$

(b) $^-12 \div ^-4$

Solution

(a) $14 \div ^-2 = ^-7$

> First ignore the signs and work out $14 \div 2 = 7$.
> Then use the rules above to work out the sign of the answer.

(b) $^-12 \div ^-4 = 3$

> First ignore the signs and work out $12 \div 4 = 3$.
> Then use the rules above to work out the sign of the answer.

① Work out these.
   (a) 15 ÷ 5   **(b)** 15 ÷ ⁻5   **(c)** ⁻15 ÷ 5   **(d)** ⁻15 ÷ ⁻5
   (e) 11 ÷ ⁻1   **(f)** ⁻8 ÷ ⁻4   **(g)** ⁻18 ÷ 3   **(h)** 24 ÷ ⁻6
   (i) 14 ÷ ⁻1   **(j)** ⁻42 ÷ 7   **(k)** ⁻64 ÷ ⁻8   **(l)** ⁻54 ÷ ⁻9

② Work out the value of these fractions.

   (a) $\frac{18}{-3}$ **(b)** $\frac{-12}{-6}$ **(c)** $\frac{-50}{5}$ **(d)** $\frac{-67}{-67}$ **(e)** $\frac{100}{-25}$

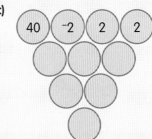

Remember
$\frac{18}{-3}$ means
18 ÷ ⁻3.

③ Work out these.
   (a) 6 × 5 ÷ ⁻2   **(b)** ⁻3 × 4 ÷ ⁻2   **(c)** 10 × ⁻5 ÷ ⁻2   **(d)** ⁻6 ÷ ⁻3 × ⁻8

④ Use the fact that ⁻448 ÷ 28 = ⁻16 to write down the answers to these calculations.
   (a) ⁻448 ÷ ⁻28   **(b)** 448 ÷ ⁻28   **(c)** ⁻16 × 28

⑤ **Puzzle**

In these puzzles each number is divided by the number on its right to get the number in the circle below.

Copy and complete the puzzles.

(a)

⁻32   ⁻8   4

(b)

⁻54   6   ⁻2

(c)

40   ⁻2   2   2

⑥ **Puzzle**

Copy and complete these multiplication tables.

(a)

×	⁻3		
	⁻18		
2		16	
		⁻8	⁻5

(b)

×	2			⁻4
		6		
⁻2		⁻6		
6			⁻6	
				4

10 Two-dimensional shapes

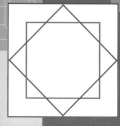

Coming up ...

● symmetry of shapes
● properties of triangles and quadrilaterals
● solving problems about triangles and quadrilaterals
● congruent shapes
● finding the midpoint of a line using coordinates

Chapter starter

This pattern is made from three squares.

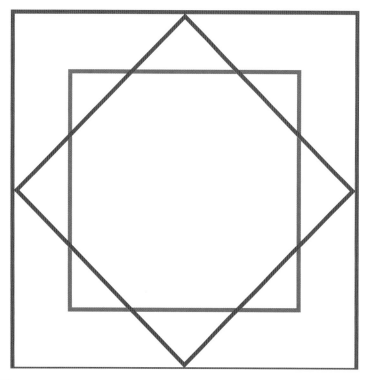

1 How many right-angled triangles can you find in the shape?

2 What other shapes can you find?

Do you remember?

● the properties of triangles and quadrilaterals
● how to recognise reflection and rotation symmetry
● how to recognise right angles
● that angles on a straight line add up to 180°
● that the angles in a triangle add up to 180°
● that angles at a point add up to 360°
● how to recognise parallel lines
● the properties of angles associated with parallel lines
● the meaning of congruent
● how to plot and read coordinates in all four quadrants
● how to find the mean
● how to divide a negative number by a positive number

Key words

reflection
symmetry
line of symmetry
axis of symmetry
mirror line
rotation
symmetry
triangle
equilateral
triangle
isosceles triangle
scalene triangle
right-angled
triangle
quadrilateral
scalene
quadrilateral

square
rectangle
parallelogram
rhombus
kite
trapezium
isosceles
trapezium
arrowhead
line of symmetry
bisect
diagonal
tessellation
congruent
midpoint
line segment

Some shapes have **reflection symmetry**.

This triangle has one **line of symmetry**.

You can check for reflection symmetry by tracing and seeing if you can fold the tracing so that one half fits exactly over the other half.

Note
A line of symmetry is sometimes called an **axis of symmetry** or a **mirror line**.

A parallelogram has **rotation symmetry** of order 2.

You can check for rotation symmetry by tracing and turning the tracing round to see if it fits exactly on top of the original drawing.

Look at the triangle again.

It only looks the same if you turn it through a full turn back to its original position.

It does not have rotation symmetry.

You say it has rotation symmetry of order 1.

Look at the parallelogram again.

You cannot fold it in half so that one half fits exactly over the other.

It has no lines of symmetry.

A rhombus has two lines of reflection symmetry and rotation symmetry of order 2.

A regular heptagon has seven sides.

It has seven lines of symmetry and rotation symmetry of order 7.

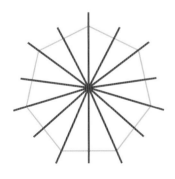

1. Copy these shapes.
   On your drawings, mark any lines of symmetry.
   Write down the order of rotation symmetry under each shape.

(a)

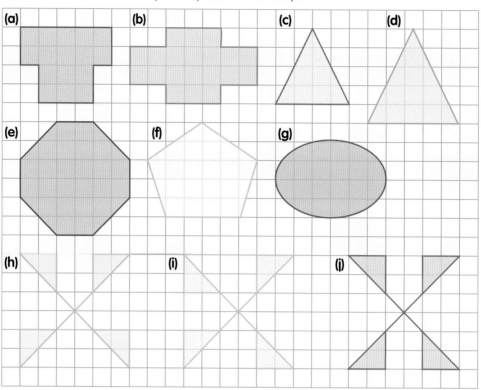

2. Copy these diagrams.
   Colour in three squares on each diagram to give it the symmetry stated.

(a)

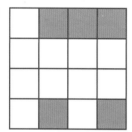

Two lines of reflection symmetry

Rotation symmetry of order 2

(b)

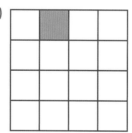

No lines of reflection symmetry

Rotation symmetry of order 4

(c)

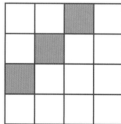
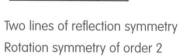

Two lines of reflection symmetry

Rotation symmetry of order 2

(d)

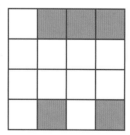

One line of reflection symmetry

Rotation symmetry of order 1

(e)

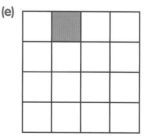

Two lines of reflection symmetry

Rotation symmetry of order 2

(f)

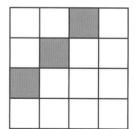

One line of reflection symmetry

Rotation symmetry of order 1

Continued...

Continued ...

10.2 Triangles and quadrilaterals

Look at triangle ABC.

- ● AC is a line of symmetry
- ● AC **bisects** BD, so BC and CD are equal.
- ● The two sides AB and AD are equal.
- ● Angle ACB and ACD are right angles, as they are equal and half of angle BCD, which is a straight line.
- ● The two angles ABC and ADC are equal.

A rhombus ABCD can be folded along the line AC and along the line BD to show that both diagonals are lines of symmetry.

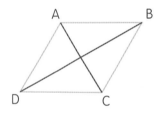

The rhombus can be folded along AC and then along BD without opening it to produce a right-angled triangle.

This tells you a number of things about rhombuses.

- ● All four sides of a rhombus are equal.
- ● The diagonals are both lines of symmetry.
- ● The diagonals bisect each other.
- ● The diagonals cross at right angles.
- ● The diagonals bisect the angles.

Investigation

Try folding other quadrilaterals to see what you can discover.

Copy the table on the next page.

Use your results to complete the table.

For each shape, include a diagram with the diagonals drawn in.

Write 'Yes' or 'No' in columns 2 to 4 and the correct number in the last two columns.

Shape	Diagonals are equal?	Diagonals bisect each other?	Diagonals cross at right angles?	Number of lines of symmetry	Order of rotation symmetry
Square					
Rectangle					
Parallelogram					
Rhombus					
Kite					
Isosceles trapezium					
Trapezium					
Arrowhead					
Scalene quadrilateral					

Now try these 10.2

① Cut a square into two identical pieces with one straight cut.
Here are three different ways.
Arrange the two pieces in a different way.
You must only put equal sides together and the shapes cannot overlap.

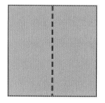  

So you can do this …   … but you cannot do this.

   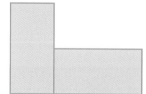

What different shapes can you make?

② You have two identical isosceles triangles.
Join the triangles by putting equal sides together.
What different shapes can you make?
Draw and name each one.

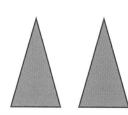

Continued …

③ Puzzle

For each group of four shapes, think of a fact which makes the **red** one the odd one out.
Give as many different reasons as you can.

For example: **Rectangle**, Rhombus, Square, Kite
Possible answers:
The rectangle is the only one whose diagonals do not cross at right angles.
The rectangle is the only one that does not have two equal sides next to each other.

(a) Rectangle, Parallelogram, **Square,** Trapezium
(b) Rectangle, **Triangle,** Square, Trapezium
(c) Rectangle, Parallelogram, Kite, **Trapezium**
(d) **Rectangle,** Parallelogram, Trapezium, Rhombus
(e) Equilateral triangle, Square, **Rectangle,** Rhombus.

④ How many different quadrilaterals can you make on a 3 by 3 pinboard?
Draw them all.
Label each one square, rectangle, parallelogram, rhombus, kite, trapezium,
arrowhead or scalene.

10.3 Solving problems

To solve a problem, you need to be able to explain how you got your answer.

Jordan says

I can make a
tessellation pattern
with any triangle.

Megan doesn't believe him.
He proves it like this.

'I draw a triangle – it can be any triangle – like this, for example.'

'Then I draw another one, exactly the same, and rotate it through 180°.
I attach it to the first one.'

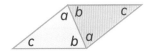

Continued ...

'I can make a row of triangles by repeating this pattern.

Each vertex has angles of $a + b + c$, which are the angles of the triangle, or 180°, so the top and bottom of my pattern are straight lines.'

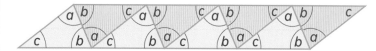

'So now I can put lots of rows together to complete my tessellation.'

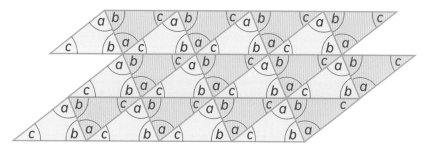

You should be able to see lots of vertically opposite angles, corresponding angles and alternate angles.

Now try these 10.3

1 Bethany draws a quadrilateral ABCD on her computer.

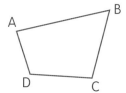

She copies the quadrilateral, rotates it through 180° and drags it next to the first one.

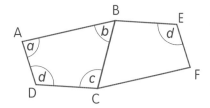

(a) Copy the diagram showing the two quadrilaterals.
Label the angles in the copied quadrilateral a, b and c.
(Angle d has been done for you.)
(b) What do you notice about angles ABC and BCF?
(c) What does this tell you about the lines AB and CF?

2 In the diagram, triangles ABC and BCD are isosceles triangles.

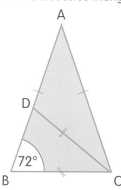

(a) Make a sketch of the diagram and calculate these angles.
Explain your reasoning.
(i) Angle BDC
(ii) Angle BCD
(iii) Angle BCA
(iv) Angle DCA
(v) Angle ADC
(vi) Angle DAC
(b) What can you say about triangle ADC?

Continued...

❸ Puzzle

This tessellation is made of regular octagons and squares.

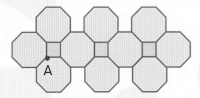

(a) Look at the vertex marked A.
Work out the size of each interior angle of a regular octagon.

(b) Now use this tessellation of equilateral triangles, squares and hexagons to work out the size of each interior angle of a regular hexagon.

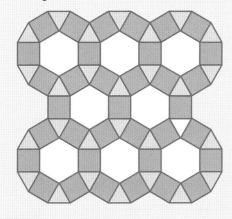

❹ Work out the size of the angles marked with letters in this diagram.
Explain how you worked them out.

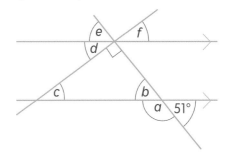

❺ Brain strain

An isosceles triangle has one angle which is 60° greater than the size of the two equal angles.

What is the size of each angle?

10.4 Congruent shapes

In Year 7 you learnt that **congruent** shapes are exactly the same shape and size.

ABCD is a parallelogram.

The diagonal AC divides the parallelogram into two triangles.

Triangles ACD and CAB look like congruent triangles but are they?

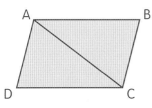 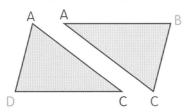

Think about the sides.

AD = BC   because opposite sides of a parallelogram are equal.
DC = AB   because opposite sides of a parallelogram are equal.
AC = AC   because it is the same line.

Continued ···

Think about the angles.

Angle ADC = Angle CBA   because opposite angles of a parallelogram are equal.

Angle DAC = Angle BCA   because they are alternate angles on parallel lines.

Angle DCA = Angle BAC   because they are alternate angles on parallel lines.

So the triangles have three pairs of equal sides and three pairs of equal angles.

If the sides are equal and the angles are equal then the shapes must be congruent.

Now try these 10.4

1. Match these triangles into pairs that are congruent.

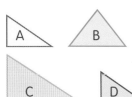

2. (a) In how many different ways can you divide a 4 by 3 pinboard into two congruent parts?
   One way is shown as an example.
   (b) What about a 4 by 4 pinboard?
   (c) How many ways can you divide a 4 by 4 pinboard into *four* congruent parts?
   One way is shown as an example.

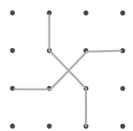

3 Puzzle

(a) Each of these shapes can be divided into two congruent parts.
    See if you can find out how.

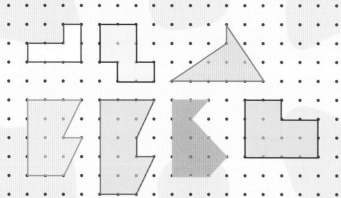

(b) Make up your own puzzle like the one above.
    Try to make up some easy ones and some difficult ones.
    Test them on a friend.

On the grid, AB is a straight line.

More properly it is called a **line segment**.

The line can be continued in both directions but you are only interested in the segment between the points A and B.

CD is also a straight line segment.

The point A is (1, 1) and the point B is (5, 3).

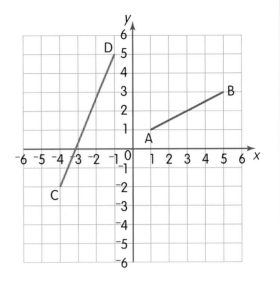

The point halfway along AB is called the **midpoint of AB**.

It is quite easy to see that it is (3, 2).

Look at the line segment AB more closely.

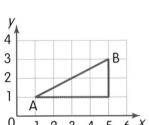

The red line shows that the x coordinate of the midpoint has to be halfway between 1 and 5.

To find the number halfway between 1 and 5, you find the mean.

Add them together and divide by 2.

(1 + 5) ÷ 2 = 3

The blue line shows that the y coordinate of the midpoint has to be halfway between 1 and 3.

(1 + 3) ÷ 2 = 2

So the midpoint is (3, 2).

Example

Find the midpoint of the line segment CD.

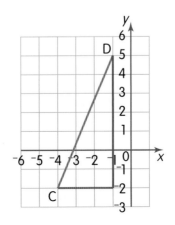

Continued...

Solution

The midpoint of a line segment is
(the mean of the *x* coordinates, the mean of the *y* coordinates).

The point C is (⁻4, ⁻2) and the point D is (⁻1, 5).

The mean of the *x* coordinates is (⁻4 + ⁻1) ÷ 2 = ⁻5 ÷ 2 = ⁻2.5.

The mean of the *y* coordinates is (⁻2 + 5) ÷ 2 = 3 ÷ 2 = 1.5.

So the midpoint of CD is (⁻2.5, 1.5).

Remember
When you divide a negative number by a positive number the result is a negative number.

Now try these 10.5

❶ Calculate the midpoint of each of the line segments, AB, CD and EF in the diagram.
Check that your answers are actually on the lines.

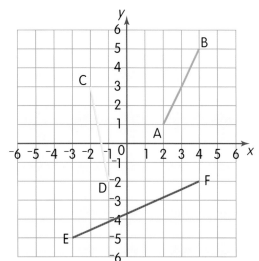

❷ M, N, P, Q and R are points on a grid.
M is (4, 1), N is (5, 5), P is (⁻2, 6), Q is (⁻1, 10) and R is (⁻7, 5).
Calculate the midpoints of these lines.

  (a) MN   **(b)** MQ   **(c)** NP
  (d) MR   **(e)** NQ

Now check your answers by drawing.

❸ Puzzle

The point (3, ⁻2) is halfway between the points (6, 1) and (0, ⁻5).

Find five more pairs of points that complete this sentence.

The point (3, ⁻2) is halfway between the points (□, □) and (□, □).

❹ Miles has messed up his homework.
Every answer is wrong!
Find his mistakes and work out the correct answers.

Homework
Find the midpoints of the lines joining each of these pairs of points.
(a) (3, 5) and (7, 9)
(b) (−2, 4) and (3, 4)
(c) (−5, 3) and (−2, −6)
(d) (1, 3) and (4, 2)

(a) (3 + 5) ÷ 2 = 8 ÷ 2 = 4
   (7 + 9) ÷ 2 = 16 ÷ 2 = 8
   Answer: (4, 8)

(b) (−2 + 3) ÷ 2 = −1 ÷ 2 = −0.5
   (4 + 4) ÷ 2 = 8 ÷ 2 = 4
   Answer: (−0.5, 4)

(c) (−5 + −2) ÷ 2 = −3 ÷ 2 = −1.5
   (3 + −6) ÷ 2 = −9 ÷ 2 = −4.5
   Answer: (−1.5, −4.5)

(d) (1 × 4) ÷ 2 = 4 ÷ 2 = 2
   (3 × 2) ÷ 2 = 6 ÷ 2 = 3
   Answer: (2, 3)

Continued ...

5 Say whether each statement is true or false. For the false statements, work out the correct answers.

(a) The midpoint of (3, 5) and (4, 2) is (3.5, 3.5).

(b) The midpoint of (2, 5) and (4, 6) is (3.5, 5).

(c) The midpoint of (⁻2, 4) and (4, 2) is (⁻1, 3).

(d) The midpoint of (⁻4, ⁻1) and (5, ⁻3) is (0.5, ⁻1).

6 Brain strain

Copy and complete these statements.

(a) (2, 5) is halfway between (0, 0) and (□, □).

(b) (2, ⁻5) is halfway between (⁻1, 2) and (□, □).

(c) (2, 5) is halfway between (⁻3, ⁻1) and (□, □).

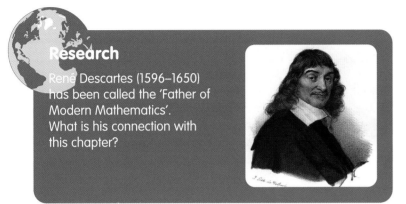

Research

René Descartes (1596–1650) has been called the 'Father of Modern Mathematics'. What is his connection with this chapter?

# 11 Transformations

Subject links
● art
● design and technology

Coming up ...

◗ transforming shapes by reflection, rotation and translation
◗ transforming shapes by combinations of reflections, rotations and translations

Do you remember?

● how to transform shapes by reflections, rotations and translations
● how to recognise and describe reflections, rotations and translations
● how to plot and read coordinates in all four quadrants

Chapter starter

Look at these tessellations. They are all made from the same shape.

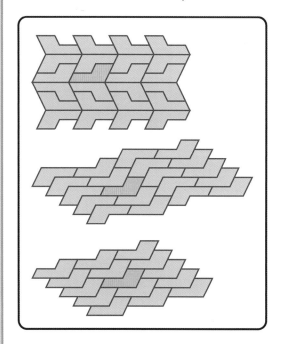

Imagine you were trying to describe them over the phone to a friend.

Your friend knows what the hexagon looks like that makes them, but does not know how they are fitted together.

1 How could you describe them so that your friend could draw them without seeing them?

2 What are the differences between the three tessellations?

Key words

centre of rotation
transformation
object
image
congruent
reflect
reflection
rotate
rotation
translate
translation

Remember
You can use tracing paper to help you draw and recognise transformations.

In Year 7 you learnt about **transformations**.

A transformation is a way of changing the position of a shape.

Reflection

A shape can be reflected.

The result is how it appears in a mirror.

In the diagram, flag A had been reflected in the line $x = 4$.

The image is flag B.

The flag appears to have been turned over.

The object and image are the same distance from the mirror line.

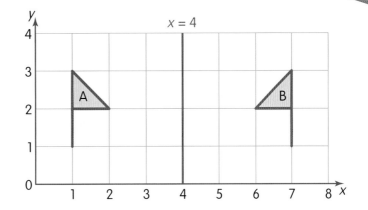

Rotation

A shape can be rotated.

The result is how it appears after being turned through a given angle.

In the diagram, flag A has been rotated through 90° anticlockwise about the point (0, 0).

The image is flag C.

It is as if flag A was drawn on a wheel with its centre at (0, 0) and the wheel is then turned 90° anticlockwise.

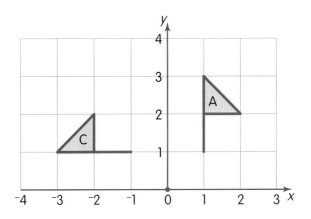

Translation

A shape can be translated.

The result is how it appears after a slide from one place to another.

In the diagram, flag A has been translated one square to the right and three squares down.

The image is flag D

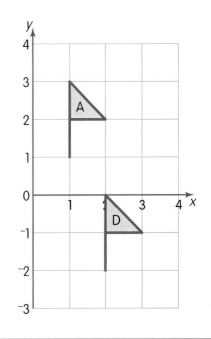

When you perform a reflection, a rotation or a translation, the object and the image are **congruent**.

You change the position of the object but not its size or shape.

1 Copy these shapes.
Reflect the shapes in the red mirror lines.

(a)

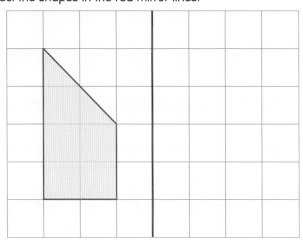

(b)

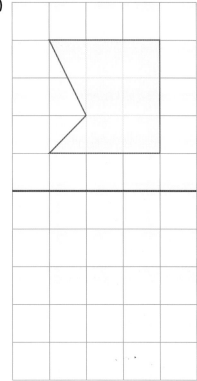

(c)

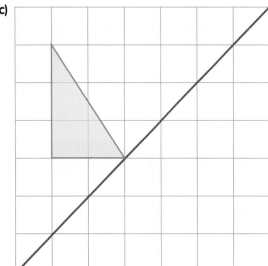

2 Copy these shapes.
Rotate the shapes about the centres of rotation, marked •, by the angles given.

(a) 90° anticlockwise

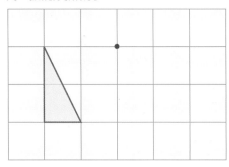

(b) 90° clockwise

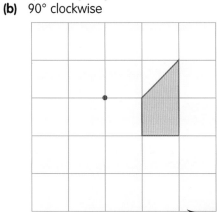

Continued ...

(c) 180° clockwise

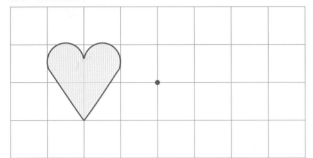

(d) 90° anticlockwise

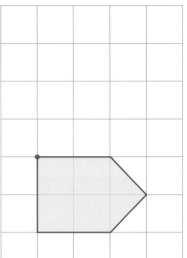

③ Puzzle

Something has fallen apart!

Follow the instructions to put it back together.

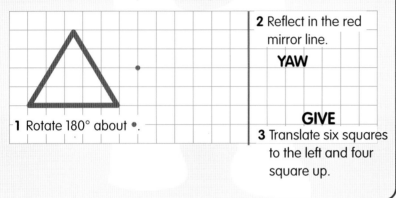

1 Rotate 180° about •.

2 Reflect in the red mirror line.

YAW

GIVE

3 Translate six squares to the left and four square up.

Investigation

Charlie says that rectangle A can be transformed into rectangle B with a reflection.
Ella says it is a rotation.

Lois says it is a translation.

Luke says they are all correct. It could be any one of these.

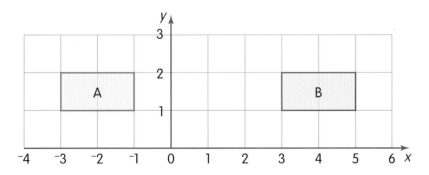

❶ Draw a transformation which could be a reflection or a rotation but not a translation.

❷ Investigate further.

In the diagram, flag A is reflected in the x axis on to flag B.

Flag B is then reflected in the y axis on to flag C.

The mirror lines are shown in red.

Flag A can be transformed into flag C directly by rotating it through 180° about the origin (0, 0).

Check this with tracing paper.

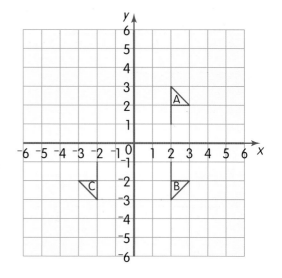

Now try these 11.2

1 (a) Copy this diagram.

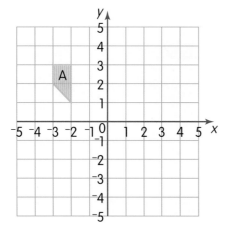

(b) Rotate trapezium A through 90° anticlockwise about the origin.
Label the image B.
(c) Rotate trapezium B through 180° anticlockwise about the origin.
Label the image C.
(d) What single transformation would transform trapezium A directly into trapezium C?

2 (a) Copy the diagram in question 1 again.
(b) Reflect trapezium A in the y axis.
Label the image B.
(c) Reflect trapezium B in the x axis.
Label the image C.
(d) What single transformation would transform trapezium A directly into trapezium C?

Continued ...

3 **(a)** Copy the diagram in question **1** again.
  (b) Translate trapezium A three squares to the right and one square up.
     Label the image B.
  (c) Rotate trapezium B through 90° clockwise about the point (2, 1).
     Label the image C.
  (d) What single transformation would transform trapezium A directly into trapezium C?

4 **(a)** Copy this diagram.

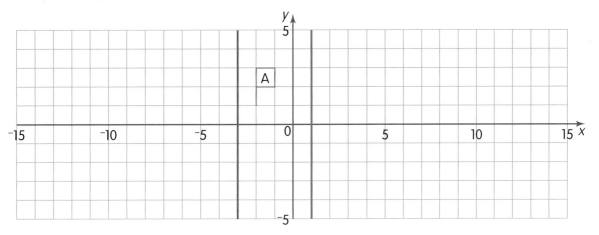

  (b) Reflect flag A in the red line, $x = ^-3$.
     Label the image B.
  (c) Reflect flag B in the green line, $x = 1$.
     Label the image C.
  (d) What translation transforms flag A directly into C?
  (e) How far apart are the lines $x = ^-3$ and $x = 1$?
  (f) Repeat the question with different vertical mirror lines.
     What is the connection between the translation of the flag A into flag C
     and the distance between the two vertical mirror lines?

5 **(a)** Copy this diagram.

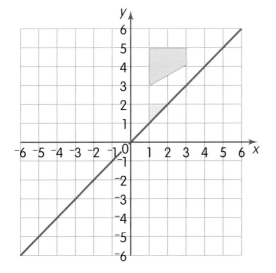

  (b) Reflect the shapes in the red line, $y = x$.
  (c) Reflect the complete pattern in the x axis.
  (d) Rotate the complete pattern through 180° about the origin.

6 Puzzle

Copy and complete the sentences below for this diagram.

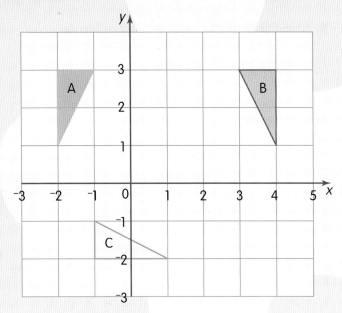

(a) Triangle A can be transformed into triangle B by a reflection in the *y* axis followed by a translation of

[　] squares [　　　　] and [　] squares [　　　　].

(b) Triangle A can be transformed into triangle C by a rotation through 90° anticlockwise about the origin

followed by a translation of [　] squares [　　　　] and [　] squares [　　　　].

(c) Triangle C can be transformed into triangle B by a rotation through 90° clockwise about the point (2, 0)

followed by a reflection in the line *x* = [　].

7 Brain strain

Look at the diagram in question **6** again.

Can you find the single transformation that transforms

(a) triangle A into triangle B
(b) triangle A into triangle C
(c) triangle C into triangle B?

12 Area

Subject links
- design and technology
- geography
- science

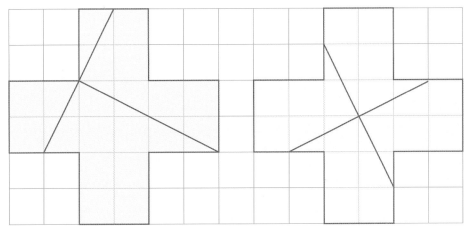

Coming up ...

- finding the area of a parallelogram, a triangle and a trapezium
- finding the area of compound shapes

Chapter starter

1. Copy these shapes on to squared paper.

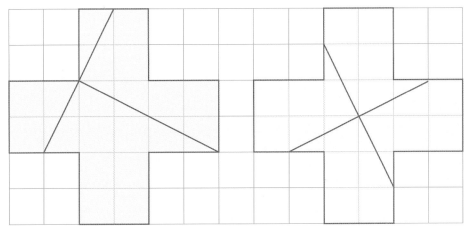

2. Cut each shape into four pieces along the lines.
3. Rearrange each set of four pieces to make a square.

Do you remember?

- how to find the area of a rectangle
- the meaning of congruent, perpendicular and parallel
- how to substitute numbers into a formula
- how to measure lines to the nearest millimetre
- how to convert between metric units
- about the order of operations

Key words

area
base
perpendicular height
centimetre (cm)
square centimetre (cm²)
parallelogram
triangle
trapezium
parallel
congruent
compound shape

The area of a shape is how much space it occupies.

You know that the area of a rectangle can be calculated by multiplying the length by the width, as this works out how many squares it takes to fill it.

This rectangle is 6 cm long and 4 cm wide.

Its area is length × width = 6 cm × 4 cm = 24 cm².

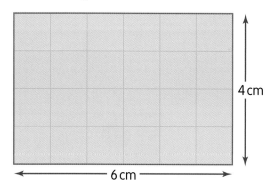

4 cm

6 cm

You can cut a triangle from one end of the rectangle and move it to the other end.

It makes a parallelogram but the area is unchanged.

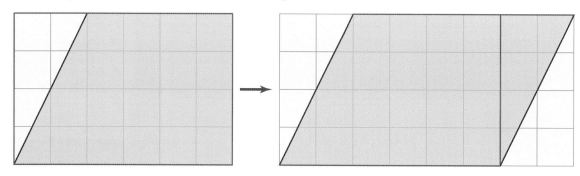

So the parallelogram has a base of 6 cm and a height of 4 cm.

It has an area of 24 cm².

This parallelogram is made from the same rectangle.

So it also has an area of 6 cm × 4 cm = 24 cm².

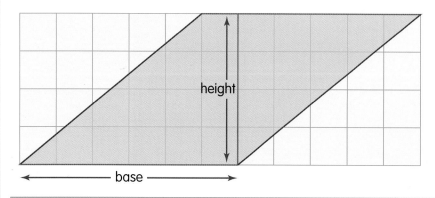

height

base

The length of the sloping side is not important when calculating the area. The lengths to be multiplied are perpendicular (or at right angles) to each other.

The area of a parallelogram = base × perpendicular height or *A = b × h*.

1. Calculate the area of these parallelograms.

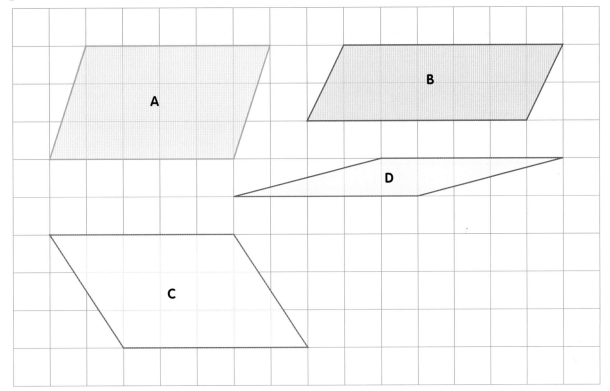

2. Calculate the area of these parallelograms.

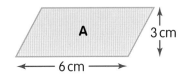 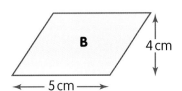 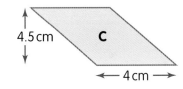

3. Calculate the area of these parallelograms.
   (a) Base = 8 cm, height = 6 cm
   (b) Base = 4.5 cm, height = 4 cm
   (c) Base = 5.4 cm, height = 4.7 cm

4. (a) Measure the base and height of this parallelogram.
   Use your measurements to calculate the area.
   (b) Robert thought the area was 25 cm².
   Explain his mistake.
   (c) Find the perimeter of the parallelogram.

Continued ...

⑤ Puzzle

A parallelogram has a base of 8 cm and an area of 56 cm².

What is the perpendicular height of the parallelogram?

⑥ Puzzle

Draw three different parallelograms with an area of 3 cm².

⑦ Puzzle

Two parallelograms, A and B, have the same area.

Parallelogram A is 2 cm longer than parallelogram B.

Parallelogram A is 8 cm long.

Parallelogram B has a height of 4 cm.

(a) How long is parallelogram B?
(b) What is the area of parallelogram B?
(c) What is the height of parallelogram A?

---

⑧ Tony is designing a logo.

He starts with two squares, one with sides of 4 cm and one with sides of 6 cm.

He colours the square in blue and the two parallelograms in red.

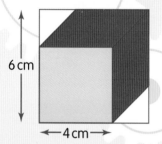

He then creates his logo to look like three cubes stuck together.

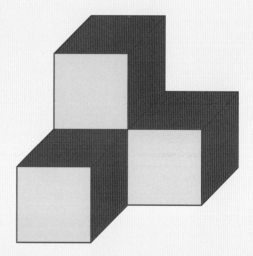

In the real, full size drawing of the three cubes, what area is red?

When a parallelogram is cut in half along a diagonal, it produces two congruent triangles.

You know that the formula for the area of the parallelogram is Area = $b \times h$.

The triangle is exactly half the parallelogram, so the formula for the area of a triangle is
Area = $b \times h \div 2$.

You can write

> **The area of a triangle = $\frac{1}{2}$ × base × perpendicular height or $A = \frac{1}{2}bh$.**

Continued ...

Even obtuse-angled triangles are half a parallelogram.

Two of these triangles …   … make this parallelogram

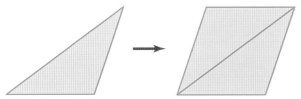

Note that the perpendicular height of an obtuse-angled triangle does not meet the base.

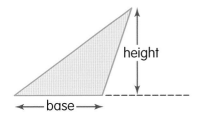

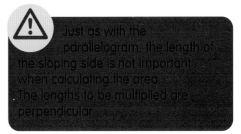

Just as with the parallelogram, the length of the sloping side is not important when calculating the area. The lengths to be multiplied are perpendicular.

Don't forget to divide by two when finding the area of a triangle!

Now try these 12.2

① Calculate the area of these triangles.

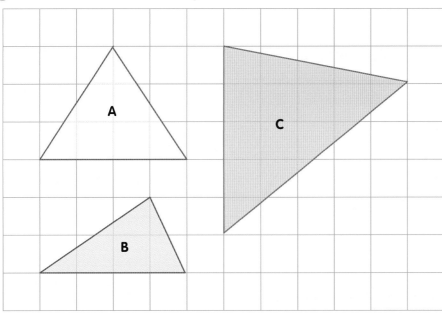

Continued …

2 Calculate the area of these triangles.

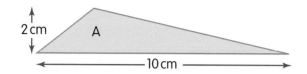

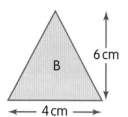

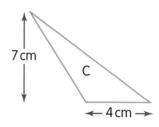

3 Take measurements from this triangle to calculate its perimeter and area.

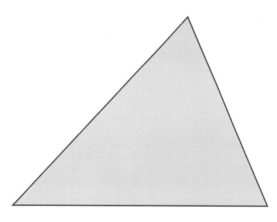

4 **(a)** Calculate the area of these triangles.
    (i) Triangle ACD
    (ii) Triangle ABD
    (iii) Triangle BDE
  (b) Check that your answers add up to the area of the parallelogram ABEC.

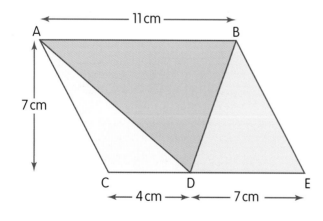

5 **Puzzle**

Split this rectangle into four triangles with areas of $5\,cm^2$, $6\,cm^2$, $9\,cm^2$ and $10\,cm^2$.

Hint
Use the dot!

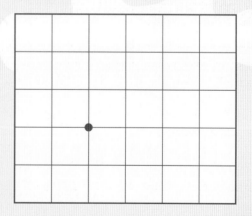

Continued ...

6 Lee is entering a sailing competition.
He wants to make a sail for his boat.

The rules of the competition are that the area of the sail must be no more than 6 m².

Lee's sail is a triangle.

He wants it to be 3 m high.

What length of base should he use?

7 In the picture, the triangle is painted on the road. It is 150 cm wide and 2 m tall.

(a) How wide is the triangle in metres?

(b) What is the area of the triangle in metres squared (m²)?

(c) What is the height of the triangle in centimetres?

(d) What is the area of the triangle in centimetres squared (cm²)?

With a friend

The pins on this 4 by 4 pinboard are 1 cm apart.

Use a pinboard or spotty paper to make a triangle with an area of 1 cm².

Draw the triangle.

Now your friend makes a different triangle with the same area.

(It must be a new shape, not just a reflection, rotation or translation of yours.)

Continue until neither of you can make any new triangles.

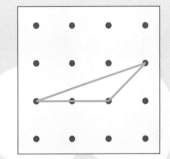

12.3 The area of a trapezium

In the same way that a parallelogram can be split into two congruent triangles, it can also be cut into two congruent trapeziums.

The length of the base of the parallelogram, $a + b$, is equal to the sum of the parallel sides of one of the trapeziums.

The area of the parallelogram is base × height or $(a + b) \times h$.

The area of each trapezium is half of that or $\frac{1}{2}(a + b)h$.

$\frac{1}{2}(a + b)$ is the average of the parallel sides, so you can write

Area of a trapezium = the average of the parallel sides × height or $\frac{1}{2}(a + b)h$.

1 Find the area of these trapeziums.

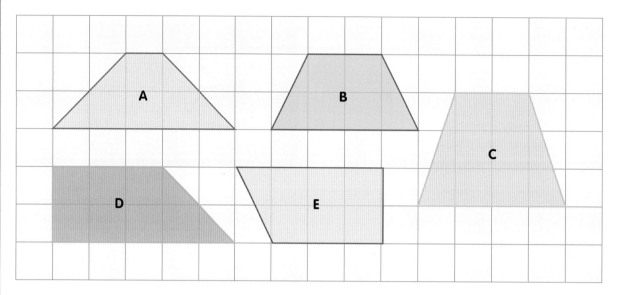

2 Find the area of these trapeziums.

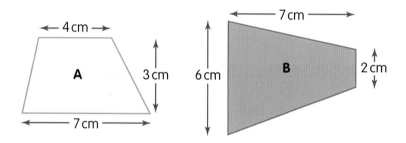

3 By taking appropriate measurements, find the perimeter and area of this trapezium.

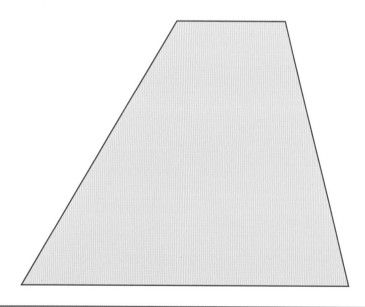

Continued...

④ Sally has a water feature in the shape of a trapezium.

Here is a sketch of it.

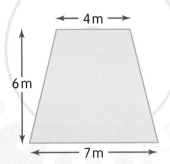

She wants to cover half of the surface with lily pads.

A lily pad has an area of about 0.25 m².

How many lily pads does she need?

⑤ Look at this picture frame.

It is made of four trapeziums.

The frame is a 40 cm square and the picture is a 20 cm square.

The height of each trapezium is 10 cm.

(a) What is the area of each trapezium?

(b) What is the total area of the frame?

---

⑥ **Puzzle**

Draw these shapes each with an area of 8 cm².

(a) A rectangle   **(b)** A parallelogram   **(c)** A triangle   **(d)** A trapezium

⑦ **Brain strain**

Draw a square with an area of 8 cm².

12.4 The area of compound shapes

A **compound shape** is made from two or more other shapes.

Here is an example.

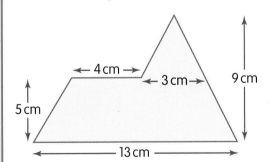

To find the area of a compound shape you must split it into ones whose area you can find, triangles, rectangles, parallelograms and trapeziums, and then add the areas together.

Example

Find the area of the shape above.

Continued ...

Solution

Split the shape into a triangle and a trapezium.

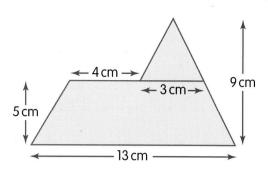

The triangle has a base of 3 cm.

It has a height of (9 cm − 5 cm) = 4 cm.

So the area of the triangle = base × height ÷ 2
$$= 3 \text{ cm} \times 4 \text{ cm} \div 2$$
$$= 6 \text{ cm}^2.$$

You must take care when reading the lengths of the shapes and calculating any missing lengths.

The length of the longer parallel side of the trapezium is 13 cm.

The length of the shorter parallel side of the trapezium is (3 cm + 4 cm) = 7 cm.

It has a height of 5 cm.

So the area of the trapezium $= \frac{1}{2}(a + b) \times h$
$$= \frac{1}{2}(7 + 13) \times 5$$
$$= 50 \text{ cm}^2.$$

The total area = 6 cm² + 50 cm² = 56 cm².

Now try these 12.4

1. Find the area of these shapes.

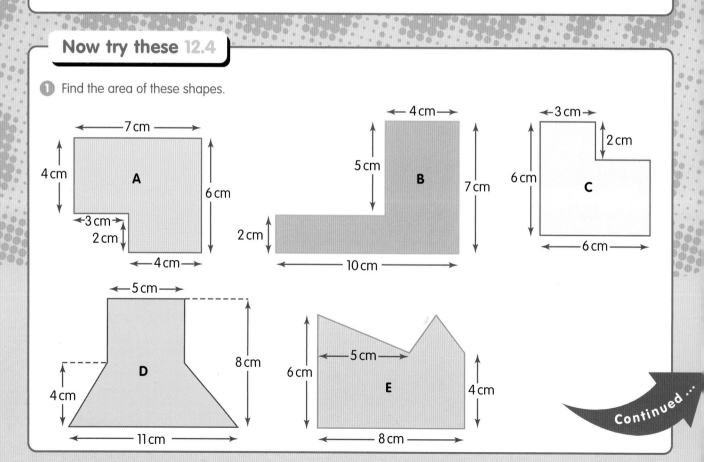

Continued ...

2 Find the perimeter of shape A in question **1**.

3 Fred wants to build a shed.

Here is a sketch of the end of the shed.

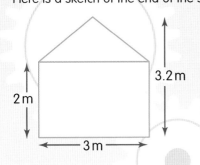

He needs to know how much timber to buy.

Calculate the area of the end of the shed.

4 The parallelogram BCED has an area of 24 cm².

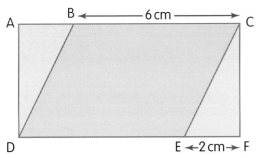

What is the area of the rectangle ACFD?

5 Look at this diagram.

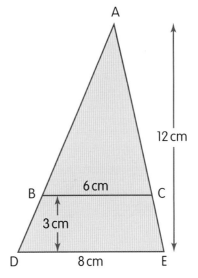

(a) Find the area of triangle ADE.
(b) Find the area of triangle ABC.
(c) Find the area of the trapezium BCED.
(d) Check that your answers to parts
    (b) and (c) add up to your answer to part (a).

6 **Puzzle**

The tangram is a Chinese puzzle dating back to 1813.

It consists of seven pieces.

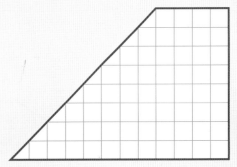

(a) Copy the tangram on to centimetre squared paper.

(b) Calculate the area of each of the seven pieces.

(c) Check that your answers to part (b) add up to 64 cm², the area of the square.

(d) Rearrange the pieces to make this trapezium.

(e) Check that this trapezium and the square you started with have the same area.

Continued ...

7 A tin lid is in the shape of a regular octagon.

The dimensions are shown in the diagram below.

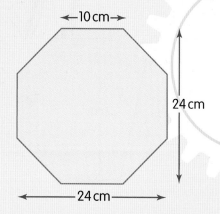

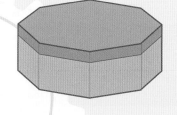

← 10 cm →

24 cm

← 24 cm →

Hint
The height of the trapeziums is not 10 cm.

Copy the diagram.

Split the octagon into a rectangle and two trapeziums.

Calculate the area of the tin lid.

Investigation

1 Use a pinboard or spotty paper.

Create a shape with just one pin inside it.

Count the number of pins on the perimeter.

In the example there are seven.

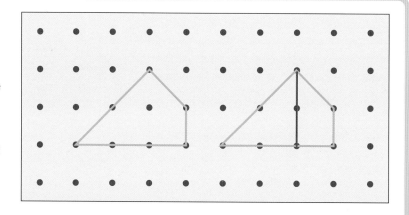

Calculate the area of the shape by splitting it into rectangles, triangles and trapeziums.

In the example, the shape has been split into a triangle and a trapezium.

Area of triangle = $2 \times 2 \div 2 = 2\,cm^2$

Area of trapezium = $(2 + 1) \div 2 \times 1 = 1.5\,cm^2$

Total area = $3.5\,cm^2$

2 Repeat for different shapes, making sure that there is only one pin inside the shape.

3 Find the rule connecting the number of pins on the perimeter and the area.

4 Investigate further.

13 Constructions and loci

Subject links
- design and technology
- geography

Coming up ...

- constructing a triangle given the length of all three sides (SSS)
- bisecting lines and angles
- constructing perpendiculars
- finding simple loci

Do you remember?

- how to measure and draw lines to the nearest millimetre
- how to use a protractor to draw and measure angles
- the properties of a rhombus
- the properties of special triangles
- how to construct a triangle given the length of a side and the size of two angles (ASA)
- how to construct a triangle given the length of two sides and the size of the angle between them (SAS)
- the meaning of perpendicular and parallel

Chapter starter

1 Use a pair of compasses to draw a circle.

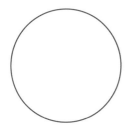

2 Put the point of your compasses on the circle and draw another circle, exactly the same size.

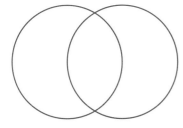

3 Use a point where the two circles cross as the centre of the next circle.

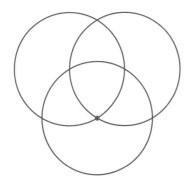

4 Continue in the same way around the original circle to make this pattern.

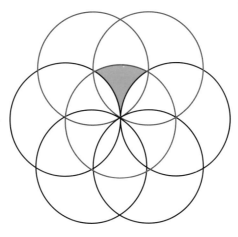

5 The blue section is inside three circles, which are coloured blue here to show you.

Colour your pattern using these rules.

- Sections inside just one circle: colour green.
- Sections inside two circles: colour red.
- Sections inside three circles: colour blue.
- Sections inside four circles: colour yellow.

Key words

construct	perpendicular
construction	bisect
compasses	bisector
straight edge	perpendicular bisector
triangle	
angle	rhombus
vertex (plural: vertices)	locus (plural: loci)
arc	

In Year 7 you learnt how to draw triangles when you are given two sides and the angle between them and when you are given two angles and the side between them.

What if you wanted to draw a triangle like this?

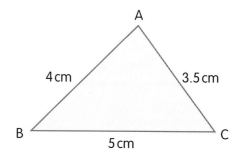

You might start by drawing a side BC of 5 cm.

But then, where do you draw the 4 cm side AB?

You do not know at what angle to draw the line AB.

It has to be 4 cm long but A also has to be 3.5 cm from C.

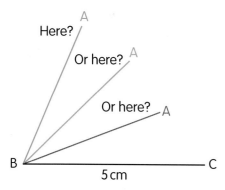

This is how to construct a triangle given the length of all three sides, the **side-side-side** case or **SSS** for short.

> **You will need**
> ruler
> compasses

❶ Draw the line BC 5 cm long. ← You will get the best result if you make the longest side the base.

❷ Then open your compasses so they are exactly 4 cm wide. Put the point on B and draw an arc.

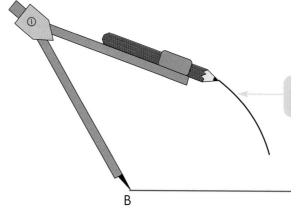

All points on the arc are 4 cm from B so the line AB has to go from B to some point on the arc.

Continued ···

3 Now open your compasses to 3.5 cm.
Draw an arc from C to cross the first arc.

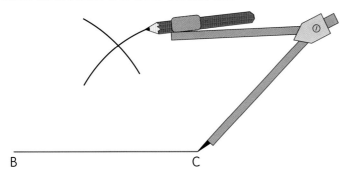

B   C

4 Draw lines from points B and C to point A to complete the triangle.

Note
Do not rub out your construction marks.

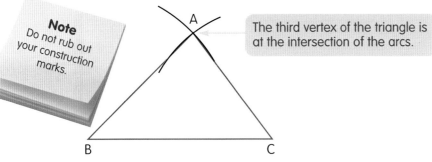

The third vertex of the triangle is at the intersection of the arcs.

B   C

Now try these 13.1

You will need
ruler
compasses

1 Make accurate drawings of these triangles.

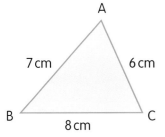

7 cm   A   6 cm

B   8 cm   C

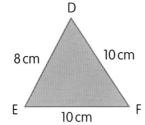

D

8 cm   10 cm

E   10 cm   F

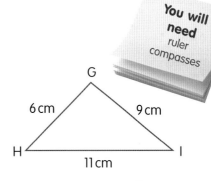

G

6 cm   9 cm

H   11 cm   I

2 **(a)** Construct an equilateral triangle with sides of 11 cm.
   (b) Construct an isosceles triangle with two sides of 8 cm and one side of 12 cm.

Hint
Draw a sketch first.

3 Puzzle

Try to construct a triangle with sides of 14 cm, 8 cm and 5 cm.

What happens?

Can you make up a rule about the lengths of sides of triangles?

Continued ...

4 Tony wants to make a wooden rhombus.

It needs to have sides of 8 cm and a short diagonal of 9 cm.

Draw a template for him like the one in the diagram.

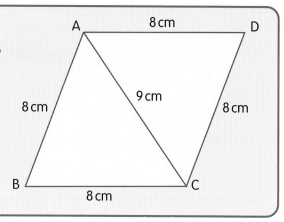

13.2 Constructing a perpendicular bisector

Ben, Lewis and Cara were playing a game.

In their game, Ben and Lewis had to be the same distance away from Cara.

Cara said, 'If I stand in the centre of the circle and you two boys stand on the circle, you will both be the same distance from me'.

The boys realised that they could move anywhere around the circle and they would always be the same distance from Cara.

> **Note**
> You could say the boys are **equidistant** from Cara.
> They are always the same distance from her.

After a while, Cara got bored just standing still at the centre of the circle.

She suggested that the boys stand still and she would move, but always staying the same distance from each of them.

The boys stood at the ends of a line and Cara moved forwards and backwards along the red path.

Continued ..

Cara realised that her path **bisected** the line between Ben and Lewis.

Her path and their line were **perpendicular**.

Her path is the **perpendicular bisector** of the line.

It divides the line into two equal lengths and is at right angles to it.

This is how to construct the perpendicular bisector of a line using just a straight edge and a pair of compasses.

1 Draw a line.

2 Open your compasses to more than half the length of the line.
Put the point of your compasses on one end of the line and draw two arcs, one on either side of the line.

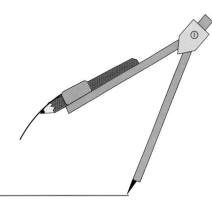

3 Keep your compasses open to the same distance.
Put the point of your compasses on the other end of the line.
Draw two more arcs to cut the first two.

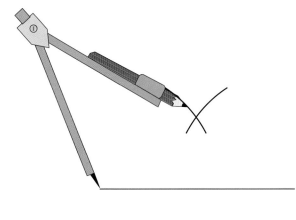

4 To draw the perpendicular bisector, join the points where the arcs cross.

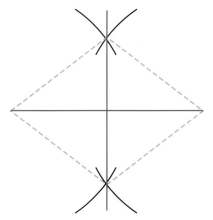

As you keep your compasses open to the same distance, the blue shape is a rhombus.
The diagonals of a rhombus bisect at right angles.

Continued...

With a friend

Draw a line 12 cm long.

Use a straight edge and a pair of compasses to construct the perpendicular bisector. Ask your friend to check your drawing by measuring.

The bisector should cut the line exactly at 6 cm and the lines should meet at right angles.

Now try these 13.2

You will need
straight edge
compasses
ruler

❶ Draw a large right-angled triangle.
Construct the perpendicular bisector of the shortest side.
Now construct the perpendicular bisector of the next shortest side.
Where do the perpendicular bisectors cross each other?

❷ Draw a large acute-angled triangle.
Construct the perpendicular bisector of each side.
If your constructions are accurate, all three perpendicular bisectors should cross at a point.
Use this point as the centre of a circle.
Draw the circle so that it just touches all three vertices of the triangle.

❸ Puzzle

What happens if you repeat question **2** with an obtuse-angled triangle?

❹ Brain strain

Draw a large circle.

Now draw a quadrilateral so that each vertex is on the circle.

Construct the perpendicular bisector of one of the sides.

What happens?

Construct the perpendicular bisectors of the other sides.

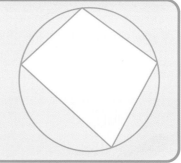

❺ Follow these instructions to construct an isosceles triangle with a base of 8 cm and a height of 10 cm.
  (a) Draw a horizontal line 8 cm long.
  Label it AB.
  (b) Draw the perpendicular bisector of AB and extend it to a point 10 cm above the line.
  (c) Join the end of the perpendicular bisector to A and B.

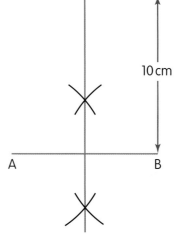

10 cm

A   B

Continued

6 A cabinet maker is making a chest of drawers.

The drawers are in rows of two.

She makes a rectangular base and needs to divide it exactly down the middle.

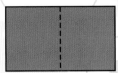

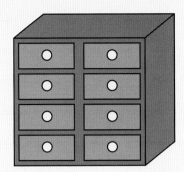

Draw a rectangle 14 cm long and 8 cm wide to represent the base.

Construct a perpendicular bisector of one of the long sides to mark in the dividing line.

ICT task

Use dynamic geometry software to draw a line.
Then draw two circles with the same radius using the ends of the line as the centres.
Draw two more pairs of circles from each end of the line.
What can you say about the points where the circles intersect?

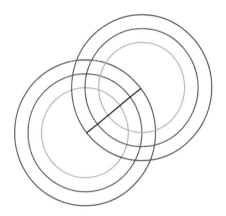

13.3 Other constructions

You will need
straight edge
compasses

Constructing an angle bisector

You can use another fact about the diagonals of a rhombus to bisect an angle.

1 Start with an angle you want to bisect.

Continued…

2 Put the point of your compasses on the vertex of the angle and draw arcs at equal distances along each line of the angle.

3 Keep your compasses open to the same distance. Draw intersecting arcs from where the first arcs cross the lines of the angle.

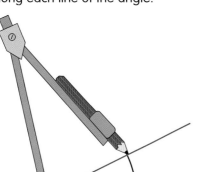

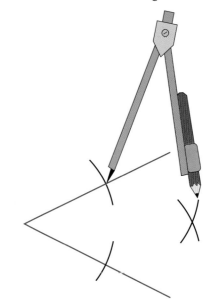

4 Finally, draw a line from the point of the angle through the intersection of the second set of arcs.

This is the **angle bisector**.

This construction works because the diagonal of a rhombus bisects the angle.
Can you see the imaginary rhombus?

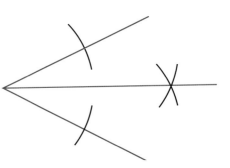

With a friend

Draw an acute angle.

Construct the bisector of the angle.

Ask your friend to measure your angle and check that your bisector really does cut it in half.

Constructing a perpendicular from a point to a line

The shortest distance from a point to a line is the perpendicular distance.

You draw a perpendicular line from a point to a line by drawing another imaginary rhombus.

1 Put the point of your compasses on the point, labelled A.
Draw two arcs crossing the line.

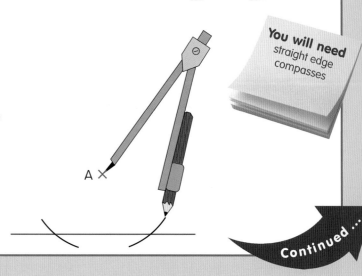

You will need
straight edge
compasses

Continued ...

2 Keep your compasses open to the same distance. From each point where the arcs cross the line, draw another arc.
Where these second two arcs cross is the fourth vertex of the imaginary rhombus.

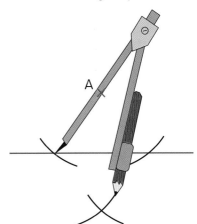

3 Finally, join the points on either side of the line to draw the perpendicular.

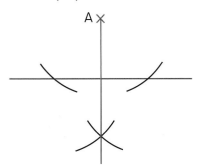

Constructing a perpendicular from a point on a line

This is a method of constructing a right angle at a point on a line.

Instead of drawing a rhombus, this time you use an imaginary isosceles triangle.

1 Put the point of your compasses on the point, labelled A.
Draw two arcs at equal distances on the line either side of A.

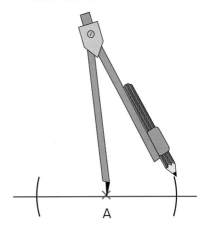

2 Open the compasses wider.
Put the point of your compasses where one of the arcs you have just drawn crosses the line.
Draw an arc.
Keep your compasses open to the same distance.
Repeat at the other arc on the line by drawing another arc on the same side of the line and crossing the one you have just drawn.

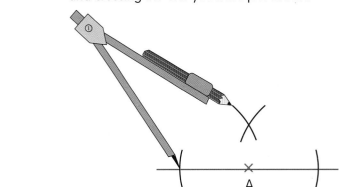

3 Join the point where the second set of arcs cross to the point on the line to draw the perpendicular.
Can you see the imaginary isosceles triangle?

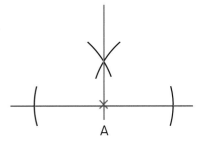

You will need
straight edge
compasses
ruler
protractor

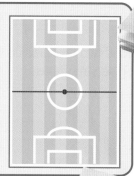

① Joe is making a miniature football stadium for his child's birthday.

He has painted the first touchline (one of the long sides) of the pitch, which is 10 cm long.

Draw a line 10 cm long and help Joe mark the halfway line by measuring halfway along the line, and then constructing a perpendicular at that point.

② Puzzle

(a) Make an accurate drawing of this triangle.
(b) Construct the bisector of angle BAC.
(c) Now construct the bisector of angle ACB.
(d) Find out what is special about the point where these two bisectors cross.

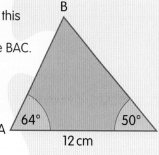

Do you remember?
This is an ASA triangle.
You have been given two angles and the side between them.
This is how to draw it.
• Draw AC 12 cm long.
• Measure and draw an angle of 64° at A.
• Now measure and draw an angle of 50° at C.
• B is at the point where the two lines meet.

③ (a) Make an accurate drawing of this triangle.
(b) Construct a perpendicular from A to BC.
(c) Measure the height of the perpendicular.
(d) Find the area of the triangle.

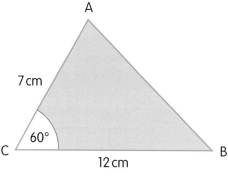

Do you remember?
This is an SAS triangle.
You have been given two sides and the angle between them.
This is how to draw it.
• Draw BC 12 cm long.
• Measure an angle of 60° at C.
• Draw the line AC 7 cm long.
• Join the points A and B to complete the triangle.

④ (a) Draw an isosceles triangle ABC so that AB = AC = 12 cm and angle BAC = 70°.
(b) Bisect angle BAC.
(c) Check by measuring that your angle bisector really does divide angle BAC into two angles of 35° each.
(d) Check by measuring that your angle bisector really does divide side BC into two equal parts.

Hint
Draw a sketch first.

⑤ (a) Construct an equilateral triangle ABC with sides of 11 cm.
(b) Construct the perpendicular from the vertex A to the line BC.
(c) Construct the perpendicular bisector of AC.
(d) Bisect angle ACB.

Note
The plural of locus is loci.

A **locus** is a path or route followed by a moving point.

Some loci can be seen.

FOR EXAMPLE The path of a paint brush is visible, as it leaves a trail of paint behind it.
A sparkler briefly leaves a light trail.

Other loci cannot be seen as they leave no trail.

FOR EXAMPLE The end of a pendulum leaves no trail.
A child's head as she goes down a slide leaves no trail.

Imagine a dog on a lead 2 metres long, running around a boy.

If the boy stands still and the dog pulls tight on the lead, the dog will run in a circle with a radius of 2 m.

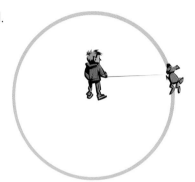

A group of girls are listening to music on a mobile phone.

They all sit so that they are 2 metres away from the phone.

They are sitting in a circle with a radius of 2 m.

Both of these examples describe a locus which is a circle with a radius of 2 m.

A locus can be thought of in two different ways: either as the path of a moving point (the dog) or a set of points (the girls).

Example

Draw the locus of points which are 2 cm away from a line 4 cm long.

Solution

Draw a line 4 cm long. ───────────

Draw some points 2 cm from the line and join them.

The red dotted line shows the locus of points 2 cm from the original line.

You will need
ruler
compasses
counters

1 (a) Follow this route on the map.

Start at A.

Go past the Town Hall.

At the end of the Town Hall, turn left.

Keep going until you come to the roundabout (R).

Turn right at the roundabout and then keep going.

Where do you end up?

(b) Charlie is standing at B looking towards the Sports Centre.

Write down a route to direct him from B to J.

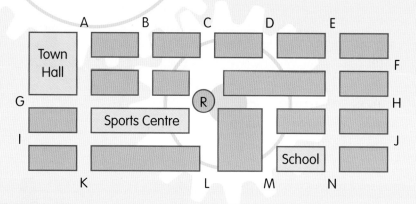

2 Mark a cross in the centre of a piece of paper.
Place some counters so that they are 10 cm away from the cross.
What shape do the counters make?

3 Draw a line AB 8 cm long.
Construct the perpendicular bisector of AB.
Choose any point on the perpendicular bisector.
Label it X.
Measure the distances XA and XB.
What do you notice?

Hint
Use your answer to question **3** to help you.

4 Mark two points, P and Q, 6 cm apart.
Draw the locus of points which are the same distance from P and Q.

5 The rules of football state that when a penalty is taken, all the players apart from the kicker and the goalkeeper must be

1 inside the field of play
2 outside the penalty area
3 behind the penalty mark

Look at the diagram of part of a football pitch.

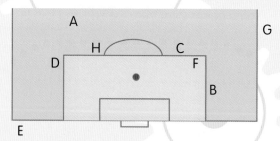

Which of the players, labelled A to H, are standing in the correct place?

For each of the others, say which rules they are breaking, rule 1, 2 or 3.

Continued ...

6 Draw a line AB 7 cm long.
Place some counters so that they are all exactly 5 cm from the line AB.
What shape do the counters make?

7 Brain strain

Draw two parallel lines 6 cm apart.

Label them AB and CD.

Place some counters so that they twice as far from AB as they are from CD.

What shape do the counters make?

ICT task

Adam Howell wrote his initials using Logo.

1 Use Logo to copy his initials.
Write down the instructions that you use.

2 Use Logo to write your own initials.
Write down the instructions that you use.

Subject links
- science

$$b + 2c + d$$

Coming up ...

- substituting numbers into an expression
- simplifying expressions by collecting like terms
- multiplying a single term over a bracket

Chapter starter

1 Look at this number wall.

The number in each brick is found by adding together the two bricks underneath it.

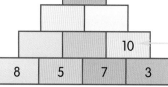

$7 + 3 = 10$

(a) Copy and complete the number wall.

(b) Rearrange the bottom row of bricks. What happens to the total in the top brick?

(c) Arrange the bottom row of bricks to give
(i) the greatest total   **(ii)** the smallest total

(d) Investigate for other numbers in the bottom row.

2 This algebra wall uses letter symbols for the numbers in the bottom row.

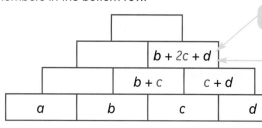

Remember $c + c = 2c$.

In each brick just write down how many lots of a, b, c, and d there are.

(a) Copy and complete the algebra wall.

(b) Investigate algebra walls with five bricks on the bottom row.

(c) Look at the expressions in the yellow bricks. What patterns do you notice?

(d) Investigate further.

Research

Find out about Pascal and Pascal's triangle. What similarities do you notice between the algebra walls in the Chapter starter and Pascal's triangle? Make a poster to show what you find.

Hint
The number in front of a letter symbol is called a **coefficient**. The coefficients of $1b + 2c + 1d$ are 1, 2, 1.

Do you remember?

- BIDMAS
- how to use algebraic notation
- how to substitute integers into simple expressions
- how to collect like terms
- the meaning of the words variable, term and expression
- what indices are and how to use them
- how to add/subtract and multiply/divide negative numbers

Key words

algebraic expression

substitute

evaluate

simplify

simplest form

like terms

brackets

expand

verify

An **algebraic expression** is an expression which contains letter terms (variables).

So $7 + 2 \times 5 - 3$ is an **expression**.

$3a + 2b - 7$ is an **algebraic expression**.

It contains 3 **terms**. ← '3a', '2b' and '7'

You learnt how to **substitute** positive integers into simple expressions in Year 7.

You can also substitute negative integers into expressions.

You use the same order of operations in algebra as you do when you are just working with numbers.

> **Remember**
> You can use the 'word' **BIDMAS** to help you remember the order of operations.
> **B**rackets first.
> Then **I**ndices.
> **D**ivision and **M**ultiplication next.
> And finally, **A**ddition and **S**ubtraction.

Example

Find the value of $3a + 2b$ when $a = 6$ and $b = {}^-5$.

Solution

When $a = 6$ and $b = {}^-5$

then $3a + 2b = 3 \times a + 2 \times b$ ← $3a$ means $3 \times a$ or 3 lots of a or $a + a + a$.

$\qquad = 3 \times 6 + 2 \times {}^-5$ ← Multiply first. Remember a negative number multiplied by a positive number gives a negative number.

$\qquad = 18 + {}^-10$

$\qquad = 8$

Remember that $a \times a$ can be written as a^2. ← You say 'a squared'

$3a^2$ means $3 \times a^2$ or 3 lots of a^2 or $a^2 + a^2 + a^2$.

You say '$3a$ squared'

> **Note**
> **Evaluate** means work out the value of.

Example

(a) Evaluate $4(8 + a)$ when $a = 2$.
(b) Evaluate $7 + 5a^2$ when $a = 3$.

Solution

(a) Substitute $a = 2$ into $4 \times (8 + a)$. ← Remember $4(8 + a)$ means 4 lots of '8 + a'

$\qquad = 4 \times (8 + 2)$ ← Work out the brackets first.

$\qquad = 4 \times 10$

$\qquad = 40$

(b) Substitute $a = 3$ into $7 + 5 \times a^2$ ← Write in the '×' sign.

$\qquad = 7 + 5 \times 3^2$

$\qquad = 7 + 5 \times 9$ ← A square is a power or an index. Work out the square first. 3^2 means 3×3.

$\qquad = 7 + 45$

$\qquad = 52$

Continued...

You don't need to use the '÷' sign when writing an expression.

Instead, '6 divided by x' or '$6 \div x$' is written as $\dfrac{6}{x}$.

Also 'n divided by 2' or 'half of n' is written as $\dfrac{n}{2}$.

Example

Evaluate $\dfrac{2n + 1}{n + 4}$ when $n = 3$.

Solution

Substitute $n = 3$ into $\dfrac{2n + 1}{n + 4}$

$$= \dfrac{2 \times 3 + 1}{3 + 4}$$

$$= \dfrac{6 + 1}{7}$$

Work out the 'top' and 'bottom' parts separately first.

$$= \dfrac{7}{7}$$

$$= 1$$

And then divide.

Now try these 14.1

1 Evaluate $5x^2$ when
   (a) $x = 1$
   (b) $x = 2$
   (c) $x = 3$.

2 When $y = 5$ evaluate these.
   (a) $2y + 5$
   (b) $7(2y + 5)$
   (c) y^2
   (d) $3y^2$
   (e) $y^2 + 4$
   (f) $40 - y^2$
   (g) y^3
   (h) $2y^3$
   (i) $5 + 4y^3$

3 **(a)** Evaluate these expressions when $n = 2$, $n = 3$ and $n = 4$.
   (i) $\dfrac{n}{n}$
   (ii) $\dfrac{2n}{n}$
   (iii) $\dfrac{3n}{n}$
   (b) What do you notice?
   (c) What does $\dfrac{4n}{n}$ equal?

4 Look at Chloe's maths homework.
What mistakes has she made?
What should the answers be?

> When $x = 3$ then
>
> (a) $4x^2 = 4 \times 3^2 = 12^2 = 144$ ✗
>
> (b) $10 - x^2 = 10 - 3^2 = 7^2 = 49$ ✗
>
> (c) $5(x - 2) = 5(3 - 2) = 15 - 2 = 13$ ✗

5 When $a = {}^-2$, $b = {}^-3$ and $c = {}^-4$ evaluate these.
   (a) $2a$
   (b) $a + b$
   (c) $5 + c$
   (d) ab
   (e) $c - b$
   (f) $4 + 3c$
   (g) $a(b - 2c)$
   (h) abc

6 Brain strain

Evaluate $\dfrac{a + b}{2a}$ when
   (a) $a = 3$ and $b = 9$
   (b) $a = 2$ and $b = 10$
   (c) $a = 1$ and $b = 7$
   (d) $a = 5$ and $b = 0$.

You can **simplify** an expression by combining **like terms.**

Like terms contain exactly the same letter symbols.

Example

Simplify $\quad a + 8b - 2a - 7b + 3a.$

Solution

Simplify $\quad a + 8b - 2a - 7b + 3a$ ← Collect like terms.
Keep the sign ('+' or '−') with the term that follows it.

$\quad\quad\quad = a - 2a + 3a + 8b - 7b$

$\quad\quad\quad = 2a + b$ ← Remember $1b$ is written as b.

You cannot simplify this any further because a and b are unlike terms.

$2a + b$ is the **simplest form**.

Example

Simplify $\quad 6x + 5 + 4y - 3 + 2y - 4x - 1.$

Solution

Simplify $\quad 6x + 5 + 4y - 3 + 2y - 4x - 1$ ← Collect together like letter terms and number terms.

$\quad\quad\quad = 6x - 4x + 4y + 2y + 5 - 3 - 1$

$\quad\quad\quad = 2x + 6y + 1$

Now try these 14.2

1 Simplify these.
(a) $4a - 3a + 2a - a$
(b) $10b + 5b - 4b$
(c) $7c - 3c - 3c$
(d) $8d - 6d + 2d - 4d$

2 Simplify these.
(a) $4e + 3 + 2e + 5$
(b) $6 + 3f - 4 - 2f + 1$
(c) $8g + 4 - 5g - 3 + 2g$
(d) $7h - 4h + 3 - 2h - 3$

3 Simplify these.
(a) $6s + 3t + 5t - 4s$
(b) $12u - 2v + 6u + 3v + 4v$
(c) $w + 2x + 3w + 4x + 5w$
(d) $6y + 8z - 4y + 3y - 5z - 3z$

4 (a) Work out the value of these expressions when $n = 5$, $n = 10$ and $n = 30$.

(i) $\dfrac{2n}{2}$ (ii) $\dfrac{4n}{2}$ (iii) $\dfrac{6n}{2}$

(b) Use your answers to help you simplify $\dfrac{10n}{2}$.

Continued ...

5 **(i)** Write down an expression for the perimeter of each of these shapes.
(ii) Simplify each of your expressions.

(a)

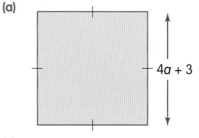

$4a + 3$

Remember
The marks on the sides tell you that they are equal length.

(b)

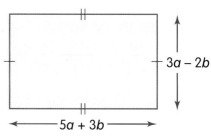

$3a - 2b$

$5a + 3b$

(c)

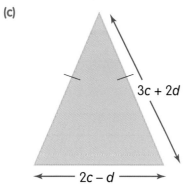

$3c + 2d$

$2c - d$

(d)

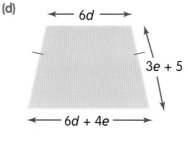

$6d$

$3e + 5$

$6d + 4e$

---

6 Brain strain

The expression in each brick is made by adding the expressions in the two bricks beneath it.

Work out the missing expressions.

(a)

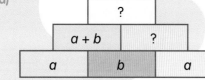

| ? |
| $a + b$ | ? |
| a | b | a |

(b)

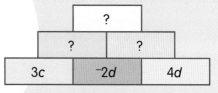

| ? |
| ? | ? |
| $3c$ | ^-2d | $4d$ |

(c)

| ? |
| $a - 2b$ | ? |
| a | ? | $4b$ |

(d)

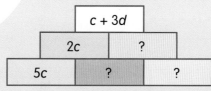

| $c + 3d$ |
| $2c$ | ? |
| $5c$ | ? | ? |

(e)

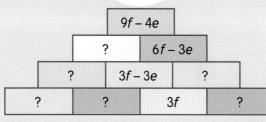

| $9f - 4e$ |
?	$6f - 3e$
?	$3f - 3e$	?
?	?	$3f$	?

Choose values for the letter terms and substitute them into each expression to verify that your answers are right.

7 Brain strain

Find an expression for the missing lengths in this shape.

Simplify each of your expressions.

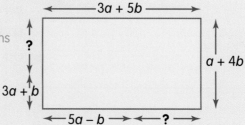

$3a + 5b$

?

$a + 4b$

$3a + b$

$5a - b$?

Remember that $3(4a - 7)$ means $3 \times (4a - 7)$.

You can write this expression without the bracket by multiplying each term inside the bracket by 3.

This is called **expanding**.

Example

Expand these.

(a) $3(4a - 7)$

(b) $t(s - u)$

Solution

(a) You can use the grid method that you met in Year 7.

×	$4a$	$^-7$
3	$3 \times 4a = 12a$	$3 \times {}^-7 = {}^-21$

$3(4a - 7) = 12a - 21$ ← Note that the sign is '−' because $3 \times {}^-7 = {}^-21$.

(b) You may like to use this arrow method instead.

$t(s - u) = t \times s + t \times {}^-u$

$\qquad\qquad = st - tu$ ← Note that the sign is '−' because $t \times {}^-u = {}^-tu$

Write st not ts.
When you write algebraic expressions, you write the letters in a term in alphabetical order.

When you simplify an expression you may have to expand some brackets first.

Example

Simplify $3(4x - 5) + 2(3 - x)$.

Remember
You can use the grid method if you prefer.

Solution

Deal with each bracket separately.

$3(4x - 5) = 3 \times 4x + 3 \times {}^-5$

$\qquad\qquad = 12x - 15$

$2(3 - x) = 2 \times 3 + 2 \times {}^-x$

$\qquad\quad = 6 - 2x$

Then add $12x - 15$ and $6 - 2x$.

$12x - 15 + 6 - 2x$

$= 12x - 2x - 15 + 6$

$= 10x - 9$

So $3(4x - 5) + 2(3 - x) = 10x - 9$

Continued ...

Check

When $x = 2$, $\quad 3(4x - 5) + 2(3 - x) = 3(4 \times 2 - 5) + 2(3 - 2)$

$$= 3(8 - 5) + 2 \times 1$$

$$= 3 \times 3 + 2$$

$$= 9 + 2$$

$$= 11$$

When $x = 2$, $\quad 10x - 9 = 10 \times 2 - 9$

$$= 20 - 9$$

$$= 11 \checkmark$$

Now try these 14.3

1 Write each of these using correct algebraic notation.
   (a) $a \times 3$ **(b)** ba **(c)** yzx
   (d) $4 \times 2 \times n$ **(e)** $5 \times t \times 3$ **(f)** $2 \times g \times 6 \times f$

2 Expand the brackets.
   (a) $4(2 + u)$ **(b)** $7(v - 3)$ **(c)** $3(1 - w)$
   (d) $8(3x + 4)$ **(e)** $2(5y - 7)$ **(f)** $6(1 - 4z)$

3 Expand the brackets.
   (a) $a(3 + b)$ **(b)** $x(y - 4)$ **(c)** $s(t - u)$
   (d) $n(5 - m)$ **(e)** $h(f + 2g)$ **(f)** $d(2c - 7)$

4 Simplify these expressions.
   (a) $2(a + 3) + 4(a + 7)$ **(b)** $3(b - 5) + 5(2b + 3)$
   (c) $7(2c + 1) + 3(4 - c)$ **(d)** $3(d - 2) + 2(4 - d)$

5 Brain strain

(a) Su Ling and Tom are simplifying $4(x + 3) - 2(x + 1)$.

The answer is $2x + 14$.

No – it is $2x + 10$.

Su Ling   Tom

   (i) Substitute $x = 2$ into each of the three expressions.
   (ii) Who has definitely got the wrong answer?
        Give a reason for your answer.
   (iii) Simplify $4(x + 3) - 2(x + 1)$.
         Are either of them right?
(b) Simplify these expressions.
   (i) $3(y + 2) - 2(y + 1)$ **(ii)** $5(3 + 2z) - 3(z + 4)$

Continued ...

⑥ Brain strain

Find an expression for the area of each of these shapes.

Write each expression in its simplest form.

(a)
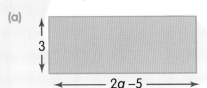

(b)
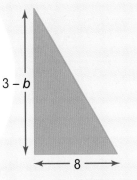

(c)
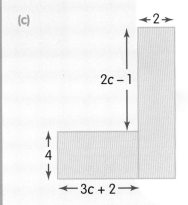

(d)
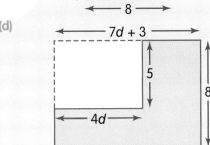

Can you find two different ways to work this one out?

⑦ Puzzle

Try this 'mind reading' puzzle.

Think of a number between 1 and 9 and add 3.
Multiply your answer by 5 and subtract 6.
Double your answer and add on any number between 1 and 9.
What is your answer?
Your numbers were ... and ... .

You can easily work out the numbers your friend has thought of by subtracting 18.

How does this help?

Why does this puzzle work?

Make up your own puzzle.

?	12	?
?	?	8
?	?	3

Coming up ...

representing functions as mapping diagrams and algebraically
finding the rule for a function machine

Chapter starter

Copy the function machines and fill in the missing numbers and rules.

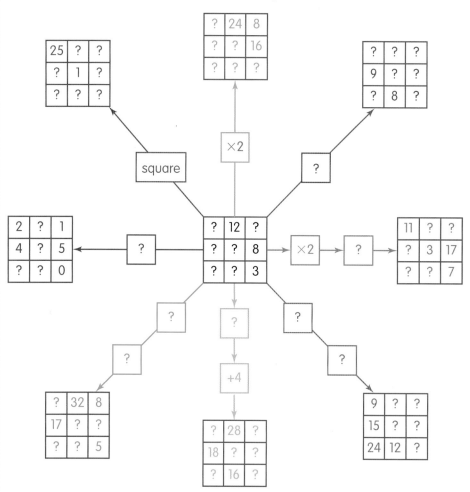

Do you remember?
- how to use function machines
- how to use algebraic notation
- how to substitute numbers into expressions
- how to find a rule for a sequence

Key words

function
function machine
input
output
linear function
mapping diagram
mapping

15.1 Functions and mapping diagrams

Look at this function machine.

input, x ⟶ [× 2] ⟶ [+ 1] ⟶ **output**

The **rule** can be written as a **function**.

> A function is a rule which turns one number (the input) into another number (the output).

$$x \to 2x + 1$$

So when $x = 4$ then $4 \to 2 \times 4 + 1$.

So $4 \to 9$.

> You say '4 maps to 9'.

You can make a table of values like this.

Input	x	0	1	2	3	4
Output	$x \to 2x + 1$	1	3	5	7	9

+2   +2   +2   +2

The outputs are increasing by the same amount each time. This tells you that $x \to 2x + 1$ is a **linear function**.

> Its graph will be a straight line. See Chapter 26 for more about this.

You can draw a **mapping diagram** to represent a function.

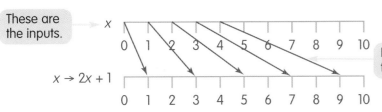

These are the inputs.

Draw an arrow to the output.

Note
The outputs are a linear sequence.

Now try these 15.1

1. For each of the following functions
   (i) copy and complete the rule

   $x \to$ [?]

   (ii) copy and complete the table of values

Input	x	0	1	2	3	4	5
Output	$x \to ?$						

   (iii) decide whether the function is linear, giving a reason for your answer.

   (a) input ⟶ [× 4] ⟶ [− 3] ⟶ output

   (b) input ⟶ [÷ 2] ⟶ [+ 2] ⟶ output

   (c) input ⟶ [× 3] ⟶ [− 6] ⟶ output

Continued...

2 Draw a mapping diagram for each of these functions.
Include at least five arrows on each of your mapping diagrams.

(a) $x \to x + 2$ (b) $x \to x - 2$ (c) $x \to x + 3$ (d) $x \to x - 1$

3 (a) Look at your mapping diagrams from question **2**.
What do you notice?

(b) Harry sketches a mapping diagram for the function $x \to x - 5$.

Is Harry right?
Give two reasons for your answer.

(c) Here is part of the mapping diagram for the function $x \to x + 4$.

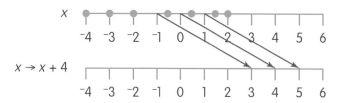

On a copy, draw arrows from the points marked ● to complete the mapping.

4 (a) Draw a mapping diagram for the function $x \to 2x$.
Include at least four arrows on your mapping diagram.

(b) Extend the arrows on your mapping diagram backwards as shown.

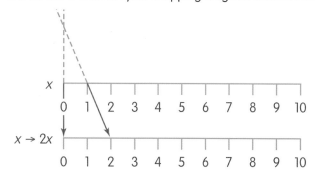

(c) Now draw a mapping diagram for the function $x \to 3x$.
Extend the arrows on your mapping diagram backwards.

(d) What do you notice?

5 Brain strain

Copy these mapping diagrams.
Draw arrows from the points marked ● to complete the diagrams.

(a)

Continued ...

(b)

$x \to 4x + 1$

(c)

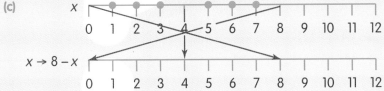

$x \to 8 - x$

❻ Brain strain

Draw a mapping diagram for each of these functions.

Include at least four arrows on each of your mapping diagrams.

(a) $x \to 2x + 3$ (b) $x \to 3x - 1$

ICT task

A function has the rule $x \to 6x - 3$.
Open a new spreadsheet to make a table of inputs and outputs for the function.
● Insert the headings and formulae as shown.

	A		
1	x	x → 6x – 3	Differences
	0	=6*A2-3	
3	=A2+0.5		=B3-B2

Remember, your spreadsheet will show the answer not the formula.

Remember to start each formula with '='.

● Copy the formulae in cells **A3**, **B2** and **C3** to the other cells in those columns.

Highlight the cell you want to copy. Click on the square at the bottom right of the cell and drag to highlight other cells in that column.

❶ What patterns do you notice?

❷ Change the formula in cell A3 to =A2-0.5.
Copy it down the column.
What happens?

❸ Change the entries in column A to produce
(i)   whole numbers
(ii) even numbers
(iii) odd numbers.
What patterns do you notice?

❹ Is the function linear?
How do you know?

❺ Choose your own functions and investigate further.

You can look at the differences between the outputs to help you work out the rule for a function machine.

> **Note**
> This is the same technique you used to find the rule for a sequence.

Example

Find the rule for this function machine.

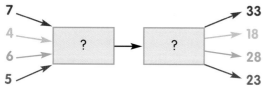

Write the rule as a **mapping**.

> **Note**
> A **mapping** is another name for a function. A mapping or function is written using algebra. The input and the output are separated by an arrow.

Solution

First put the inputs and outputs in order.

Inputs ... 4 5 6 7

Outputs ... 18 23 28 33

> The outputs are increasing by 5 so the rule is based on the 5 times table.

Differences: +5 +5 +5 +5

5 times table: ... 20, 25, 30, 35

> The first input is 4 so start the 5 times table at 4 × 5.

The rule for the 5 times table is $x \to 5x$.

Each output is 2 less than the 5 times table.

So the rule is $x \to 5x - 2$.

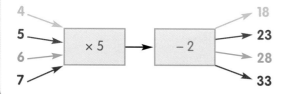

Check

$x = 4$: $5 \times 4 - 2 = 18$ ✓

$x = 5$: $5 \times 5 - 2 = 23$ ✓

$x = 6$: $5 \times 6 - 2 = 28$ ✓

$x = 7$: $5 \times 7 - 2 = 33$ ✓

Now try these 15.2

① Find the rule for each of these function machines.
Write each rule as a mapping.

(a)

(b)
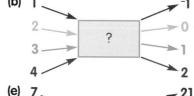

(c)
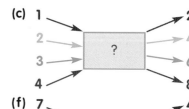

(d)
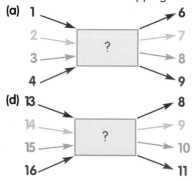

(e)
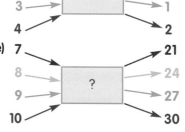

(f)
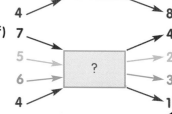

Continued ...

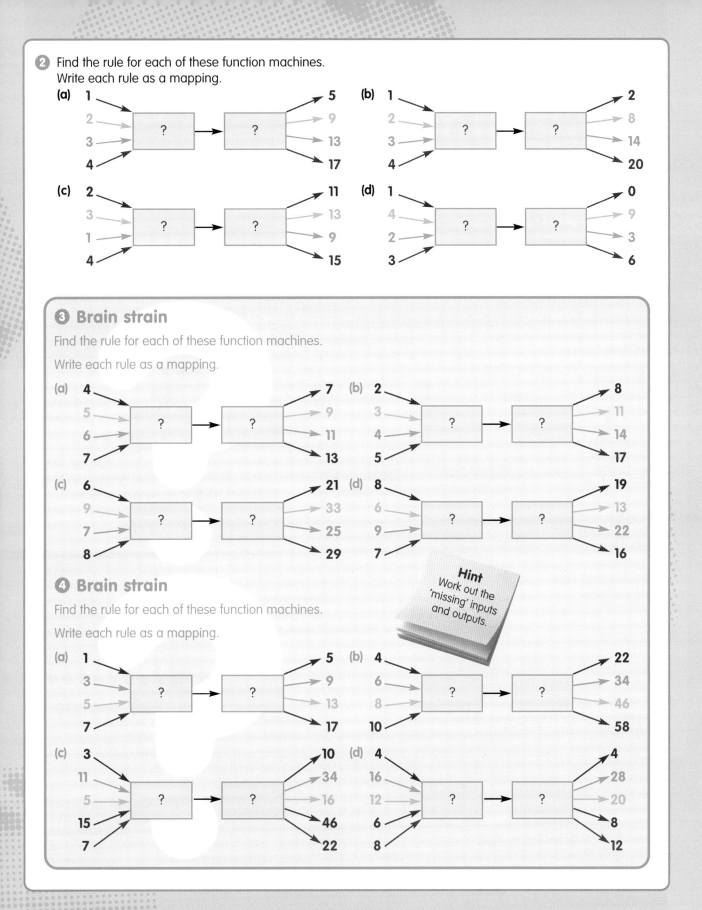

2 Find the rule for each of these function machines.
Write each rule as a mapping.

(a)
1 → ? → ? → 5
2 → → 9
3 → → 13
4 → → 17

(b)
1 → ? → ? → 2
2 → → 8
3 → → 14
4 → → 20

(c)
2 → ? → ? → 11
3 → → 13
1 → → 9
4 → → 15

(d)
1 → ? → ? → 0
4 → → 9
2 → → 3
3 → → 6

❸ Brain strain

Find the rule for each of these function machines.

Write each rule as a mapping.

(a)
4 → ? → ? → 7
5 → → 9
6 → → 11
7 → → 13

(b)
2 → ? → ? → 8
3 → → 11
4 → → 14
5 → → 17

(c)
6 → ? → ? → 21
9 → → 33
7 → → 25
8 → → 29

(d)
8 → ? → ? → 19
6 → → 13
9 → → 22
7 → → 16

❹ Brain strain

Find the rule for each of these function machines.

Write each rule as a mapping.

Hint
Work out the 'missing' inputs and outputs.

(a)
1 → ? → ? → 5
3 → → 9
5 → → 13
7 → → 17

(b)
4 → ? → ? → 22
6 → → 34
8 → → 46
10 → → 58

(c)
3 → ? → ? → 10
11 → → 34
5 → → 16
15 → → 46
7 → → 22

(d)
4 → ? → ? → 4
16 → → 28
12 → → 20
6 → → 8
8 → → 12

16 Scatter graphs

Coming up ...

- drawing scatter graphs
- interpreting scatter graphs

Chapter starter

1. Here is a list of ten maths questions.
   You have to answer them as quickly as possible.
   Ask a friend to time you.
   Then find out how many out of ten you got right.
   No calculators allowed!

(a) 47 + 74	**(b)** 106 − 47	**(c)** 36 × 4
(d) 245 ÷ 7	**(e)** 75% of 180	**(f)** $\frac{1}{2}$ of 85
(g) 1.2 − 0.88	**(h)** 2 + 3 × 4	**(i)** 5 × 4 × 3 × 2 × 1 × 0

2. Do you think that the people who got more right did the test more quickly than those who got fewer right?
   Give one reason why this might happen.
   Give one reason why this might not happen.

3. Look at the results for everyone in your class.
   Is there a pattern in the times and the scores?
   Does your score fit any pattern?

Do you remember?
- how to interpret two-way tables
- how to plot coordinates
- how to label axes and scales on graphs
- how to read scales on graphs

Key words
variable
scatter graph
scatter diagram

In the Chapter starter you collected two sets of data about the same situation.

The number of correct answers is one **variable** and the time taken to do the questions is the second variable.

Sam scored 6 out of 10 and it took him 450 seconds to do the questions.

You can plot the point (6, 450) to show Sam's data on a graph.

For each person you can plot a point on the graph.

You do not join up the points on this sort of graph.

The graph is called a **scatter graph** or **scatter diagram** because it shows you how the data is scattered about.

You can look for patterns in the data using a scatter graph, as you will see in the next section.

Example

There are ten babies under one year old in the village of Chittlesford.

The table shows the age in months and weight to the nearest kilogram of each baby.

Plot the data on a scatter graph.

Baby	A	B	C	D	E	F	G	H	I	J
Age (months)	3	11	8	6	3	4	10	7	5	1
Weight (kg)	6	10	9	8	7	6	11	5	7	4

Solution

Baby	A	B	C	D	E	F	G	H	I	J
Age (months)	3	11	8	6	3	4	10	7	5	1
Weight (kg)	6	10	9	8	7	6	11	5	7	4

There are ten babies so there will be ten coordinates to plot.

These are the x coordinates.

These are the y coordinates.

The first point to plot is (3, 6).

Continued...

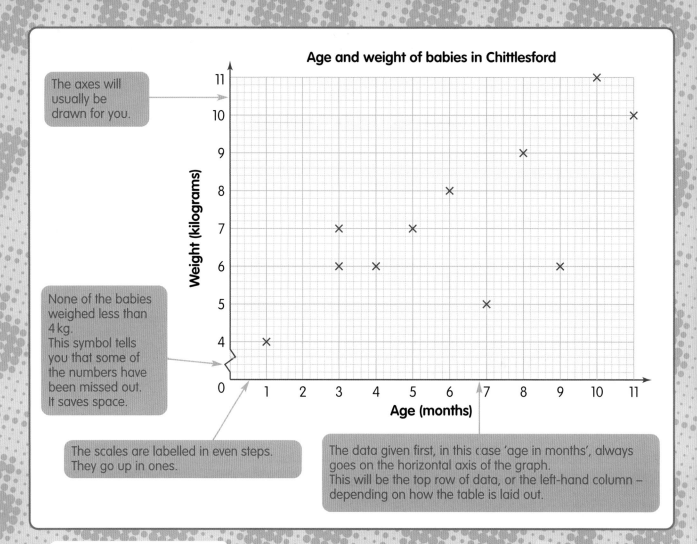

Age and weight of babies in Chittlesford

The axes will usually be drawn for you.

None of the babies weighed less than 4 kg.
This symbol tells you that some of the numbers have been missed out.
It saves space.

The scales are labelled in even steps. They go up in ones.

The data given first, in this case 'age in months', always goes on the horizontal axis of the graph.
This will be the top row of data, or the left-hand column – depending on how the table is laid out.

Now try these 16.1

Note
Keep your graphs safe because you will need them again later.

1. The table shows the number of points scored by the home team and the number of points scored by the away team in eight games of rugby.

Game	1	2	3	4	5	6	7	8
Home team points	21	14	36	8	32	23	18	16
Away team points	13	18	6	20	15	19	15	9

(a) The coordinate for game 1 is (21, 13). List the coordinates for each of the other seven games.

(b) Copy these axes. Plot the coordinates you listed in part (a) to draw a scatter graph of the data.

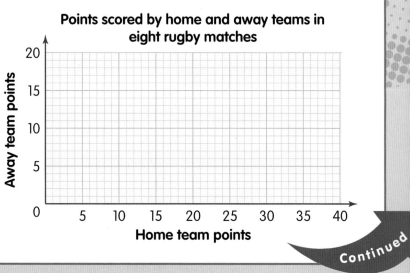

Points scored by home and away teams in eight rugby matches

Continued

② Alice recorded the number of ice creams she sold in her shop for 14 days.
She also noted the maximum temperature each day.

Day	Temperature (°C)	Number of ice creams sold
1	21	42
2	18	26
3	16	10
4	19	22
5	22	48
6	24	50
7	27	68
8	29	72
9	30	88
10	26	70
11	21	32
12	21	38
13	18	21
14	15	12

(a) List the coordinates you need to plot to draw a scatter graph.

(b) Copy these axes.
Plot the coordinates you listed in part (a) to draw a scatter graph of the data.

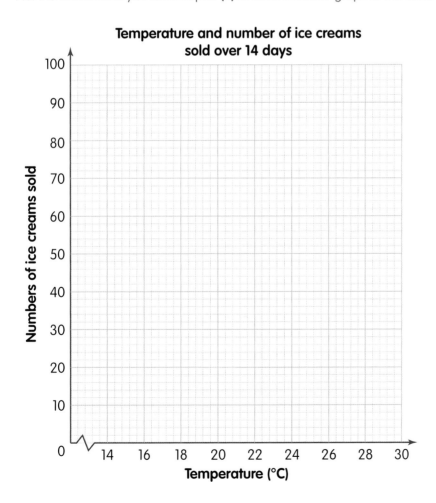

Temperature and number of ice creams sold over 14 days

Continued...

ICT task

Simon has recorded the shoe sizes and heights of eight boys in his class.
He records the data in an Excel spreadsheet.
You are going to use the Chart Wizard to create a scatter graph for this data.

	A	B	C	D	E	F	G	H	I
1	Shoe size	6	5.5	7.5	7	7	8.5	6.5	5
2	Height (cm)	128	131	148	140	155	137	143	120

1 Enter Simon's data in your own spreadsheet.

2 Select the data. ← Click on cell B1 and drag to select all the data cells.

3 Open the Chart Wizard. ← Open the 'Insert' menu and choose 'Chart...'

Step 1 On the 'Standard Types' tab, choose 'XY (Scatter)'.
Click on 'Next'.

Step 2 On the 'Series' tab, type a suitable title for the graph in the 'Name' box.
Click on 'Next'.

Step 3 On the 'Titles' tab, type suitable labels for the axis in the two 'Value' boxes.
Click on 'Next' ←

Step 4 Choose where you want to put your spreadsheet.
Click on 'Finish'.

Before you click on 'Next', you might want to go to the 'Legend' tab and uncheck the 'Show legend' tickbox.

16.2 Interpreting scatter graphs

A scatter graph can tell you whether there is a relationship between the two variables that have been plotted.

With a friend

Look back at the scatter graph on page 138.

You can see that the points make a pattern from the bottom left of the graph to the top right.

The scatter graph shows that as a baby's weight increases then its age increases.

Tom

No, the scatter graph shows that as a baby's age increases then its weight increases.

Alisha

Don't argue – you are both saying the same thing!

Megan

Continued

1 Who is right?
Explain your answer clearly.

Baby Jack is 7 months old and weighs 5 kg.

2 Think of a reason why his weight doesn't follow the same pattern as the other babies.

3 Look at the scatter graph carefully.
Write down a sensible estimate for the weight of a typical 7 month old baby.
Explain how you made your estimate.

Now try these 16.2

1 Look at the scatter graphs you drew for Now try these 16.1.
Decide which of these statements are true.
(a) **A**   A team that does well in a home match does badly in an away match.
 B   A team that does badly in a home match does badly in an away match.
 C   There is no pattern between how well a team does at home and how well it does away.
(b) **A**   When the temperature increases then the number of ice creams sold increases.
 B   When the number of ice creams sold increases then the temperature increases.
 C   Statements **A** and **B** both mean the same.
(c) Explain your answer to part **(b)** carefully.

2 Look at the following graphs.
Decide which graph (**A**, **B** or **C**) matches each of the following stories.

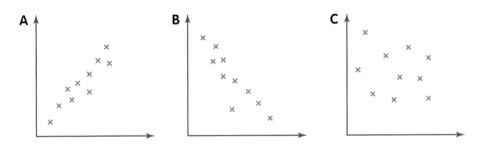

Graph ☐ shows cost of a car and age of car.

Graph ☐ shows IQ and height of secondary school pupils.

Graph ☐ shows the weight and length of killer whales.

Continued ...

3 This scatter graph shows the amount of time a group of 13-year-olds spent playing a video game and their high scores.

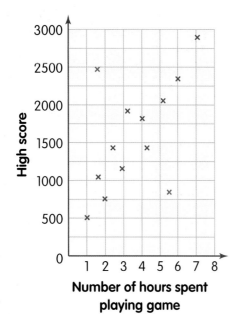

Number of hours spent playing game

(a) Copy and complete the sentence:
The more hours you spend playing a computer game the ....

(b) The points marked in green and red do not follow the pattern.
Give a reason for this.

17 Probability

Subject links
- PHSE
- geography
- science

21

Coming up ...

- finding the probability of an event not happening
- comparing experimental and theoretical probabilities
- recording all the outcomes of two events

Chapter starter

In each National Lottery draw there are balls numbered 1 to 49 spinning around a machine.

Six balls are chosen at random to give the winning numbers for a draw.

If you have three or more of the winning numbers you win a prize.

Over a long period of time all the numbers from 1 to 49 should be chosen about the same number of times.

Do you remember?
- how to calculate theoretical probabilities
- that an event that is certain has a probability of 1
- how to write one number as a fraction of another
- how to subtract fractions and decimals from 1
- how to estimate experimental probabilities
- how to order decimals
- how to round decimals to two decimal places
- what triangular numbers are
- what odd and even numbers are
- what square numbers are

① Use the internet or BBC Ceefax to get the winning numbers for draws for the previous
   (a) 2 months
   (b) 6 months
   (c) 1 year.

② How evenly do the numbers appear over each time period?

③ Do some numbers seem to appear more in a Wednesday draw than a Saturday draw?

④ Why do the numbers not all appear exactly the same number of times?

Key words
outcome

event

equally likely

probability

theoretical probability

experimental probability

relative frequency

estimate

trial

experiment

fair

biased

sample space diagram

random

In Year 7 you learnt that for situations such as rolling a dice, where the different possible outcomes are equally likely, you can calculate a probability.

FOR EXAMPLE   There is one way of rolling a 6 with an ordinary dice.

There are six equally likely outcomes.

So the probability of rolling a 6 is $\frac{1}{6}$.

Now look at the probability of the event 'rolling a 6' not happening.
You can either roll a 6 or not roll a 6.
There are no other possibilities.
So it is certain that the event will either happen or not happen.
Something that is certain has a probability of 1.

You can use this fact to work out the probability of an event not happening when you are given the probability of it happening.

FOR EXAMPLE   The probability of not rolling a 6 = 1 – the probability of rolling a 6

$$= 1 - \frac{1}{6}$$

$$= \frac{5}{6}$$

You can check this.
There are five outcomes that are not 6: 1, 2, 3, 4 and 5.
There are six equally likely outcomes.
So the probability of not rolling a 6 is $\frac{5}{6}$. ✔

As an event can either happen or not happen, the probabilities of it either happening or not happening are always going to add up to 1.
This is true even if the probability of the event is estimated from observed results rather than calculated.

Example

The probability that it will rain tomorrow is estimated to be 0.6.
Estimate the probability that it will *not* rain tomorrow.

Solution

The probability of an event not happening = 1 – the probability of it happening
The probability that it will not rain = 1 – 0.6
$$= 0.4$$

Now try these 17.1

1 A coin is tossed.
What is the probability of not getting a tail?

2 The probability it will snow on Christmas Day is 0.07.
What is the probability it will not snow on Christmas Day?

3 An ordinary fair dice is rolled.
(a) What is the probability of getting a triangular number?
(b) What is the probability of not getting a triangular number?

4 In a survey of Year 8 pupils, 89 out of 100 had their own email address.
Estimate the probability that a Year 8 pupil does *not* have their own email address.

5 Puzzle

A bag contains some numbered counters.
There are these counters.

There are also some counters with 5 on them.
The probability of not getting a 5 is $\frac{3}{7}$.
How many counters are there with a 5 on them?

6 Brain strain

The probability that United win a game is 0.57.

The probability that United draw a game is 0.30.

Work out the probability that United lose a game.

Investigation

Carry out a survey to estimate the probability that a Year 8 pupil does not have their own email address.

Collect your data with information about the gender of the pupils you ask so that you can also look for differences in the estimated probability for boys and girls.

17.2 Comparing experimental and theoretical probabilities

You learnt in Year 7 that you can estimate the probability of an event by doing an experiment or by looking at data already collected.

You use this formula.

The experimental probability of an event = $\dfrac{\text{the number of times the event happens}}{\text{the number of trials}}$

If you are estimating the probability of getting a 6 when you roll a dice, a **trial** is one roll of the dice.

Another name for the experimental probability of an event is the **relative frequency**.

The more trials you do in your experiment, the better your estimate of the probability is likely to be.

Continued ...

You can do experiments to test if coins, spinners or dice are fair or biased.

You compare the relative frequency of the event with its theoretical probability.

Example

Abby, Becky and Chloe are estimating the probability of a spinner landing on the number 1.

They suspect the spinner is biased.

The table shows how many spins each girl did and the number of times the outcome was 1.

Name	Number of spins	Number of times outcome was 1	Estimate of probability of landing on 1
Abby	12	3	0.25
Becky	100	17	
Chloe	50	12	

(a) Calculate the experimental probability of landing on 1 using
    (i) Becky's results
    (ii) Chloe's results.
(b) Abby says that her data proves the spinner is fair.
    Explain why she might be wrong.
(c) Which girl's data gives the best estimate of the probability of landing on 1?
    Explain your answer.
(d) Use the data to find the best possible estimate of the probability of landing on 1.
(e) Do you think the spinner is biased?
    Give reasons for your answer.

Solution

(a) (i) The estimated probability of an event $= \dfrac{\text{the number of times the event happens}}{\text{the number of trials}}$

    Estimated probability of the spinner landing on $1 = 17 \div 100$
    $= 0.17$

    (ii) The estimated probability of an event $= \dfrac{\text{the number of times the event happens}}{\text{the number of trials}}$

    Estimated probability of the spinner landing on $1 = 12 \div 50$
    $= 0.24$

(b) Abby's estimate is exactly the value of the theoretical probability of landing on 1 if the spinner was fair.
However, Abby has only spun the spinner 12 times.
This does not give enough data to draw reliable conclusions.

(c) Becky's data will give the best estimate as she has carried out the most spins.

Continued ...

(d) The best estimate is obtained by combining the data collected by all three girls.

In total 162 spins were carried out.

The spinner landed on 1 a total of 32 times.

The estimated probability of an event = $\dfrac{\text{the number of times the event happens}}{\text{the number of trials}}$

Estimated probability of the spinner landing on 1 = 32 ÷ 162

= 0.20 (to 2 decimal places)

(e) Altogether 162 spins were carried out.

This should give a reliable estimate of the probability.

The value of 0.20 is quite a long way from the theoretical probability of 0.25.

So the spinner might be biased, landing on 1 less often than expected.

Now try these 17.2

1 A fair coin is tossed and lands on heads five times in a row.

What is the probability of a head on the sixth toss?

2 Four boys are estimating the probability of getting a red ball out of a bag.

They each take one ball at random from the bag, note whether it is red and then return the ball to the bag.

The table shows their results.

Name	Number of trials	Number of times a red ball was obtained
Oliver	400	18
Richard	100	6
Nathan	60	3
Connor	80	5

(a) For each boy, work out the experimental probability of getting a red ball.

(b) Which boy's estimate is likely to be the best estimate of the actual probability of getting a red ball?

Explain your answer.

(c) Combine the data to get an even better estimate for this probability.

❸ Brain strain

Altogether there are 40 balls in the bag in question **2**.

Use your answer to part **(c)** of question **2** to estimate *how many* of these are red.

4 **(a)** A coin is tossed ten times and shows heads eight times.

Explain why this does not have to mean that the coin is biased.

(b) A coin is tossed 100 times and shows heads 80 times.

Explain why this almost certainly means that the coin is biased.

Investigation

How random are the phone numbers in a telephone directory?

You would probably expect the last digit of a telephone number to be equally likely to be 0, 1, 2, 3, 4, 5, 6, 7, 8 or 9, but is this true?

❶ Choose a page of telephone numbers at random and record the value of the last digit for ten numbers.

Comment on your result.

❷ Repeat part **1** until you have recorded data on 100 numbers.

Comment on your result.

❸ Do you expect the results to be different for the first digit of the numbers?

Explain your answer.

For one event it is usually fairly easy to list all the possible outcomes.

For example, when an ordinary dice is rolled the possible outcomes are 1, 2, 3, 4, 5 and 6.

It is more difficult when there are two things happening.

Example

Two ordinary dice, one red and one blue, are rolled.

(a) Find all the possible outcomes.
(b) Find the probability of rolling
    (i) a 4 on the red dice and a 3 on the blue dice
    (ii) a 4 and a 3.

Solution

(a) You can use a list.

1, 1	2, 1	3, 1	4, 1	5, 1	6, 1
1, 2	2, 2	3, 2	4, 2	5, 2	6, 2
1, 3	2, 3	3, 3	4, 3	5, 3	6, 3
1, 4	2, 4	3, 4	4, 4	5, 4	6, 4
1, 5	2, 5	3, 5	4, 5	5, 5	6, 5
1, 6	2, 6	3, 6	4, 6	5, 6	6, 6

Hint
Be systematic.
List things in a sensible order.

Or you can use a table.

Tables like this are called **sample space diagrams**.

Blue dice \ Red dice	1	2	3	4	5	6
1	✓	✓	✓	✓	✓	✓
2	✓	✓	✓	✓	✓	✓
3	✓	✓	✓	✓	✓	✓
4	✓	✓	✓	✓	✓	✓
5	✓	✓	✓	✓	✓	✓
6	✓	✓	✓	✓	✓	✓

(b) (i) Count the number of outcomes.
    There are 36 equally likely outcomes when two dice are rolled.
    The probability of any one outcome is $\frac{1}{36}$.
    So the probability of rolling a 4 on the red dice and a 3 on the blue dice is $\frac{1}{36}$.
    (ii) There are two ways to get a 4 and 3.
    You can get a 4 on the red dice and a 3 on the blue dice
    or you can get a 4 on the blue dice and a 3 on the red dice.
    So the probability of rolling a 4 and a 3 is $\frac{2}{36}$ or $\frac{1}{18}$.

Continued …

Sometimes you have to combine the result of two events.

For example, you may have to add the scores on two dice.

In this case, the different totals are *not* equally likely.

However, you can still use a list or table to find probabilities.

Example

Two dice are rolled and the scores are added together.

(a) Find all the possible totals.
(b) Find the probability of getting a total
    (i) of 2
    (ii) of 8
    (iii) which is an odd number
    (iv) which is a number below 10.

Solution

(a)

		First dice					
+		**1**	**2**	**3**	**4**	**5**	**6**
Second dice	**1**	2	3	4	5	6	7
	2	3	4	5	6	7	8
	3	4	5	6	7	8	9
	4	5	6	7	8	9	10
	5	6	7	8	9	10	11
	6	7	8	9	10	11	12

The possible totals are 2, 3, 4, 5, 6, 7, 8, 9, 10, 11 and 12.

(b) **(i)** Probability of getting a total of 2 $= \frac{1}{36}$

> There is just one way of getting a total of 2.
>
> There are 36 possible outcomes.

    (ii) Probability of getting a total of 8 $= \frac{5}{36}$

> There are five ways of getting a total of 8.

    (iii) Probability of getting a total which is an odd number $= \frac{18}{36}$

> There are 18 ways of getting a total which is an odd number.

$$= \frac{1}{2}$$

> It is good practice to give your answer in its lowest terms.

    (iv) Probability of getting a total which is a number below 10 $= \frac{30}{36}$

> There are 30 ways of getting a total less than 10.

$$= \frac{5}{6}$$

① Two coins are tossed.
   Use H to stand for heads and T to stand for tails.
   (a) List all the possible outcomes.
   (b) Use a table to show all the possible outcomes.
   (c) Find the probability of getting one head and one tail.

② For her lunch Lydia chooses a sandwich from cheese (C), ham (H) or
   tuna (T) and a piece of fruit from apple (A), banana (B) and orange (O).
   (a) Use the letters to make a list or table showing all the possible
       combinations of sandwich and fruit Lydia can have.
   (b) Lydia chooses her sandwich and fruit at random.
       Find the probability she has
       (i) a cheese sandwich and an orange
       (ii) a ham sandwich and not a banana
       (iii) a tuna sandwich.

③ Two four-sided dice, each numbered 1, 2, 3 and 4, are rolled.
   The two scores are added together.
   (a) Draw a table to show all the possible totals.
   (b) What is the probability of getting a total of 6?
   (c) What is the probability of getting a total which is a square number?
   (d) What is the probability of *not* getting a total of 4?

④ **Brain strain**

A restaurant offers five courses.

These are starter (S), sorbet (I), main course (M),
dessert (D) and cheese and biscuits (C).

As a special offer three courses can be bought for
£20.

(a) List all the possible sets of three courses.
(b) Explain why these sets of three courses are not
    equally likely to be chosen by a customer.

⑤ **Brain strain**

If a card is picked at random from a full pack there
are 52 possible outcomes.

Devise a short way of listing all 52.

With a friend

Three ordinary dice are rolled and the scores added.

① The totals cannot be shown in a simple table.
   Why not?

② How many different outcomes are there?

③ Discuss how a table can be designed to
   show all the possible outcomes when three
   dice are rolled.

Subject links
- PHSE
- design and technology

Coming up ...

- using equivalent fractions to order fractions
- adding and subtracting fractions
- multiplying an integer by a fraction
- finding a fraction of a quantity
- dividing an integer by a fraction

Do you remember?

- how to read and write fractions
- how to write one number as a fraction of another
- how to convert a fraction to a decimal
- how to find the factors of a number
- how to add, subtract, multiply and divide integers

Chapter starter

1 (a) Colour a copy of this rectangle so it is

$\frac{1}{3}$ red $\frac{1}{6}$ blue $\frac{1}{8}$ yellow.

(b) What fraction of the rectangle have you coloured altogether?

(c) What fraction is not coloured?

2 Find what fraction of these shapes is coloured

(i) red   **(ii)** blue   **(iii)** yellow.

(a)

(b)

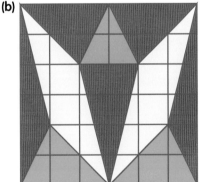

3 $\frac{1}{2}$, $\frac{1}{3}$, $\frac{1}{12}$ and $\frac{1}{15}$ are examples of unit fractions.

They are called unit fractions because they have a numerator of 1.
Make a copy of the rectangle in question **1**.
Colour the *whole* of the rectangle using unit fractions.
Use a different colour for each unit fraction.
You may not use any fraction more than once.
How many different answers can you find?

4 Draw your own rectangles.
Can you colour them using only unit fractions?
Investigate further.

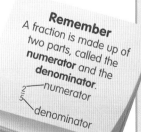

Remember
A fraction is made up of two parts, called the **numerator** and the **denominator**.

$\frac{2}{5}$ — numerator
— denominator

Key words

fraction

numerator

denominator

unit fraction

equivalent fraction

simplify

cancel

simplest form

lowest terms

common denominator

lowest common denominator

improper fraction

mixed number

integer

Remember a **fraction** is a number such as $\frac{4}{7}$ or $\frac{9}{5}$.

It is written as a **numerator** over a **denominator**.

You can show a fraction on a number line.

These number lines show different ways of writing 0.75 as a fraction.

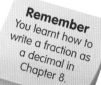

Remember
You learnt how to write a fraction as a decimal in Chapter 8.

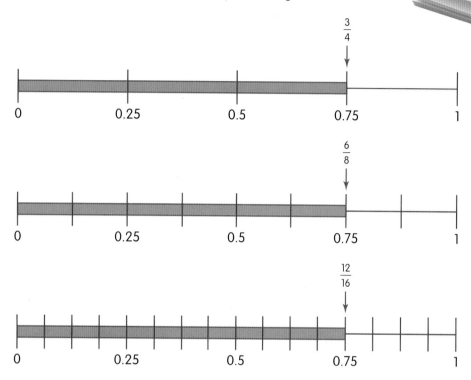

$\frac{3}{4}$, $\frac{6}{8}$ and $\frac{12}{16}$ all have the same value.

You say that they are **equivalent fractions**.

Equivalent fractions can be found by multiplying or dividing the numerator *and* denominator by the *same number*.

Here are some more fractions which are equivalent to $\frac{3}{4}$. ← They are all equal to 0.75.

$$\frac{3}{4} = \frac{15}{20} \quad \frac{3}{4} = \frac{75}{100} \quad \frac{36}{48} = \frac{3}{4}$$

×5   ×25   ÷12

Note
There are an infinite number of fractions equivalent to $\frac{3}{4}$.

You can **simplify** a fraction by dividing the numerator and denominator by the same number.

This is called **cancelling**.

When you find an equivalent fraction which uses the smallest possible numbers then the fraction is in its **simplest form** or **lowest terms**.

Continued…

Example

Simplify $\frac{72}{132}$.

Solution

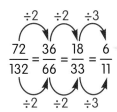

$$\frac{72}{132} = \frac{36}{66} = \frac{18}{33} = \frac{6}{11}$$

There is no number (other than 1) that divides exactly into both 6 and 11 so you stop here.

You can do this in one step.

$$\frac{72}{132} = \frac{6}{11}$$

(÷12)

You can compare fractions by writing them all with a **common denominator**.

Example

Write these fractions in order of size.

$\frac{3}{4}$ $\frac{1}{2}$ $\frac{7}{12}$ $\frac{2}{3}$

Write the smallest fraction first.

Solution

Look at the denominators.

2, 3, 4 and 12 are all factors of 12.

So you can write them all with a denominator of 12.

$$\frac{3}{4} = \frac{9}{12} \quad\quad \frac{1}{2} = \frac{6}{12} \quad\quad \frac{7}{12} \quad\quad \frac{2}{3} = \frac{8}{12}$$

(×3)   (×6)   (×4)

In order of size, they are

$\frac{6}{12}$	$\frac{7}{12}$	$\frac{8}{12}$	$\frac{9}{12}$
↓	↓	↓	↓
$\frac{1}{2}$	$\frac{7}{12}$	$\frac{2}{3}$	$\frac{3}{4}$.

Write the fractions as they appear in the question.

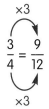

Continued ...

Fractions can be used to show numbers which are greater than 1.

This shows $\frac{9}{5}$.

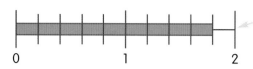

There are 5 fifths in a whole one.

This shows $\frac{8}{3}$.

There are 3 thirds in a whole one.
6 thirds make two whole ones.

Fractions like $\frac{9}{5}$ and $\frac{8}{3}$ are called top heavy or **improper fractions**.

They can also be written as **mixed numbers**.

FOR EXAMPLE $\quad \frac{9}{5} = 1\frac{4}{5} \qquad \frac{8}{3} = 2\frac{2}{3}$

You simplify an improper fraction by writing it as a mixed number
with the fraction part in its lowest terms.

FOR EXAMPLE $\quad \frac{22}{4} = 5\frac{2}{4} = 5\frac{1}{2}$

Example

Write these numbers in order
of size.

$\frac{7}{5} \qquad 2\frac{1}{8} \qquad 3\frac{1}{4} \qquad \frac{11}{8}$

Write the largest number first.

Solution

Convert the improper fractions to mixed numbers.

$\frac{7}{5} = 1\frac{2}{5} \quad 2\frac{1}{8} \qquad 3\frac{1}{4} \qquad \frac{11}{8} = 1\frac{3}{8}$

Comparing the whole numbers, the two largest numbers are $3\frac{1}{4}$ and $2\frac{1}{8}$.

To compare $1\frac{2}{5}$ and $1\frac{3}{8}$, convert $\frac{2}{5}$ and $\frac{3}{8}$ to fractions with a common
denominator.

$$\begin{array}{cc} \overset{\times 8}{\frown} & \overset{\times 5}{\frown} \\ \dfrac{2}{5} = \dfrac{16}{40} & \dfrac{3}{8} = \dfrac{15}{40} \\ \underset{\times 8}{\smile} & \underset{\times 5}{\smile} \end{array}$$

In order of size, the numbers are

$3\frac{1}{4} \qquad 2\frac{1}{8} \qquad 1\frac{16}{40} \qquad 1\frac{15}{40}$

$\downarrow \qquad\quad \downarrow \qquad\quad \downarrow \qquad\quad \downarrow$

$3\frac{1}{4} \qquad 2\frac{1}{8} \qquad \frac{7}{5} \qquad \frac{11}{8}.$

Write the fractions as they
appear in the question.

① Write each set of fractions in order of size. Write the smallest fraction first.

(a) $\frac{3}{5}$ $\frac{7}{15}$ $\frac{7}{10}$

(b) $\frac{5}{7}$ $\frac{9}{14}$ $\frac{3}{4}$

(c) $\frac{9}{12}$ $\frac{5}{6}$ $\frac{22}{24}$ $\frac{7}{8}$

(d) $\frac{3}{4}$ $\frac{5}{6}$ $\frac{7}{9}$ $\frac{13}{18}$

② Write these improper fractions as mixed numbers.

(a) $\frac{8}{5}$

(b) $\frac{7}{2}$

(c) $\frac{11}{9}$

(d) $\frac{13}{8}$

(e) $\frac{11}{3}$

(f) $\frac{30}{13}$

③ Write these mixed numbers as improper fractions.

(a) $1\frac{3}{4}$

(b) $2\frac{1}{2}$

(c) $4\frac{3}{5}$

(d) $2\frac{4}{7}$

(e) $3\frac{1}{9}$

(f) $5\frac{3}{8}$

④ Write each set of fractions in order of size. Write the largest fraction first.

(a) $1\frac{1}{2}$ $\frac{5}{3}$ $\frac{9}{4}$

(b) $\frac{23}{10}$ $\frac{12}{5}$ $2\frac{1}{2}$

(c) $3\frac{5}{6}$ $\frac{31}{8}$ $4\frac{1}{12}$ $\frac{15}{4}$

(d) $1\frac{2}{3}$ $1\frac{5}{9}$ $\frac{7}{4}$ $\frac{19}{12}$

⑤ Here are Sam's end of year exam results.
In which subject did he do best?
In which subject did he do worst?
Give reasons for your answers.

Maths	$\frac{55}{70}$
History	$\frac{16}{20}$
Science	$\frac{30}{35}$
French	$\frac{21}{28}$

⑥ Brain strain

Four friends are discussing how much water they drink each day.

Alisha says

I drink one and three-fifths of a litre.

Jack says

I drink one and three-quarters of a litre.

Megan says

I drink one and two-thirds of a litre.

Jordan says

I drink more than any of you. I drink one and seven-tenths of a litre.

(a) Is Jordan correct?
(b) Who drinks the least amount of water?
Explain your answers.

Look at this number line.

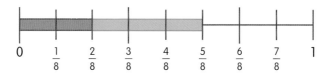

It shows that $\frac{2}{8} + \frac{3}{8} = \frac{5}{8}$.

You can also see that $\frac{5}{8} - \frac{3}{8} = \frac{2}{8}$.

When fractions have different denominators you can't add them directly.

To add $\frac{1}{2}$ and $\frac{1}{3}$ you have to rewrite them so they have a common denominator.

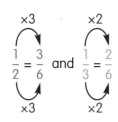

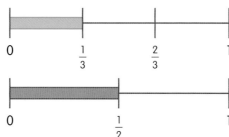

$\frac{3}{6} + \frac{2}{6} = \frac{5}{6}$

Example

Work out these.

(a) $\frac{7}{15} + \frac{2}{15}$ **(b)** $\frac{5}{6} - \frac{1}{4}$ **(c)** $\frac{3}{4} + \frac{1}{2}$

Solution

(a) $\frac{7}{15} + \frac{2}{15} = \frac{9}{15}$

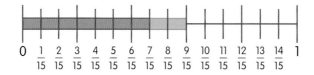

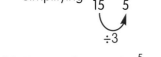

Simplifying $\frac{9}{15} = \frac{3}{5}$

(b) You need to rewrite $\frac{5}{6}$ and $\frac{1}{4}$ so they have a common denominator.

Look for a number that both 6 and 4 divide into.

$6 \times 2 = 12$ and $4 \times 3 = 12$

12 is the **lowest common denominator**. ◄————

> You can also work out $4 \times 6 = 24$ so both fractions can be written as 'twenty-fourths' but it is better to use the lowest common denominator if you can.

$$\frac{5}{6} = \frac{10}{12} \qquad \frac{1}{4} = \frac{3}{12}$$

×2 ×3

×2 ×3

Continued ...

$$\frac{5}{6} - \frac{1}{4} = \frac{10}{12} - \frac{3}{12}$$
$$= \frac{7}{12}$$

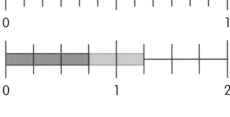

(c) $\frac{3}{4} + \frac{1}{2} = \frac{3}{4} + \frac{2}{4}$
$$= \frac{5}{4}$$
$$= 1\frac{1}{4}$$

Now try these 18.2

① Use copies of this number line to work out these.

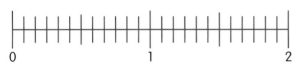

(a) $\frac{1}{4} + \frac{2}{4}$ **(b)** $\frac{5}{12} - \frac{1}{12}$ **(c)** $\frac{3}{6} + \frac{4}{6}$

(d) $\frac{1}{6} + \frac{1}{2}$ **(e)** $\frac{2}{3} - \frac{1}{4}$ **(f)** $\frac{5}{6} - \frac{1}{12}$

(g) $\frac{5}{12} + \frac{1}{2}$ **(h)** $\frac{1}{2} + \frac{1}{3} + \frac{1}{4}$ **(i)** $\frac{1}{2} + \frac{1}{12} - \frac{1}{4}$

② Work out these.

(a) $\frac{3}{5} + \frac{1}{10}$ **(b)** $\frac{5}{8} - \frac{1}{4}$ **(c)** $\frac{3}{5} + \frac{4}{5}$

(d) $\frac{7}{8} - \frac{1}{2}$ **(e)** $\frac{11}{15} - \frac{1}{3}$ **(f)** $\frac{2}{3} - \frac{1}{9}$

(g) $\frac{3}{4} + \frac{1}{5}$ **(h)** $\frac{4}{5} - \frac{1}{2}$ **(i)** $\frac{3}{4} - \frac{1}{2} - \frac{1}{8}$

③ Check your answers to questions **1** and **2** using your calculator.

Calculators vary! Find out how to enter fractions on your calculator.

④ Puzzle

Remember
Unit fractions have a numerator of 1.

The Egyptians only used unit fractions when writing fractions.

They never used the same unit fraction more than once.

So they wrote $\frac{3}{4}$ as $\frac{1}{2} + \frac{1}{4}$ ✔

but not as $\frac{1}{4} + \frac{1}{4} + \frac{1}{4}$. ✗

Write the following using unit fractions.

(a) $\frac{7}{12}$ **(b)** $\frac{3}{10}$ **(c)** $\frac{5}{12}$

(d) $\frac{9}{20}$ **(e)** $\frac{8}{15}$ **(f)** $\frac{19}{20}$

⑤ Brain strain

Tom has a bag of sweets.

He gives $\frac{2}{5}$ of the sweets to his brother and $\frac{1}{4}$ of the sweets to his sister.

What fraction of the bag of sweets does Tom have left?

⑥ Puzzle

Use four different digits to make this sum correct.

$$\frac{\square}{\square} + \frac{\square}{\square} = 1$$

Find three different answers.

This number line shows that $6 \times \frac{2}{3} = 4$.

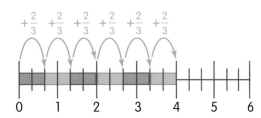

Remember
You can use repeated addition for multiplication.

As it doesn't matter which order you multiply you also know that $\frac{2}{3} \times 6 = 4$.

The number line also shows that $\frac{2}{3}$ of 6 = 4. ← To shade $\frac{2}{3}$ of this number line you need to shade up to 4.

$6 \times \frac{2}{3}$, $\frac{2}{3} \times 6$ and $\frac{2}{3}$ of 6 are all different ways of writing the same thing.

You can also work out $\frac{2}{3}$ of 6 by finding $\frac{1}{3}$ of 6 and then doubling your answer.

$\frac{1}{3}$ of 6 = 2. ← Finding $\frac{1}{3}$ is the same as dividing by 3.

So $\quad \frac{2}{3}$ of 6 = 4.

Example

Work out $4 \times \frac{5}{6}$.

Solution

You can use a number line.

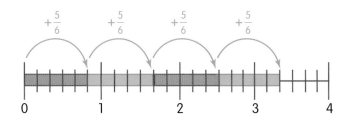

This shows that $4 \times \frac{5}{6} = 3\frac{2}{6}$. ← Remember $4 \times \frac{5}{6}$ is the same as $\frac{5}{6} \times 4$ or $\frac{5}{6}$ of 4.

$3\frac{2}{6}$ cancels to $3\frac{1}{3}$.

Alternatively you can use the method you learnt in Year 7.

$\frac{5}{6} \times 4 = \frac{20}{6}$ ← Multiply the numerator of the fraction by the integer.
← The denominator doesn't change.

$\frac{20}{6}$ cancels to $\frac{10}{3}$.

$\frac{10}{3} = 3\frac{1}{3}$

Continued ..

Example

Owen buys 10 tins of cat food on Monday.

By Saturday his cat has eaten $\frac{2}{3}$ of the food.

How many tins has the cat eaten by Saturday?

Solution

Work out $\frac{2}{3}$ of 10. ← Remember $\frac{2}{3}$ of 10 is the same as $\frac{2}{3} \times 10$.

$\frac{2}{3} \times 10 = \frac{20}{3}$

$\frac{20}{3} = 6\frac{2}{3}$

Now try these 18.3

① Work out these.

(a) $\frac{1}{5}$ of 20   (b) $\frac{1}{3} \times 12$ (c) $60 \times \frac{1}{10}$ (d) $\frac{2}{5} \times 30$ (e) $\frac{5}{7}$ of 63   (f) $72 \times \frac{11}{12}$

② Use copies of this number line to help you work out these.

(a) $5 \times \frac{1}{2}$ (b) $\frac{5}{6}$ of 2   (c) $\frac{3}{4}$ of 3   (d) $\frac{7}{12} \times 4$ (e) $\frac{2}{3} \times 4$ (f) $7 \times \frac{5}{12}$

③ Work out these.

(a) $3 \times \frac{2}{5}$ (b) $\frac{3}{10}$ of 7   (c) $\frac{6}{15} \times 3$ (d) $\frac{3}{7} \times 12$ (e) $\frac{7}{24} \times 10$ (f) $30 \times \frac{5}{6}$

④ Check your answers to questions **1**, **2** and **3** using your calculator.

⑤ A race is 300 metres long.
Steve led for two-thirds of the race.
For how many metres was he in the lead?

⑥ Tom has a 700MB CD.
He has used $\frac{3}{7}$ of the memory.
Is there enough room on the CD for him to store 150MB of pictures?

⑦ Molly gets £14 in pocket money each month.
She spends $\frac{5}{8}$ of her money and saves the rest.
How much does she save?

⑧ Brain strain

Iona does 12 hours homework one week.

$\frac{2}{5}$ of the time was spent doing English homework.

How long did she spend doing English homework?

⑨ Brain strain

Copy and complete these statements.

(a) $\frac{5}{7}$ of 63 = $\dfrac{3}{\boxed{}}$ of 60   (b) $\frac{7}{8}$ of 80 = $\dfrac{\boxed{}}{10}$ of 100

(c) $\frac{5}{9}$ of 81 = $\frac{5}{8}$ of $\boxed{}$ (d) $\frac{3}{5}$ of 30 = $\dfrac{\boxed{}}{\boxed{}}$ of 40

⑩ Brain strain

Work out these.

(a) $\frac{7}{6} \times 2$ (b) $1\frac{1}{3} \times 2$

(c) $1\frac{3}{4} \times 3$ (d) $2 \times 1\frac{5}{12}$

(e) $1\frac{1}{4} \times 7$ (f) $8 \times 2\frac{2}{3}$

Hint
One way to tackle questions involving mixed numbers is to convert them to improper fractions.

$2 \div \frac{1}{3}$ means 'how many thirds are there in 2?'

You can work it out using repeated addition or multiplying up.

This number line shows that $\frac{1}{3}$ goes into 2 six times.

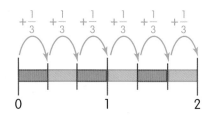

Note
This number line also shows
$2 = 6 \times \frac{1}{3}$ and
$2 = \frac{1}{3} \times 6$.

So $2 \div \frac{1}{3} = 6$.

You can also work out $2 \div \frac{1}{3}$ by reasoning that

      there are 3 thirds in 1 whole

so   there are 6 thirds in 2 wholes

Example

Work out $4 \div \frac{2}{5}$.

Solution

Draw a number line.

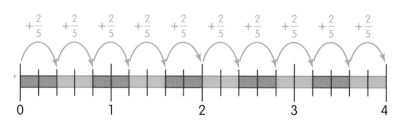

The number line shows that there are 10 'two-fifths' in 4.

So $4 \div \frac{2}{5} = 10$.

Now try these 18.4

1
  (a) How many halves are there in 1?
  (b) How many halves are there in 3?
  (c) How many quarters are there in 1?
  (d) How many quarters are there in 5?
  (e) How many sevenths are there in 1?
  (f) How many sevenths are there in 4?

2 Use copies of this number line to help you work out these.

  (a) $1 \div \frac{1}{3}$ **(b)** $2 \div \frac{1}{2}$ **(c)** $3 \div \frac{1}{4}$ **(d)** $3 \div \frac{2}{6}$ **(e)** $3 \div \frac{3}{4}$ **(f)** $3 \div \frac{6}{12}$

3 Brain strain

(a) Copy and complete these.
  $120 \times \frac{1}{6} = 20$ so $20 \div \frac{1}{6} = ?$
  $60 \times \frac{2}{6} = 20$ so $20 \div \frac{2}{6} = ?$
  $40 \times \frac{3}{6} = 20$ so $20 \div \frac{3}{6} = ?$

(b) What are the next two lines in the pattern?

19 Percentages, fractions and decimals

Subject links
- PHSE
- science
- geography
- design and technology

Coming up ...

- writing one number as a percentage of another
- comparing fractions, decimals and percentages
- finding a percentage of an amount
- finding percentage increases and decreases

Do you remember?
- that percentage means 'out of a hundred'
- how to write one number as a fraction of another
- how to find equivalent fractions
- how to convert between decimals and fractions
- how to find a fraction of an amount
- how to multiply and divide by 100
- how to add, subtract, multiply and divide integers and decimals

Chapter starter

① **(a)** Estimate the percentage of the file that has downloaded.

(b) What percentage is left to download?

② **(a)** Estimate the percentage of the pie chart that is
   (i) red
   (ii) blue
   (iii) yellow.

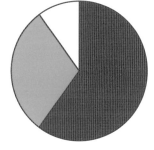

(b) What do your three estimates add up to.

③ Where have you seen percentages used in everyday life? Write down at least three situations.

Key words

percentage
per cent
convert
equivalent fraction
cancel
profit
loss
percentage profit
percentage loss
unitary method
percentage increase
percentage decrease

'Per cent' means 'out of a hundred' so 39% means 39-hundredths or $\frac{39}{100}$ or 0.39.

Similarly, 7% means seven-hundredths or $\frac{7}{100}$ or 0.07.

To write one number as a percentage of another, you first write it as a fraction.

Then you convert it to a percentage by writing an equivalent fraction with a denominator of 100.

> **Remember**
> Equivalent fractions are equal in value.

Example

What is 23 as a percentage of 50?

Solution

23 as a fraction of 50 is $\frac{23}{50}$.

> First, write 23 as a fraction of 50.

$$\overset{\times 2}{\underset{\times 2}{\frac{23}{50} = \frac{46}{100}}}$$

> Then convert to an equivalent fraction that has a denominator of 100. In this case, you multiply the numerator and the denominator by 2.

So 23 as a percentage of 50 is 46%.

Example

A jigsaw should have 300 pieces.

However, 15 pieces are missing.

(a) What percentage of the pieces are missing?
(b) What percentage of the pieces are not missing?

Solution

(a) As a fraction, $\frac{15}{300}$ of the pieces are missing.

$$\overset{\div 3}{\underset{\div 3}{\frac{15}{300} = \frac{5}{100}}}$$

> Convert to an equivalent fraction that has a denominator of 100.
> In this case, you divide the numerator and the denominator by 3.

> **Remember**
> 100% = 1 whole one

So 15 as a percentage of 300 is 5%.
5% of the pieces are missing.

(b) The percentage not missing must be 100% − 5% = 95%.

Continued ...

Example

Write 16 as a percentage of 40.

Solution

16 as a fraction of 40 = $\frac{16}{40}$.

40 cannot be multiplied in an easy way to make 100.

However, $\frac{16}{40}$ can be cancelled to make an equivalent fraction with a denominator of 10.

$$\overset{\div 4}{\frac{16}{40}} = \frac{4}{10} \; {\scriptstyle \div 4}$$

You can then write another equivalent fraction that has denominator 100 quite easily.

$$\overset{\times 10}{\frac{4}{10}} = \frac{40}{100} \; {\scriptstyle \times 10}$$

So 16 as a percentage of 40 is 40%.

Profit and loss

You will often see percentages used with profit or loss.

It is important to use the right figures in your calculations.

$$\text{Percentage profit} = \frac{\text{profit}}{\text{cost price}} \times 100\%$$

$$\text{Percentage loss} = \frac{\text{loss}}{\text{cost price}} \times 100\%$$

Example

Samir sells a T-shirt on eBay.

He bought the T-shirt for £8.

He sells it for £10.

What percentage profit does he make?

Solution

Profit = selling price − cost price

$$= £10 − £8$$

$$= £2$$

$$\frac{\text{profit}}{\text{cost price}} = \frac{£2}{£8}$$

Convert to an equivalent fraction with a denominator of 100.

$$\overset{\div 2}{} \overset{\times 25}{}$$
$$\frac{2}{8} = \frac{1}{4} = \frac{25}{100}$$
$${\scriptstyle \div 2} \quad {\scriptstyle \times 25}$$

$$\text{Percentage profit} = \frac{25}{100} \times 100\%$$

$$= 25\%$$

Samir makes a 25% profit.

1. What is 11 as a percentage of 25?

2. Write 17 as a percentage of 20.

3. What is 130 as a percentage of 200?

4. Jess gets 49 marks out of 50 in a test.
What percentage did she get?

5. Ethan has saved £300.
He buys a bicycle costing £120.
What percentage of his savings does he spend on the bicycle?

6. A cricket club has 20 players.
Six of them are injured.
   (a) What percentage of the players are injured?
   (b) What percentage of the players are not injured?

7. There are 30 pupils in a class.
Nine pupils have a dog.
What percentage of the class do *not* have a dog?

8. There are 80 sweets in a bag.
16 of the sweets are toffees.
What percentage are toffees?

9. Amy's journey is 75 miles long.
She stops for petrol after 51 miles.
What percentage of her journey is left?

10. A science book has 250 pages.
30 of the pages have photographs on them.
What percentage of the pages have photographs on them?

11. A netball team played 30 matches in a season.
They won 12 of them.
What percentage of the matches did they win?

12. This is the petrol gauge in Mark's car.
The numbers indicate the amount of fuel, in litres.
The shaded area indicates the amount of petrol in the tank.

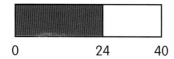

0   24   40

   (a) What fraction of the tank is full?
   Give your answer in its simplest form.
   (b) What percentage of the tank is full?

13. A fruit drink is made using 100 ml of apple juice, 150 ml of orange juice and 250 ml of grape juice.
   (a) What type of juice makes up 50% of the drink?
   (b) What percentage of the drink is apple juice?

14. Tom buys a guitar for £60.
He sells it for £84.
What percentage profit does he make?

15. Narinda buys a computer game for £40.
She gets bored with it and sells it on the internet for £28.
Work out her percentage loss.

16. **Brain strain**

Guy buys some CDs to sell at a car boot sale.

He buys 60 CDs and pays a total of £200.

At the car boot sale he sells 20 of the CDs for £4.50 each.

He reduces the price of the remaining CDs to £3 each.

At the end of the sale he still has 10 CDs left.

He sells these last 10 for £1 each.

   (a) Does Guy make a profit or a loss?
   (b) What is his percentage profit or loss?
   (c) What other costs might Guy have had to pay?

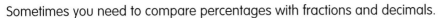

Sometimes you need to compare percentages with fractions and decimals.

A good way to do this is to convert them all to the same type of number.

For example, you could write them all as percentages.

Example

Bradley wants to buy a new computer.

He decides on a suitable model and finds its recommended retail price (RRP).

Then he finds these three special deals on the internet.

Cherie's Computers	Mike's Machines	Za's Bazaar
30% off RRP	$\frac{1}{3}$ off RRP	Pay only 0.8 of RRP

Which supplier is offering the cheapest deal?

Solution

At Cherie's Computers you would pay

$$100\% - 30\% = 70\% \text{ of the RRP.}$$

At Mike's Machines you would get

$$\frac{1}{3} = 33\tfrac{1}{3}\% \text{ off.}$$ You should learn that $\frac{1}{3} = 33\tfrac{1}{3}\%$.

So you would pay

$$100\% - 33\tfrac{1}{3}\% = 66\tfrac{2}{3}\% \text{ of the RRP.}$$

At Za's Bazaar you would pay

$$0.8 = \frac{8}{10}$$

Convert the decimal to a fraction. Then convert to an equivalent fraction with a denominator of 100.

$$\underset{\times 10}{\overset{\times 10}{\frac{8}{10} = \frac{80}{100}}}$$

$$\frac{80}{100} = 80\% \text{ of the RRP.}$$

Therefore the cheapest deal is at Mike's Machines as you pay the smallest percentage of the RRP.

1. Which of these amounts is the largest?
   28% $\frac{1}{4}$ 0.31 $\frac{3}{10}$

2. Which of these amounts is the smallest?
   $\frac{2}{3}$ 70% $\frac{3}{4}$ 0.65 $\frac{3}{5}$

3. Three children are climbing ladders in the school gym.
   The ladders are all the same height.
   Anna is $\frac{1}{3}$ of the way up ladder A.
   Beth is 30% of the way up ladder B.
   Kyle is 0.35 of the way up ladder C.
   (a) Which child is furthest up their ladder?
   (b) Which child is nearest the ground?

4. Which of these fractions is closest to 12%.
   $\frac{1}{5}$ $\frac{1}{6}$ $\frac{1}{8}$ $\frac{1}{10}$ $\frac{1}{12}$

5. A pie chart has three sections, coloured red, green and blue.
   $\frac{2}{5}$ of the pie chart has been coloured red and $\frac{1}{4}$ has been coloured green.
   The rest is blue.
   What percentage of the pie chart has been coloured
   (a) red or green
   (b) blue?

6. Arrange these amounts in order of size, smallest first.
   $\frac{2}{3}$ 55% $\frac{1}{2}$ 0.45 $\frac{3}{5}$

7. Which of these percentages is closest to $\frac{4}{5}$?
   52%   62%   72%   82%   92%

8 Puzzle

Copy and complete these.

Write one digit in each box.

(a) $\frac{7}{10}$ is the same as ☐☐ %.

(b) 15% is the same as $\frac{☐}{20}$.

(c) $\frac{1}{5}$ is the same as ☐☐ %.

9. **(a)** Write 0.3 as a percentage.
   (b) Write $\frac{17}{20}$ as a percentage.

10. Jack says

5% is the same as $\frac{1}{200}$.

Jordan says

5% is the same as $\frac{1}{20}$.

Who is correct?
Explain your answer.

You learnt how to find a percentage of an amount in Year 7 but it is an important piece of work that will be needed in the next section.

There are different ways of finding a percentage of an amount.

The examples below show you three methods.

You can use whichever method you prefer.

The method you prefer may be different depending on the numbers involved and whether or not you are allowed to use a calculator.

Example

Find 35% of 160.

Solution

This method uses your knowledge of fraction equivalents.

$$10\% \text{ of } 160 = \frac{1}{10} \text{ of } 160$$

> You should know that $10\% = \frac{1}{10}$.

$$= 160 \div 10$$

> To find $\frac{1}{10}$ of an amount you divide by 10.

$$= 16$$

$$30\% \text{ of } 160 = 3 \times 16$$

> $30\% = 3 \times 10\%$

$$= 48$$

$$5\% \text{ of } 160 = 16 \div 2$$

> $5\% = 10\% \div 2$

$$= 8$$

$$35\% \text{ of } 160 = 30\% \text{ of } 160 + 5\% \text{ of } 160$$
$$= 48 + 8$$
$$= 56$$

Example

There are 1200 pupils in a school.

3% of the pupils say they want more homework.

How many is this?

Solution

The method used in this example is called the **unitary method**.

First you find 1% of the quantity by dividing by 100.

Then you multiply by the number of per cent you are interested in.

$$1\% \text{ of } 1200 = \frac{1}{100} \text{ of } 1200$$

> $1\% = \frac{1}{100}$ and you find $\frac{1}{100}$ by dividing by 100.

$$= 1200 \div 100$$

$$= 12$$

$$3\% \text{ of } 1200 = 3 \times 12$$

> You want to find 3% so you multiply 1% by 3.

$$= 36$$

36 pupils say they want more homework.

Continued ...

Example

There are 800 people at a theme park.

65% of the people at the theme park are under 18 years old.

How many are under 18 years old?

Solution

This method involves converting the percentage to a decimal by dividing by 100.

You then multiply the decimal equivalent by the quantity.

$65\% = \frac{65}{100} = 0.65$ ← Convert the percentage to a decimal.

0.65×800 ← Multiply the decimal equivalent by the total number of people at the theme park.

$= 0.65 \times 100 \times 8$ ← $800 = 100 \times 8$

$= 65 \times 8$

$= 520$

520 people at the theme park are under 18 years old.

Now try these 19.3

1. Work out these.
   - **(a)** 10% of 60
   - **(b)** 5% of 400
   - **(c)** 8% of 600
   - **(d)** 20% of 50
   - **(e)** 30% of 150
   - **(f)** 40% of £120
   - **(g)** 15% of £40
   - **(h)** 12% of 85 km
   - **(i)** 32% of 1200 miles
   - **(j)** 2% of 3500
   - **(k)** 45% of 700
   - **(l)** 6% of £27 000

Hint
Don't forget to include the units in your answer if you are finding a fraction of a quantity.

2. At Hodder High School there are 400 boys and 500 girls.
   - **(a)** On Monday, 15% of the boys were absent.
     How many boys were absent on Monday?
   - **(b)** On the same day, 16% of the girls were absent.
     How many pupils were absent in total that day?

3. A car tyre is supposed to last for 25 000 km.
   It needs to be inspected when it has travelled 85% of this distance.
   How many kilometres can the tyre travel before it needs to be inspected?

4. Here is Sam's method for working out $17\frac{1}{2}\%$ of 360.
   Use Sam's method to work out these.
   - **(a)** $17\frac{1}{2}\%$ of £520
   - **(b)** $17\frac{1}{2}\%$ of £86.40

   > 10% of 360 = 360 ÷ 10
   >   = 36
   >
   > 5% of 360 = 36 ÷ 2
   >   = 18
   >
   > $2\frac{1}{2}\%$ of 360 = 18 ÷ 2
   >   = 9
   >
   > $17\frac{1}{2}\%$ of 360 = 10% + 5% + $2\frac{1}{2}\%$
   >   = 36 + 18 + 9
   >   = 63

Note
There is a tax added to the cost of many goods and services that we buy.
It is called **value added tax** and usually abbreviated to **VAT**.
For a long time this tax has been $17\frac{1}{2}\%$ of the pre-VAT price.

Continued ...

5 In a mathematics examination there are two parts, Section A and Section B.
Section A is out of 30 marks. Section B is out of 20 marks.
Nathan got 70% of Section A right and 60% of Section B right.
 (a) How many marks did Nathan score on Section A?
 (b) How many marks did Nathan score in total?
 (c) What was Nathan's overall percentage mark for the examination?

You can't just add the percentage scores.

6 Puzzle

Copy and complete these.
Write one digit in each box.

(a) 20% of 450 is ☐ ☐ .

(b) 10% of ☐ ☐ ☐ is 63.

(c) ☐ ☐ % of 80 is 32.

Investigation

Without using a calculator, work out 15% of 840 using each of the three methods used in the examples.

Do you get the same answer each time?

Which of the three methods do you prefer?

Give a reason for your answer.

19.4 Percentages on your calculator

When you can use a calculator, you will probably find the second or third method used in the examples most efficient.

The examples show how to use these methods with a calculator.

It is probably best to choose the method you prefer and stick to it.

Example

Work out 38% of 427.

Solution

When you use the unitary method, use your calculator to work out 1% and then to multiply by the number of per cent you require.

1% of 427 = 427 ÷ 100

      = 4.27

Work this out mentally or use your calculator.
$1\% = \frac{1}{100}$ and you find $\frac{1}{100}$ by dividing by 100.

38% of 427 = 38 × 1% of 427

      = 4.27 × 38

      = 162.26

Work this out using your calculator.

Continued ···

Example

Find 7% of 120.

Solution

When you use this method, you can convert the percentage to a decimal mentally and then use your calculator to multiply the decimal by the quantity you are working with.

$7\% = \frac{7}{100} = 0.07$ ←── Work out the decimal equivalent mentally by dividing the number of per cent by 100 or use your calculator.

7% of 120 = 0.07 × 120 ←── Work this out using your calculator.

       = 8.4

Remember
7% = 0.07
70% = 0.7

Investigation

Work out 79% of 48 using each of the methods shown above.

Do you get the same answer each time?

Which method do you prefer?

Give a reason for your answer.

Now try these 19.4

Use your preferred method to work out these.

1. 9% of 130

2. 13% of 65

3. 62% of 450

4. 95% of 450

5. 47% of £1300

6. 76% of 2500

7. 16% of 250 metres

8. 51% of 8000 euros

9. 17.5% of £80

10. 13% of 965 metres

11. 43% of 52 kg

12. 3% of £9

Percentages are often used to describe increases or decreases.

SALE! All prices reduced by 28%

Pocket money increases by 15% for 13-year-olds

To increase an amount by a percentage

● work out the value of the increase
● add this to the original amount.

Example

Chris gets £8 pocket money.

His pocket money is increased by 15% when he is 13 years old.

How much pocket money does he get when he is 13 years old?

Solution

15% of £8 = £1.20

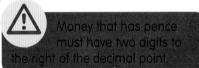

Work out 15% of £8.
Use whichever method you prefer.

Chris' pocket money goes up by £1.20.

Add this to the original amount, £8.

New amount = £8 + £1.20

= £9.20

⚠ Money that has pence must have two digits to the right of the decimal point.

In a similar way, to decrease an amount by a percentage

● work out the value of the decrease
● take this away from the original amount.

Example

A laptop computer costs £600.

In a sale the price is reduced by 28%.

What is the sale price of the laptop?

Solution

28% of £600 = £168

Work out 28% of £600.
Use whichever method you prefer.

The price of the computer goes down by £168.

Take this away from the original amount, £600.

Sale price = £600 – £168

= £432

Do not use your calculator for questions **1** to **4**.

1 Copy and complete this table.

	Original amount / quantity	Percentage increase	New amount / quantity
(a)	48	25%	
(b)	£120	10%	
(c)	£45	20%	
(d)	70	30%	
(e)	60p	35%	
(f)	£3500	80%	
(g)	68 cm	55%	

2 Copy and complete this table.

	Original amount / quantity	Percentage decrease	New amount / quantity
(a)	40	10%	
(b)	35	20%	
(c)	240	40%	
(d)	660	25%	
(e)	£160	75%	
(f)	48 metres	5%	
(g)	£7800	95%	

3 There are four children in a family.
They receive different amounts of pocket money.
Jim is the youngest. He receives 60p.
Erin receives £1.10.
Sam receives £3.
Yasmin is the oldest. She receives £4.50.
They are all given an increase of 20%.

(a) Work out how much pocket money each receives after the increase.

(b) Sam says that Yasmin received a bigger increase than he did.
Is Sam correct?
Give a reason for your answer.

4 A shop sells electrical goods.

£45

£80

£225

£3.60

BATTERY

The shop has a sale.

All prices are reduced by 20%.

(a) Work out the sale price of each item.

(b) Jess says

It would be easier if the shop just said they would decrease all the prices by £5.

Do you think that Jess's idea is a good one?
Give a reason for your answer.

Continued ...

You may use your calculator for questions **5** to **11**.

⑤ A blu-ray DVD player costs £350 on the internet.

To have it delivered costs an extra 6%.

Work out the cost of the blu-ray DVD player including delivery.

⑥ Val buys a new hockey stick for £32.

She sells it to her friend and makes an 8% loss.

How much did she sell the hockey stick for?

⑦ Tickets for a rock concert cost £20 each plus a 4% booking fee.

Niamh buys four tickets.

Work out the total cost including the booking fee.

⑧ Robert's car was worth £8000 when it was new.

However, it has now lost 70% of its value.

How much is Robert's car worth now?

⑨ A train journey usually takes 2 hours.

Due to bad weather, today's journey is expected to take 20% longer.

Work out the expected journey time today.

Give your answer in hours and minutes.

⑩ A restaurant bill after a birthday party is £72.

A service charge of 15% is added to the bill.

Work out the final bill.

⑪ Wes has savings of £150 in a bank account for a year.

The money earns interest at 3% per year.

How much is in his account after a year?

Note

When you have a savings account, the money in your account earns **interest**.

This is money added to your account by the bank or building society.

They pay a percentage of the amount in the account.

Investigation

Dan says

Increasing an amount by 200% will double the amount.

Emily says

Increasing an amount by 100% will double the amount.

(a) Who is correct?

Check your answer by increasing £30 by 100% and by 200%.

(b) How many times bigger do you make an amount if you increase it by 300%?

Give an example to explain your answer.

(c) What happens to an amount if you decrease it by 100%?

Give an example to explain your answer.

20 Ratio and proportion

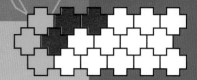

Coming up ...

- simplifying ratios
- solving problems using ratio
- dividing a quantity in a given ratio
- using the unitary method to solve problems involving direct proportion
- using graphs to solve problems involving direct proportion

Do you remember?

- how to write ratios
- how to find equivalent fractions
- how to convert between metric measures
- how to convert between units of time
- how to divide a quantity in a given ratio with two parts
- how to use the unitary method to solve problems involving percentages
- how to interpret conversion graphs

Chapter starter

1 Follow the rules to colour in these grids.
Make your designs as interesting as you can.

(a)

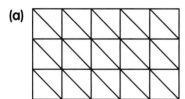

For every triangle you colour green colour 4 red

(b)

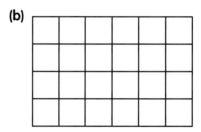

For every 3 squares you colour green colour 5 red.

(c)

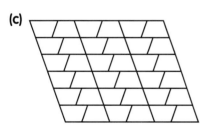

For every trapezium you colour green colour 2 red and 3 blue.

(d)

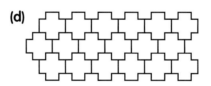

For every 2 crosses you colour green colour 4 red.

(e)

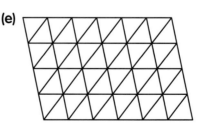

For every triangle you colour blue colour 2 red and 3 green.

Key words

ratio   simplest form

equivalent ratio   direct proporti

simplify   unitary metho

2 For each grid, write down what fraction of the whole grid is coloured in each colour.

174

Marcel is counting the animals on his small farm.

He has six pigs, twelve chickens and nine lambs.

The ratio of pigs to chickens to lambs is
6 : 12 : 9.

The ratio can be simplified to an equivalent ratio by dividing each number by 3.

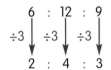

$$6 : 12 : 9$$
$$\div 3 \downarrow \quad \div 3 \downarrow \quad \div 3 \downarrow$$
$$2 : 4 : 3$$

This is the ratio in its **simplest form**.

The quantities in a ratio must have the same units.

When the ratio has been simplified the units are left out.

Example

During a week at school, Robbie has 50 minutes of RE, 2 hours 30 minutes of English and 1 hour 25 minutes of history.

Work out the ratio of the times for each subject.

Give your answer in its simplest form.

Remember
1 hour = 60 minutes

Solution

RE	:	English	:	History
50 minutes	:	2 hours 30 minutes	:	1 hour 25 minutes
50 minutes	:	150 minutes	:	85 minutes

$\div 5$ $\div 5$ $\div 5$

10	:	30	:	17

Convert all the times to minutes.

The units are left out.

1. Simplify these ratios as much as possible.
   (a) 12 : 8 : 2
   (b) 15 : 25 : 20
   (c) 33 : 44 : 66
   (d) 27 : 18 : 21
   (e) 40 : 24 : 32
   (f) 66 : 48 : 30

2. Simplify these ratios as much as possible.
   (a) £3.50 : 50p
   (b) 10 cm : 2 m
   (c) 2 hours : 90 minutes
   (d) 750 g : 2 kg
   (e) 5.2 km : 400 m
   (f) 80p : £1.50 : £2
   (g) 4 m : $2\frac{1}{2}$ m : 50 cm
   (h) 1200 ml : 3 litres : $2\frac{1}{2}$ litres
   (i) 45 minutes : 1 hour 15 minutes : 1 hour 30 minutes

3. A chef spends two and a half hours cooking.
   He then spends 40 minutes clearing up.
   Find the ratio of cooking time to clearing up time.
   Give your answer in its simplest form.

4. A drink is made by mixing 1 litre of orange juice with half a litre of pineapple juice and 250 ml of lemonade.
   Write the ratio of orange juice to pineapple juice to lemonade in its simplest form.

5. A recipe for a cake uses 600 g of butter, 1.2 kg of flour and 150 g of marzipan.
   What is the ratio of butter to flour to marzipan in its simplest form?

6. Here are the results of a race.

Position	Name	Time
1st	I M Quick	56 seconds
2nd	N O Speed	1 minute 4 seconds
3rd	B Hind	1 minute 12 seconds

Write the ratio of the times in its simplest form.

7. Anna has a piece of string 2 metres long.
   She cuts a piece of length 40 cm, so she now has two pieces of string.
   Find the ratio of the length of the shorter piece to the length of the longer piece. Give your answer in its simplest form.

20.2 Solving problems using ratio

Equivalent ratios can help you solve problems.

Example

The ratio of the ages of Seema and Kate is 5 : 4.

Seema is 15 years old.

How old is Kate?

Solution

Seema : Kate
5 : 4
×3 ×3
15 : 12

This is the ratio in its simplest form.

Seema's actual age is 15 so you find an equivalent ratio that has 15 as the first number.

Kate is 12 years old.

There can be more than two quantities in the ratio.

Example

In tubes of Twizzles there are red, blue and yellow sweets.

The ratio of red to blue to yellow sweets is 6 : 3 : 4.

There are 18 blue sweets in a large tube of Twizzles.

How many sweets are in this tube?

Continued ...

Solution

red	:	blue	:	yellow
6	:	3	:	4

×6 ↓   ×6 ↓   ×6 ↓

36	:	18	:	24

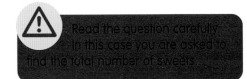

This is the ratio in its simplest form.

The actual number of blue sweets is 18 so you find an equivalent ratio that has 18 as the middle number.

There are 36 red sweets, 18 blue sweets and 24 yellow sweets.

The number of sweets in the tube is 36 + 18 + 24 = 78.

⚠ Read the question carefully. In this case you are asked to find the total number of sweets.

Now try these 20.2

1. The ratio of boys to girls in a class is 3 : 4.
   There are 15 boys.
   How many girls are there?

2. The ratio of toffees to chocolates in a box of sweets is 2 : 5.
   There are 20 chocolates.
   (a) How many toffees are there?
   (b) How many sweets are there altogether?

3. To make fizzy apple juice you mix apple juice and fizzy water in the ratio 3 : 10.
   Bradley uses 90 ml of juice.
   (a) How much water does he need?
   (b) Show that he has made less than half of a litre of fizzy apple juice.

4. To make 5 litres of Gorgeous Green paint you mix together 3 litres of blue paint with 2 litres of yellow paint.

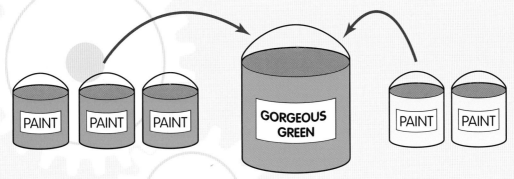

   (a) Sam uses 6 litres of blue paint.
       How much yellow paint does she need?
   (b) Edward uses 30 litres of yellow paint.
       How much blue paint does he need?

Continued ...

⑤ For a school trip, the ratio of pupils to teachers must be 8 : 1.

    (a) 96 pupils are going on a school trip.

       How many teachers are needed?

    (b) A trip has been organised for 160 pupils.

       Unfortunately there are only 16 teachers available.

       How many more teachers are needed if the trip is to take place?

⑥ The ratio of the ages of three brothers is 3 : 4 : 5.
The youngest brother is 9 years old.
Work out the ages of the other boys.

⑦ Tangy Treat cocktail mixes orange juice, lime juice and lemonade in the ratio 6 : 2 : 7.
    (a) Holly uses 20 ml of lime juice.
       How much orange juice does she need?
    (b) Alex uses 14 cl of lemonade.
       How much lime juice does he need?
    (c) Roisin is having a party and is going to make a large bowl of Tangy Treat.
       She uses 3 litres of orange juice.
       How much Tangy Treat does she make?

⑧ To make concrete you mix cement, sand and aggregate in the ratio 2 : 4 : 5.

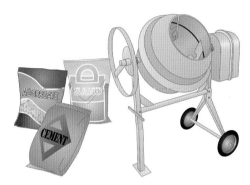

    (a) Bob uses 36 kg of sand.
       How much aggregate does he need?
    (b) Bill uses 65 kg of aggregate.
       How much concrete does he make?
    (c) Boris has 30 kg of cement, 15 kg of sand and 50 kg of aggregate.
       He wants to use all his cement to make some concrete.
       How much more sand does he need to buy?
       How much more aggregate does he need to buy?

20.3 Dividing a quantity into a given ratio

You learnt how to divide a quantity into two parts in Year 7.

You use a similar method to divide a quantity into three parts.

Example

A school has a sponsored jog to raise money for charity.

The pupils vote for which charity they want to give the money to.

They vote for an animal charity, a children's charity and an old people's charity in the ratio 7 : 3 : 2.

720 pupils voted.

How many voted for the animal charity?

Continued ...

Solution

animal charity	:	children's charity	:	old people's charity
7	:	3	:	2

$7 + 3 + 2 = 12$ ← Add the numbers in the ratio.

$720 \div 12 = 60$ ← Divide 720 into 12 equal parts.

Number voting for the animal charity = 60×7 ← Multiply by the number of parts required, 7.

$= 420$ ← Only the number who voted for the animal charity was asked for.

Now try these 20.3

① Divide £35 in the ratio 2 : 3.

② Divide $45 in the ratio 5 : 4.

③ Divide 24 metres in the ratio 1 : 2 : 3.

④ Divide 100 sweets in the ratio 2 : 5 : 3.

⑤ Divide 52 grams in the ratio 4 : 3 : 6.

⑥ Divide £77 in the ratio 1 : 8 : 2.

⑦ The three angles in a triangle are in the ratio 2 : 3 : 5. Work out the three angles.

Hint
The angles in a triangle add up to 180°.

⑧ Fatima's CD collection has pop CDs, jazz CDs and classical CDs in the ratio 8 : 2 : 1.

She has 220 CDs.
How many are pop CDs?

⑨ In a mathematics competition Gold, Silver and Bronze certificates are awarded in the ratio 2 : 3 : 4.
Altogether 540 certificates are awarded.
Work out how many of each type are awarded.

⑩ Kylie communicates by email, text message and letter.
The ratio the number of emails, text messages and letters that Kylie sends one month is 8 : 47 : 5.
She sent a total of 180 communications.
How many of each type did she send?

⑪ Tropical Delight cocktail mixes lime juice, orange juice and mango juice in the ratio 1 : 3 : 6.

How much orange juice does Luigi need to make 4 litres of Tropical Delight?

⑫ **Brain strain**

Joe, Kim and Shakira buy a house for £135 000.

Joe pays £40 000, Kim pays £50 000 and Shakira pays £45 000.

They sell the house for £202 500.

They divide the money in the ratio of the amounts they paid.

Work out how much they each receive.

Some quantities are connected so that if you double one, the other also doubles.
The quantities are in **direct proportion**.

FOR EXAMPLE   3 pens cost 45p.

6 pens cost 90p. ◄──── Doubling the number of pens doubles the cost.

30 pens cost £4.50. ◄──── If you multiply the number of pens bought by 10 then you must also multiply the cost by 10.

Quantities are also in direct proportion if when you halve one quantity the other quantity also halves.

FOR EXAMPLE   £10 is worth €13.

       £5 is worth €6.50. ◄──── Halving the number of pounds halves the number of euros.

       £1 is worth €1.30. ◄──── If you divide the number of pounds by 10 you must also divide the number of euros by 10.

You learnt about the **unitary method** in Chapter 19 when you were working with percentages.
This method can also be useful for solving problems involving direct proportion.

Example

Six pencils cost 90p.

How much do eight pencils cost?

Solution

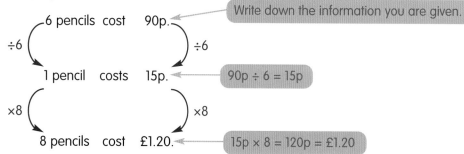

6 pencils cost 90p. ◄──── Write down the information you are given.

÷6   ÷6

1 pencil costs 15p. ◄──── 90p ÷ 6 = 15p

×8   ×8

8 pencils cost £1.20. ◄──── 15p × 8 = 120p = £1.20

Continued ...

Quantities that are in direct proportion can be shown on a graph.

All graphs that show direct proportion will be straight lines that pass through the origin, (0, 0).

Example

£1 is worth about 200 Japanese Yen.

The graph shows how many Yen amounts up to £10 are worth.

Pete takes a holiday in Tokyo.

(a) His friend says he should have about £5 in Yen for transport from the airport.
Use the graph to work out the value of £5 in Yen.

(b) Pete buys some sushi that costs 450 Yen.
Use the graph to estimate how much the sushi costs in pounds.

(c) Pete buys credit for his mobile phone and spends 3500 Yen.
Use the graph to work out how may pounds credit he buys.

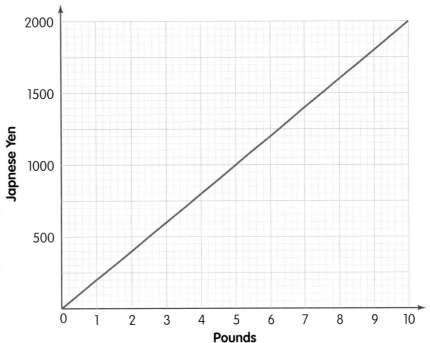

Solution

(a) See the red lines on the graph.
£5 is worth 1000 Yen.

(b) See the blue lines on the graph.
The sushi cost about £2.25.

(c) The value of 3500 Yen cannot be read directly from the graph.
However, you can break down the amount.
See the green lines on the graph.
3500 Yen = 2000 Yen + 1500 Yen
= £10 + £7.50
= £17.50
He buys £17.50 worth of credit.

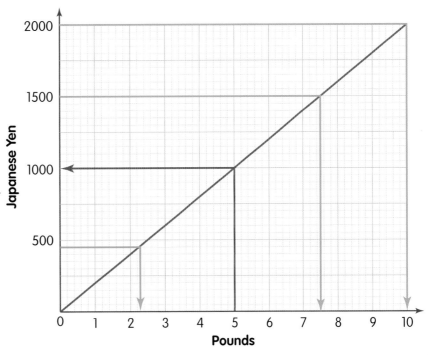

1. Five bags of crisps cost £1.40.
How much do eight bags cost?

2. It takes a toy maker 4 days to make 20 toy frogs.
How many frogs could he make in 7 days?

3. Chris is having a party.
She knows she can fill 42 cups from 6 bottles of lemonade.
She has 11 bottles of lemonade.
How many cups can she fill?

4. 36 pencils cost £4.32.
How much do 60 pencils cost?

5. 5 miles is about 8 kilometres.
On a school trip to Paris, Dan sees a road sign that says that they are 50 kilometres from Paris.
About how many miles are they from Paris?

6. £20 is worth about 39 US dollars.
Greg is going on holiday.
He takes £550 to spend.
About how many dollars does he have?

7. Sarah's guinea pigs eat 4 bags of food in 10 days.
How many days would 14 bags of food last them?

8. 12 exercise books contain 720 pages.
How many pages are there in 21 books?

9. 20 giant size packs of frozen chips weigh 15 kg.
How much do 36 packs weigh?

10. A car can travel 176 km on 16 litres of fuel.
How far can it travel on 9 litres of fuel?

11. On Christmas Eve Santa travels extremely quickly.
He takes 10 minutes to visit 18 million children.
How many children does he visit in 45 minutes?

12. A group of friends are taking part in a charity run.
They decide to all wear a T-shirt with their team name on.
The graph shows the cost of buying up to eight T-shirts.

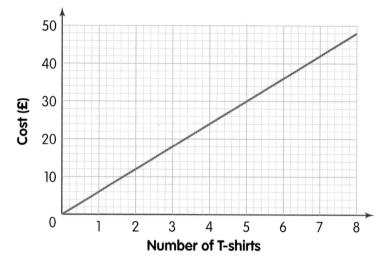

(a) Use the graph to work out the cost of 6 T-shirts.
(b) How many T-shirts can they buy for £20?
(c) What is the cost of 30 T-shirts?

13. **Brain strain**

Which of these pairs of quantities are in direct proportion?

Give reasons for your answers.

(a) The number of shirts ironed and the total time taken.
(b) The number of shirts hung on a washing line to dry and the total time for them to dry.
(c) The number of the house where you live and your mark in a mathematics examination.
(d) The time taken to run 100 metres and the speed that you run at.

21 Units of measurement

Subject links
- science
- design and technology
- geography

Coming up ...

- estimating lengths, masses and capacities
- converting between imperial units and metric units
- working with time

Do you remember?
- how to convert between metric units
- how to measure lengths, masses and capacities
- how to calculate the area of a rectangle
- how to multiply an integer by a decimal
- how to multiply an integer by a fraction

Chapter starter

According to the laws of cricket, the distance between the two sets of stumps is 20.12 metres.

The stumps are 71.1 cm tall and they are positioned so that they are 22.86 cm wide.

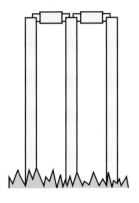

1. Why were such strange measurements chosen?
2. Investigate the measurements for the marking of a football pitch or a tennis court.

Key words

metric	estimate
length	imperial
millimetre (mm)	inch
centimetre (cm)	foot
metre (m)	yard
kilometre (km)	mile
mass	ounce (oz)
gram (g)	pound (lb)
kilogram (kg)	pint
tonne	gallon
capacity	second
millilitre (ml)	minute
centilitre (cl)	hour
litre (l)	

In Year 7 you learnt about metric units used for measuring length, mass and capacity.

When estimating, it helps to make a comparison with a quantity you already know.

Here is a reminder of how metric units are connected and some useful facts to help you when estimating.

Length

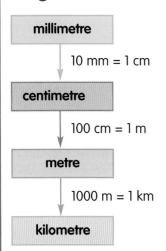

A long ruler is 30 cm long, a short one is 15 cm.

A door is about 2 m high.

A football pitch is about 100 m long.

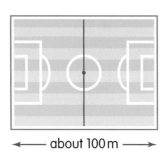

←— about 100 m —→

Mass

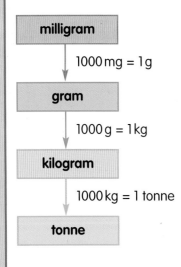

An average-sized cat has a mass of about 6 kg.

A bag of sugar has a mass of 1 kg.

A can of cola has a mass of 350 g.

A DVD in its case has a mass of about 100 g.

A small family car has a mass of about 1 tonne.

Continued…

Capacity

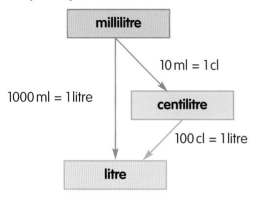

1000 ml = 1 litre

10 ml = 1 cl

100 cl = 1 litre

A bath uses about 150 litres of water.

A large bottle of lemonade holds 2 litres.

A can of cola holds 33 cl or 330 ml.

A teaspoon holds 5 ml.

To estimate the length of your classroom, imagine laying doors end to end down the classroom.

Each door is about 2 m so, if you think six doors would fit, then you estimate the length to be about 12 m.

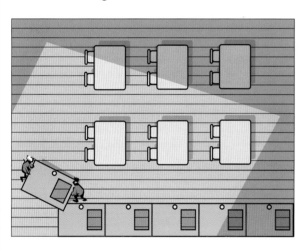

Note

In any estimating work, do not give your answers to a high degree of accuracy.
An estimate of 12 m is good but 11.83 m is not a sensible estimate, as you cannot estimate the length of a classroom to the nearest centimetre.
An estimate should always be a single answer rather than a range, so give an answer of 12 m instead of 10 to 15 m.

Now try these 21.1

With a friend

Each of you should write down estimates of all the measurements listed below.

Check by measuring.

Whoever is nearer each one gets a point. See who wins!

Estimate these lengths.

1. The length of the classroom (front to back)
2. The height of the classroom
3. The height of the door
4. The length of your table
5. The height of your table
6. The width of a window
7. The height of the board

Continued ...

① Estimate each of these.
Weigh them to check.
(a) The mass of your chair
(b) The mass of your exercise book
(c) The mass of your school bag (with all its contents)
(d) The mass of a packet of A4 paper.

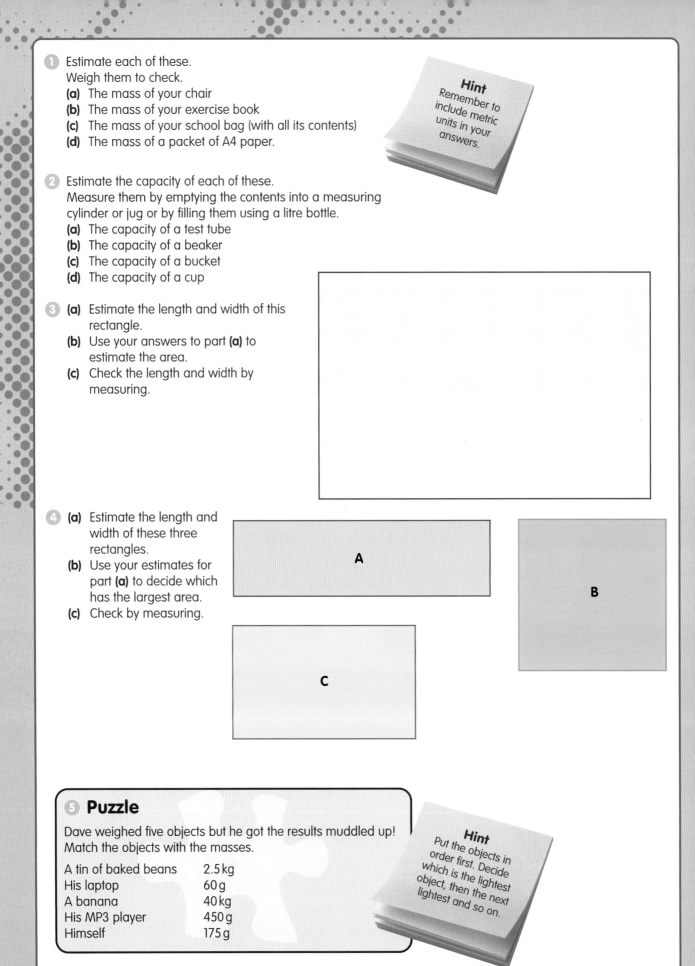

Hint
Remember to include metric units in your answers.

② Estimate the capacity of each of these.
Measure them by emptying the contents into a measuring cylinder or jug or by filling them using a litre bottle.
(a) The capacity of a test tube
(b) The capacity of a beaker
(c) The capacity of a bucket
(d) The capacity of a cup

③ (a) Estimate the length and width of this rectangle.
(b) Use your answers to part (a) to estimate the area.
(c) Check the length and width by measuring.

④ (a) Estimate the length and width of these three rectangles.
(b) Use your estimates for part (a) to decide which has the largest area.
(c) Check by measuring.

A

B

C

⑤ **Puzzle**

Dave weighed five objects but he got the results muddled up!
Match the objects with the masses.

A tin of baked beans	2.5 kg
His laptop	60 g
A banana	40 kg
His MP3 player	450 g
Himself	175 g

Hint
Put the objects in order first. Decide which is the lightest object, then the next lightest and so on.

You need to know these approximate conversions between metric and imperial units.

Length

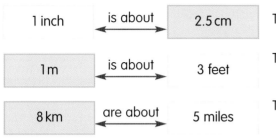

There are 12 inches in a foot.

There are 3 feet in a yard.

There are 5280 feet or 1760 yards in a mile.

Mass

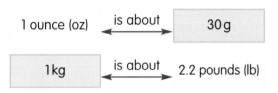

There are 16 ounces in a pound.

Capacity

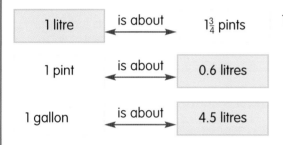

There are 8 pints in a gallon.

You need to be able to convert between metric and imperial units.

Example

(a) Mary has a four-pint bottle of milk.
How many litres this is?

(b) Harry asks his mum how far he would have to run in a marathon.
His mum knows that a marathon is 26 miles long but Harry wants to know how many kilometres this is.

Solution

(a) 1 pint is about 0.6 litres.
So 4 pints is 4 × 0.6 litres = 2.4 litres.

(b) 5 miles is about 8 km.
A marathon is 26 ÷ 5 = 5.2 lots of 5 miles.
So a marathon is 5.2 × 8 km = 41.6 km.
Because this is only an approximation, you say a marathon is about 42 km.

1. Ipswich is about 50 miles from Norwich. About how many kilometres is this?

2. **(a)** A Frenchman in England sees this road sign.

   He knows it means the maximum speed is 40 miles per hour.

   40

   He needs to know this speed in kilometres per hour.

   (i) Roughly how many kilometres are equal to 40 miles?

   (ii) What is the maximum speed in kilometres per hour?

   (b) He is travelling from Dover to North London.

   He has to travel 100 miles.

   How many kilometres is this?

   (c) His car has a petrol tank that holds 10 gallons.

   How many litres is this?

3. When Abigail was born, she weighed 8.8 lb. What is this in kilograms?

4. **(a)** Which is heavier, 500 g of chocolate or 8 oz of chocolate?

   (b) Which contains more, half a pint of milk or 400 ml of milk?

5. Cameron is cooking.

   Here is the recipe.

Italian Pudding
2 eggs
$\frac{1}{2}$ oz of castor sugar
$\frac{3}{4}$ pint of milk
2 oz of cake crumbs
$\frac{1}{2}$ lb of dates
$\frac{1}{2}$ lb of raisins
2 oz of mixed peel
1 lb of cooking apples

   Cameron does not use imperial measures.

   Convert the recipe into metric units for him.

21.3 Working with time

Jess, Dan and Mohammed have watched 13 football matches this season.

They want to work out the total amount of time they have spent watching football.

They know that a match lasts for 90 minutes.

Mohammed says

90 minutes is 1 hour 30 minutes. 13×1.30 is 16.90. That's 16 hours and 90 minutes so we've watched 17 hours 30 minutes of football.

Dan says

That's wrong! 90 minutes is $1\frac{1}{2}$ hours. You should have done $13 \times 1.5 = 19.5$ hours.

Jess says

I think it's easier to work in minutes. 13×90 is 1170 minutes. I just divide by 60 to change it into hours. $1170 \div 60$ is 19.5. That's 19 hours 50 minutes.

Continued ...

Dan tells Jess she has made a mistake at the end.

19.5 hours is $19\frac{1}{2}$ hours, or 19 hours 30 minutes.

Dan has the correct answer!

Time does not have any metric units, so it can be difficult to use a calculator when working with time if you need to mix units.

Here is a reminder of how the units of time are connected.

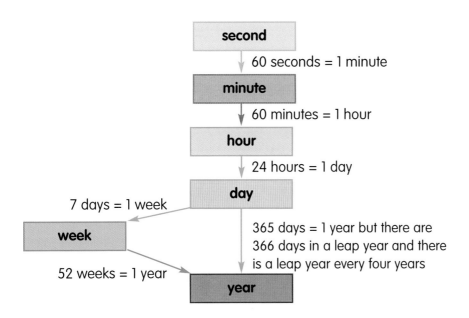

Remember also that 15 minutes is a quarter of an hour, which is 0.25 as a decimal.

30 minutes = 0.5 hours

45 minutes = 0.75 hours

Now try these 21.3

1 Work out how many
   (a) days there are in 6 weeks
   (b) seconds there are in $2\frac{1}{2}$ minutes
   (c) minutes there are in $4\frac{1}{4}$ hours
   (d) weeks there are in $4\frac{1}{2}$ years.

Remember
There is an extra day in a leap year and there is a leap year every four years.

2 Sarah is 12 years old today!
   (a) How many leap years has she lived through?
   (b) How many days old is Sarah today?
   (c) How many hours old is Sarah?

3 Joe counts that he gets 14 weeks' holiday from school every year.
   (a) How many weeks in a year does he go to school?
   (b) Estimate that he goes to school 5 days every week.
       How many days a year does he go to school?
   (c) Joe has been going to school for 8 years and he has never been
       absent! How many days has he spent at school?
   (d) School starts at 9:00 a.m. and finishes at 3:45 p.m.
       How long does Joe spend at school every week?

Continued ...

4 Owen can swim a length of the swimming pool in 1 minute 15 seconds.
  (a) How long does it take him to swim 7 lengths?
  (b) The swimming pool is 60 m long.
     How far does he swim in this time?

5 Puzzle

Match the times in the first column with the same time in the second column.

1 minute 40 seconds	2.5 minutes
3 hours 15 minutes	4.75 hours
2 minutes 30 seconds	200 seconds
4 hours 45 minutes	165 minutes
3 minutes 20 seconds	100 seconds
$\frac{1}{4}$ of an hour	105 minutes
2 hours 45 minutes	195 minutes
$1\frac{3}{4}$ hours	900 seconds

6 Brain strain

Can you live to be a million?

Nobody lives to be a million years old, but how old would you be if you lived
  (a) a million days
  (b) a million hours
  (c) a million minutes
  (d) a million seconds?

Hint Consider a year to be 365.25 days.

22 Enlargements and scale drawings

Subject links
- geography
- design and technology
- art

Coming up ...

- recognising and drawing enlargements using a scale factor
- drawing enlargements using a centre of enlargement and a scale factor
- making scale drawings
- scale factors as ratios

Chapter starter

Here are six pictures.

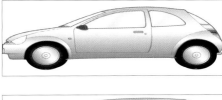

1. Measure the length and width of each rectangular frame.
2. What do rectangles A, C and F have in common?
3. What do rectangles D, E and F have in common?
4. What do rectangles A, B and D have in common?

Do you remember?

- how to multiply and divide by an integer
- the meaning of the words object and image
- how to draw and measure lines and angles
- how to plot and read coordinates in all four quadrants
- how to convert between metric units
- how to construct ASA, SAS and SSS triangles
- how to find simple loci

Key words

enlarge

enlargement

scale factor

centre of enlargement

object

image

vertex

scale drawing

scale

ratio

Kirsty has a photo taken in her karate gear.

It is 2 cm tall and 1 cm wide.

She wants a larger photo.

She decides to make it 4 cm taller and 4 cm wider.

The larger photo is 6 cm tall and 5 cm wide.

Here it is.

'That doesn't look right,' she thinks. 'I've put on a bit of weight!'

Kirsty has made the mistake of adding the same amount to both the height and the width.

She should have *multiplied* both the height and the width by the same amount.

Her original photo is 2 cm tall and 1 cm wide.

To make the photo 6 cm tall, she needs to multiply the original height by 3.

She needs to multiply the width by 3 as well.

So the width should be 3 × 1 cm = 3 cm.

> An **enlargement** of a shape always has all its measurements multiplied by the same number.
> This number is called the **scale factor**.

So Kirsty wants an enlargement with a scale factor of 3.

Continued...

Example

Is triangle DEF an enlargement of triangle ABC?

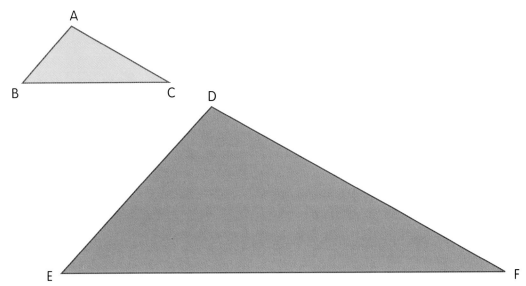

Solution

Measure the sides of triangle ABC.

AB = 2 cm   AC = 3 cm   BC = 4 cm

Measure the sides of triangle DEF.

DE = 6 cm   DF = 9 cm   EF = 12 cm

So in the triangle DEF, all the sides are three times as long as the corresponding sides in triangle ABC.

Therefore triangle DEF is an enlargement of triangle ABC.

___

As with other transformations, the original shape is called the **object** and the shape after it has been transformed is called the **image**.

Unlike other transformations, the image is *not* the same size as the object.

A shape and its enlargement are *not* congruent.

When you draw an enlargement, it helps to label the vertices with the same letter followed by a dash.

So in the image, the vertex corresponding to A is labelled A'.

The triangle DEF in the example above could be labelled A'B'C'.

To draw an enlargement, the length of each side must be multiplied by the same number (the scale factor) and all angles must stay the same.

Continued ...

Example

Draw an enlargement of this shape using a scale factor of 3.

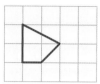

Solution

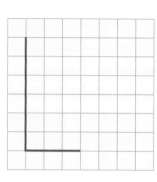

It is easiest if you start with a vertical or a horizontal line.

The horizontal line of the object is 1 cm long.

The vertical line is 2 cm long.

In the enlargement, the horizontal line needs to be 3 × 1 cm = 3 cm long.

The vertical line needs to be 3 × 2 cm = 6 cm long.

You need to be very careful to get the correct angles.

The top line slopes down one square and goes across two squares.

In the enlargement it must go down three squares and go across six squares.

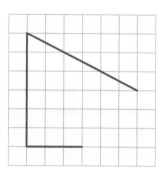

Finally, join the ends to complete the shape.

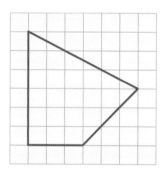

Hint
Check your drawing looks the right shape.

Now try these 22.1

① Draw enlargements of these shapes with a scale factor of 2.

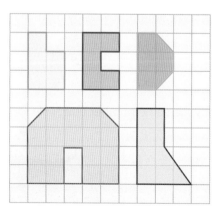

⚠ Scale factors are multiplying factors, not adding factors. So if AB = 1 cm and A'B' = 4 cm, the scale factor is not 3 (1 + 3 = 4). The scale factor is 4 (because 1 × 4 = 4).

Hint
To draw an enlargement with a scale factor of 2, make every line twice as long as it is in the original shape.

Continued ..

2 Now use a scale factor of 3 to draw enlargements of the shapes in question **1**.

3 Try this method of drawing an enlargement.
The bear is drawn on 0.5 cm squares.
Use a piece of centimetre-squared paper to produce an enlargement.
First, draw a square 8 cm long and 8 cm wide.
Then copy each square from the picture above on to the bigger squares on your paper.
You should end up with a picture twice as long and twice as wide as the original.

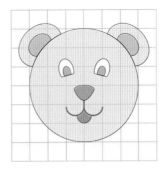

4 Look at this diagram.

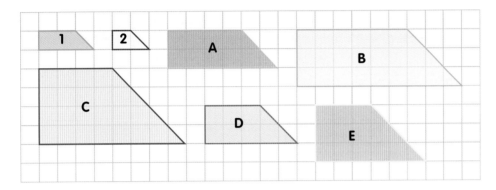

(a) Two of the shapes lettered A to E are enlargements of shape 1.
Which shapes are they and what is the scale factor of each enlargement?

(b) Two of the shapes lettered A to E are enlargements of shape 2.
Which shapes are they and what is the scale factor of each enlargement?

(c) Which shape is the odd one out?

5 Anglian Wardrobes created a logo from the company initials.

The yellow letters are an enlargement of the blue letters, with a scale factor of 2.

Design a similar logo, using your own initials.

Your design must contain your initials twice and the second set must be an enlargement of the first with a scale factor of 2.

6 Brain strain

In triangle ABC, AB = 3 cm, BC = 5 cm and AC = 6 cm.

In an enlargement, A'B' = 6 cm.

(a) What is the scale factor of the enlargement?

(b) How long are B'C' and A'C'?

Continued ...

With a friend

Draw a shape in a 4 by 3 cm grid, such as the example shown.

Your friend must draw an enlargement of your shape with a scale factor of 2.

Then you must draw an enlargement of the original shape with a scale factor of 3.

If either of you makes a mistake, that person scores a point.

Then your friend draws the starting shape, you draw the enlargement with scale factor 2 and your friend draws the enlargement with scale factor 3.

The first player to get 5 points loses.

22.2 Using a centre of enlargement

Imagine drawing a picture on a rubber sheet.

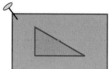

Pin the sheet at one corner.

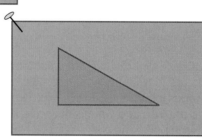

Stretch the sheet so that the drawing is enlarged with a scale factor of 2.

Each side of the triangle is twice the original length.

> Each vertex is twice as far from the pin as it was originally.

The pin has not moved.

The position of the pin is called the **centre of enlargement**.

Example

Draw an enlargement of this quadrilateral using the red dot as the centre of enlargement and with a scale factor of 3.

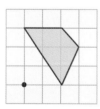

Solution

Draw lines from the centre of enlargement.

Each line must go through a vertex of the object.

Continued ...

Its length must be three times the distance from the centre of enlargement to the vertex of the object.

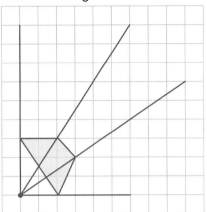

The ends of the lines mark the vertices of the image.

Join the vertices to complete the enlargement.

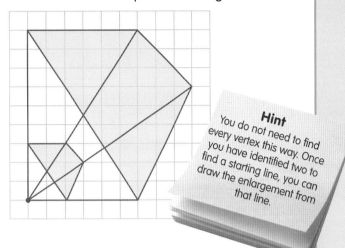

Hint
You do not need to find every vertex this way. Once you have identified two to find a starting line, you can draw the enlargement from that line.

Now try these 22.2

1. Enlarge each of these shapes using the red dot as the centre of enlargement.
   Enlarge A, B and C by a scale factor of 2.
   Enlarge D by a scale factor of 3.

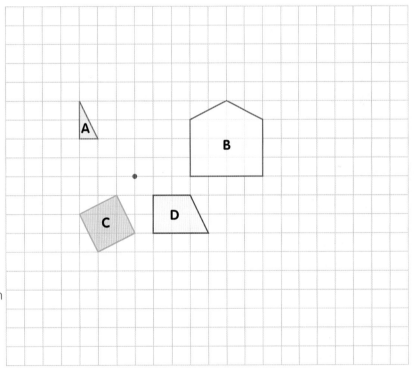

2. (a) Draw a set of axes with both the x and y axes labelled from 0 to 16.
   Plot the points A(2, 1), B(2, 3), C(3, 4) and D(3, 1).
   Join the points to create a trapezium.

   (b) Using the origin (0, 0) as the centre of enlargement, draw an enlargement of your trapezium with a scale factor of 2.
   Label the image A'B'C'D'.
   Write down the coordinates of points A', B', C' and D'.

   (c) Again using the origin as the centre of enlargement, draw an enlargement of your trapezium with a scale factor of 3.
   Label the image A"B"C"D".
   Write down the coordinates of points A", B", C" and D".

   (d) Still using the origin as the centre of enlargement, draw an enlargement of your trapezium with a scale factor of 4.
   Label the image A'"B'"C'"D'".
   Write down the coordinates of points A'", B'", C'" and D'".

Continued …

3 In the diagram, Zoe has tried to draw enlargements of shapes A, B, C and D with the centre of enlargement as shown.

She has made a mistake with two of the enlargements.

(a) Which two are wrong? What is wrong with them?

(b) What is the scale factor of the two correct enlargements?

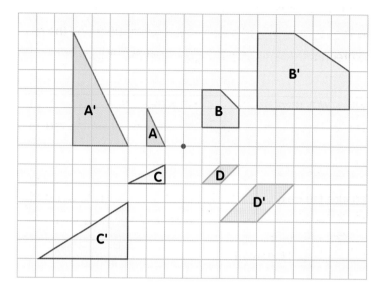

4 A teacher projects an image on to a whiteboard.

The projector is 1 m from the whiteboard. The image is too small.

It is 40 cm tall.

The teacher wants the image to be 120 cm tall.

How much further back should she move the projector?

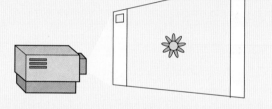

22.3 Scale drawings

A scale drawing is the same shape as the real object, but a different size.

Architects' plans are scale drawings.

Maps are also scale drawings.

Here is a scale drawing of the front of Sheila's greenhouse.

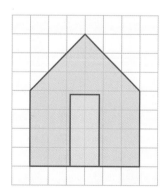

Here is a picture of the greenhouse showing its dimensions.

The side of the greenhouse is 2 m or 200 cm tall.
Sheila has drawn it 2 cm tall.

So the greenhouse is an enlargement of her drawing with a scale factor of 100 because 2 cm × 100 = 200 cm.

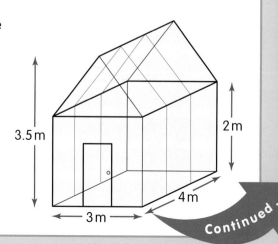

Continued

You say that the **scale** of the drawing is 1 cm to 100 cm.

This is because 1 cm on the plan represents 100 cm on the real greenhouse.

The greenhouse is 100 times bigger than the drawing.

Another way of writing the scale is 1 cm to 1 m.

This is because 1 cm on the plan represents 1 m on the real greenhouse.

Example

Measure the height of the door of the greenhouse on Sheila's drawing.

What is the real height of the door?

Solution

The door is 1.9 cm high on the drawing.

The real height of the door = 1.9 cm × 100
                            = 190 cm or 1.9 m

Example

Make a scale drawing of the side wall of Sheila's greenhouse.

Use a scale of 2 cm to 1 m.

Solution

Actual length of wall = 4 m

Length on scale drawing = 8 cm

Actual height of wall = 2 m

Height on scale drawing = 4 cm

> 1 m in real life is 2 cm on the plan.
> So 4 m in real life is
> 2 × 4 cm = 8 cm on the plan.

> 1 m in real life is 2 cm on the plan.
> So 2 m in real life is
> 2 × 2 cm = 4 cm on the plan.

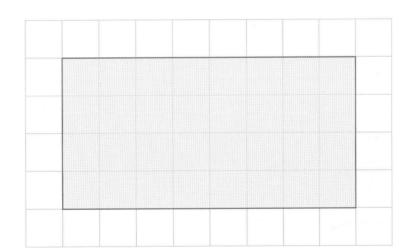

Now try these 22.3

1. Look at this diagram of a tennis court.
   Use it to make an accurate scale drawing of a tennis court.
   Use a scale of 1 cm to 1 m.

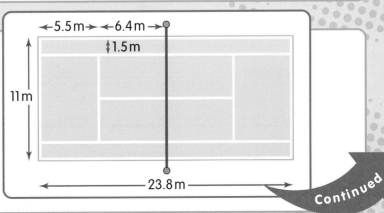

Continued ...

2 When George walks home from school, he can either walk along the roads round the park or on the path through the middle.
The plan shows the lengths of the roads around the edge of the park.

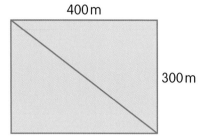

400 m

300 m

(a) Use a scale of 1 cm to 50 m to draw a scale drawing of the park.
(b) Draw in the diagonal to represent the path through the middle of the park.
Measure the diagonal on your drawing.
How long is the path through the middle of the park?

3 Make a scale drawing of each of these triangles.
Use the scale given.

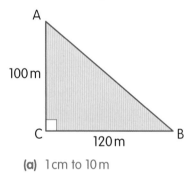

100 m
120 m

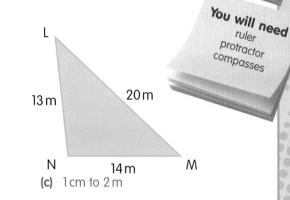

13 m   20 m
25 m   14 m

(a) 1 cm to 10 m   (b) 1 cm to 5 m   (c) 1 cm to 2 m

4 Use your drawings from question **3** to find these lengths.
(a) AB   (b) DE

Remember
You learnt how to construct triangles in Chapter 13.

You will need
ruler
protractor
compasses

22.4 Scale factors as ratios

The scale on a map will often be given as a ratio.

FOR EXAMPLE   Scale 1 : 20 000

This means that every 1 cm on the map is 20 000 cm in real life.

To make it easier to use the scale, you can convert one of the parts of the ratio to a different unit.

20 000 cm = 200 m

So a scale of 1 : 20 000 means that every 1 cm on the map is 200 m in real life.

Continued ...

Example

The map shows two villages, Podley and Croxton.

The scale is 1 : 500 000.

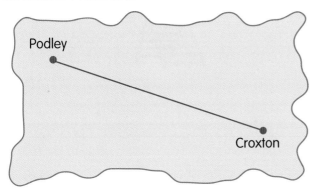

Seb runs from Podley to Croxton.

How many kilometres does he run?

Solution

On the map, Podley and Croxton are 6 cm apart. ← Measure the distance with a ruler.

1 cm on the map	represents	500 000 cm in real life.
1 cm	represents	5000 m
1 cm	represents	5 km

6 cm on the map represents 6 × 5 km = 30 km in real life.

Now try these 22.4

Remember
100 cm = 1 m
1000 m = 1 km

1. For each map scale, work out the distance that 1 cm on the map represents in real life.
   Give your answers in a sensible unit.
   (a) 1 : 100
   (b) 1 : 500
   (c) 1 : 30 000
   (d) 1 : 100 000
   (e) 1 : 200 000
   (f) 1 : 2 000 000

Continued...

② Here is a plan of a playground.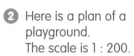
The scale is 1 : 200.
   (a) How far apart are the following?
   Give your answers in metres.
   (i) The swings and the climbing frame
   (ii) The climbing frame and the slide
   (iii) The slide and the roundabout
   (b) What are the length and width of the playground?

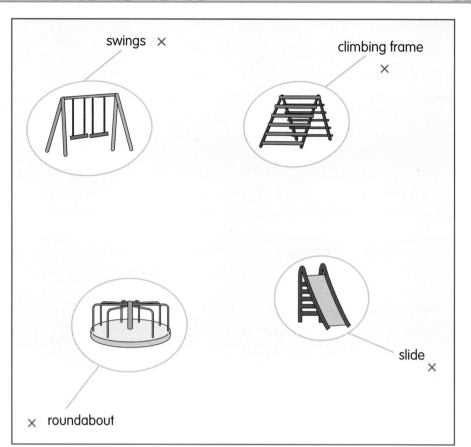

③ The map shows an orienteering course.
The scale is 1 : 50 000.
   (a) Ali ran each stage of the course:
   A to B, B to C, C to D and D to E.
   How long is each stage in real life?
   Give your answers in kilometres.
   (b) The finish line is 4.5 kilometres from E.
   How far from E is the finish line on the map?

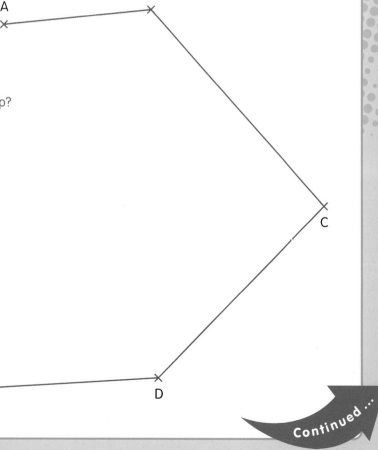

Continued...

Ratios can be used to represent any scale factor.

4 A scale model of a car is made.
The scale is 1 : 40.
(a) The height of the model is 4 cm.
What is the height of the car in real life, in metres?
(b) The length of the car in real life is 2.2 m.
What is the length of the model car?

5 A radio station in Leeds can be received up to 40 kilometres from Leeds.
The map shows the position of Leeds and four locations A, B, C and D.
The scale of the map is 1 : 1 000 000.

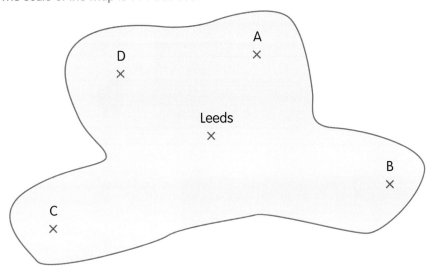

On a copy of the map, show the area that can receive the radio station.
Which of the locations A to D lie within this area?

23 Solids

Subject links
- design and technology
- science.
- art
- geography

Coming up ...

- the nets of three-dimensional shapes
- two-dimensional representations of three-dimensional shapes
- the volume of a cuboid
- the volume and surface area of a shape made of cuboids

Do you remember?
- what a prism is
- the names of three-dimensional shapes
- how to draw nets
- how to construct triangles and perpendiculars
- how to make isometric drawings
- how to calculate the areas of rectangles and shapes made out of rectangles
- how to calculate the surface area of a cuboid

Chapter starter

There are over 200 pyramids in Egypt.

The Great Pyramid is in the city of Giza in Egypt.

It was the tallest structure on Earth for more than 3200 years.

The Great Pyramid has four triangular sides and a square base.

The height of the Great Pyramid is 147 metres.

Each side of the square base is 230 metres in length.

1. Imagine looking straight at one face of the pyramid.
   You would see an isosceles triangle with a base of 230 m and a perpendicular height of 147 m.
   Make a scale drawing.
   Use a scale of 1 mm to 1 m.

2. Imagine looking at the pyramid from the ground.
   What is the maximum number of sides you could see?

3. What is the maximum number of sides you could see from the air?

4. What would the Great Pyramid look like from directly above?
   Draw a sketch of the view from above.

Key words

three-dimensional
two-dimensional
net
view
front elevation
side elevation
plan
cuboid
volume
cubic centimetre (cm^3)
cubic metre (m^3)
cubic millimetre (mm^3)
surface area
square centimetre (cm^2)
square metre (m^2)
square millimetre (mm^2)

Three-dimensional shapes can be made from a net.

To draw a net you need to be accurate.

First, draw a rough sketch of the net.

Then make an accurate drawing.

You may need to use some of the skills you learnt in Chapter 13.

Don't forget to add tabs.

If you are not sure how many tabs you need, it is better to add too many and then cut them off later when you make the model.

This is how you would make a net for this triangular prism.

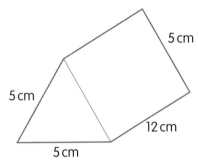

First, make a rough sketch.

● Draw the three rectangles accurately, 12 cm long and 5 cm wide.
● Then construct the two equilateral triangles. You will need to use compasses.
● Now add tabs.
● Cut out the net and make the prism.

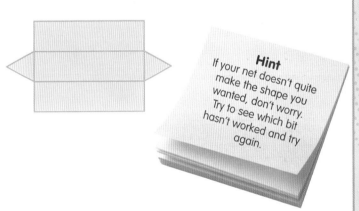

Hint
If your net doesn't quite make the shape you wanted, don't worry. Try to see which bit hasn't worked and try again.

Normally you don't have to worry about the tabs.

They are not part of the net.

Now try these 23.1

① This triangular prism has ends which are isosceles triangles.
The base of each triangle is 3 cm long and the sloping sides are 4 cm long.
The length of the prism is 8 cm.
Construct a net of this shape, cut it out and make the shape.
Make sure you draw a sketch first.

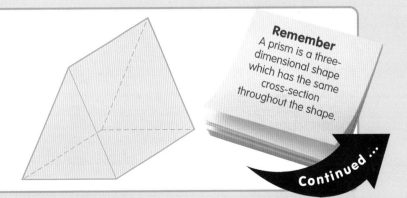

Remember
A prism is a three-dimensional shape which has the same cross-section throughout the shape.

Continued ...

2 Here is a net.

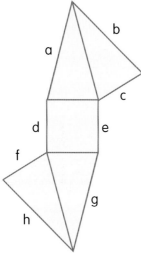

(a) What is the name of the three-dimensional shape it makes?

(b) Which edge will meet up with edge a?

(c) Pair up the other edges that will meet.

3 A tetrahedron has four faces.
In this tetrahedron, each face is an equilateral triangle with sides of 7 cm.

Dave says that there is only one possible net for a tetrahedron.
Is he right?
Try to draw some nets.

4 Look at the diagram.
Some of the shapes are nets. Some are not.
For those that are, name the shape and make a drawing on isometric paper.

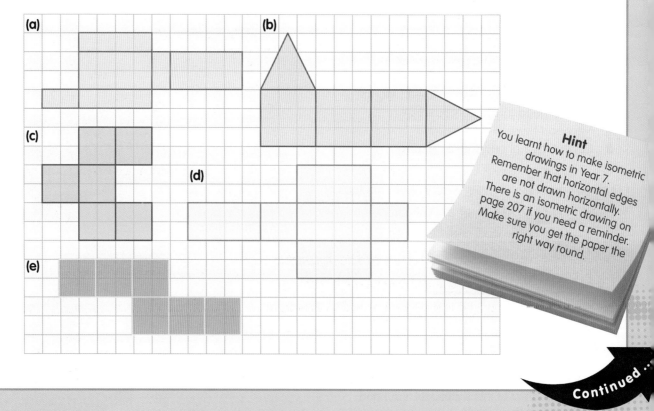

> **Hint**
> You learnt how to make isometric drawings in Year 7.
> Remember that horizontal edges are not drawn horizontally.
> There is an isometric drawing on page 207 if you need a reminder.
> Make sure you get the paper the right way round.

Continued ...

⑤ Puzzle

What shape would this net make?

Copy the net and make the shape to check you are right.

⑥ Brain strain

Make a net for this shape.

Be prepared to try one and then modify it if it doesn't work.

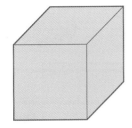

3 cm

1 cm

1 cm   1 cm

1 cm

1 cm   3 cm

1 cm

⑦ A company needs to make nets of a square-based pyramid.

The base is a 8 cm square and each isosceles triangle has two sides of 10 cm.

The net has to be made from A4 card, which is 29.7 cm long and 21 cm wide.

Design a net that will fit on A4 card.

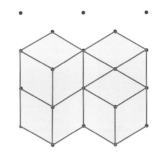

23.2 Plans and elevations

A drawing of a three-dimensional object can be misleading.

For example, this cube has a length and height of 2 cm.

The width is also supposed to be 2 cm, but it only measures about 1.4 cm.

Measure it to check!

Another type of drawing is an isometric drawing. Here is a shape made of five cubes drawn on isometric paper.

Continued ...

Sometimes it helps to draw three different views of a shape: the view looking straight at the front (the **front elevation**), the view from the right-hand side (the **side elevation**) and the view from above (the **plan**).

This shape is made of ten centimetre cubes.

Looking in the directions of the arrows, this is what you would see.

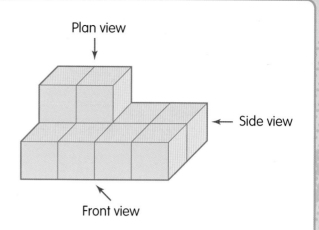

Plan view

Side view

Front view

Front elevation

Side elevation

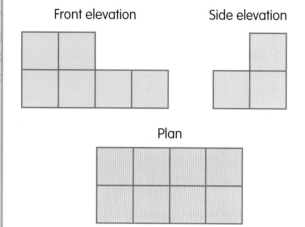

Plan

Now try these 23.2

① Make each of these shapes out of cubes.
For each shape, choose the diagram which is the front elevation, the side elevation and the plan.
Some of the views fit more than one shape.

(a)

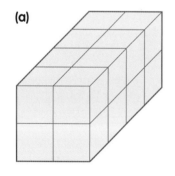

(b)

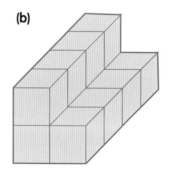

(c)

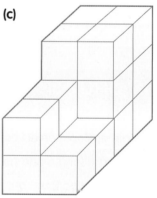

(1)

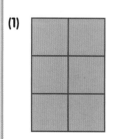

(2)

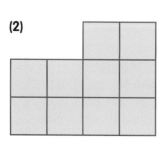

(3)

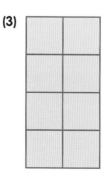

(4)

(5)

(6)

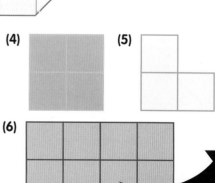

Continued

2 Make these shapes out of cubes.
Draw the front elevation, side elevation and plan of each shape.

(a) 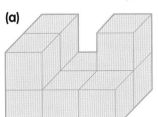   **(b)** 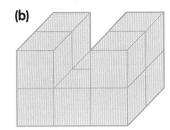   **(c)**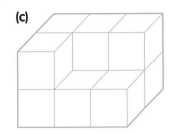

3 Make an isometric drawing of each of the shapes in question **2**.

4 Puzzle

Can you make a shape with these views?

Each shape is made of nine cubes.

(a) Front elevation   Side elevation

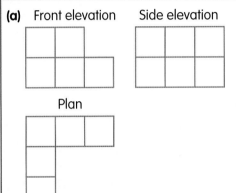

Plan

(b) Front elevation   Side elevation

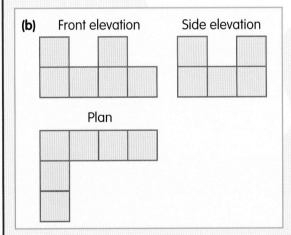

Plan

Make an isometric drawing of each shape.

5 Puzzle

All of these shapes have the same plan!

Which have the same front elevations?

Which have the same side elevations?

Make the shapes first and then draw the elevations.

A   B

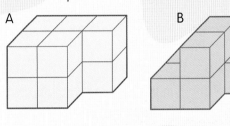

C   D

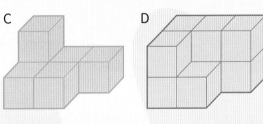

E   F

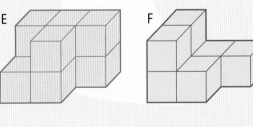

G   H

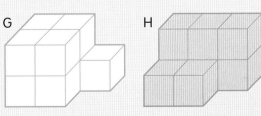

Area is the amount of two-dimensional space inside a two-dimensional shape.

A box has space inside it.

This is a three-dimensional space, which is called **volume**.

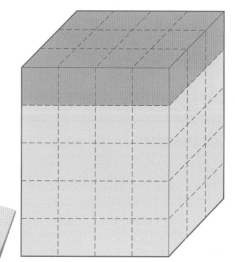

A box 4 cm long, 3 cm wide and 5 cm tall could be filled with centimetre cubes.

The top layer contains 4 × 3 = 12 centimetre cubes.

But there are five layers.

So the total number of centimetre cubes that will fill the box is 12 × 5 = 60.

Note
Volume can also be measured in metre cubes (m^3) and millimetre cubes (mm^3).

Volume can be measured in centimetre cubes.

The volume of the cuboid above is written as 60 cm^3 and read as '60 centimetres cubed' or '60 cubic centimetres'.

The number of cubes in the top layer = length × width.

This is multiplied by the height to calculate the total number of cubes.

So the volume of a cuboid = length × width × height.

You can write this as $V = l \times w \times h$.

Don't confuse volume with surface area, which you learnt about in Year 7.

Remember: the surface area is the area of all faces added together.

For this cuboid, the area of the front is 5 cm × 4 cm   = 20 cm^2.
The area of the back is the same as the front   = 20 cm^2.
The top is 4 cm × 3 cm   = 12 cm^2.
The bottom is the same as the top   = 12 cm^2.
The right-hand side is 5 cm × 3 cm   = 15 cm^2.
The left-hand side is the same as the right   = 15 cm^2.
The total surface area   = 94 cm^2.

① Calculate the volumes of these cuboids.

(a)
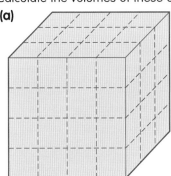

(b)
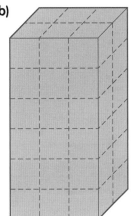

(c)
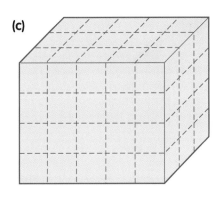

(d)
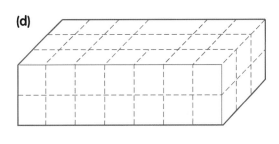

② Calculate the volumes of these cuboids.

(a)
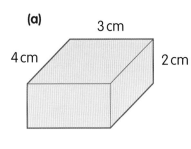

(b)
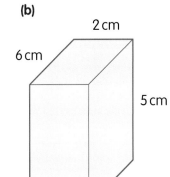

(c)
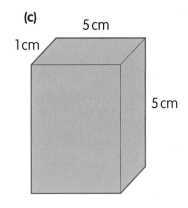

③ Find the surface area of each cuboid in question **2**.

④ Tommy has 60 centimetre cubes.
He wants to make a cuboid with them.
He makes a bottom layer 5 cm long and 2 cm wide.

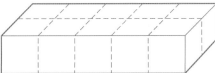

(a) How many cubes are there in this layer?
(b) He uses all 60 cubes.
How many layers high does he make the cuboid?

Continued ...

5 Copy and complete this table showing the dimensions of cuboids.

Length (cm)	Width (cm)	Height (cm)	Volume (cm³)
7	3	2	
3	4	5	
9	2	4	
4	6	2.5	
1.4	6	3	
3	4		48
5	2		100
8		4	96

6 A cube measures 4 cm × 4 cm × 4 cm.
What is the volume of the cube?

7 Ashley had a glass container that has a square base.
Each side of the base measures 8 cm.
The height of the container is 16 cm.
She wants to pour a litre of coloured water into the container.
She knows that 1 litre = 1000 cm³.
Will all of the coloured water fit into the container?

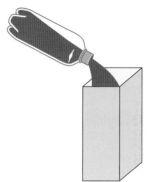

8 The Dinky Dice Company makes dice from centimetre cubes.

They are sold in boxes of 12.

The box must be in the shape of a cuboid.

(a) Find four different ways of making a cuboid out of twelve centimetre cubes.

(b) Draw a net for each cuboid.

(c) To keep costs down, the company wants to use the box with the smallest surface area, as it will use the least amount of card.
Find the area of each net.
Which one has the smallest area?

23.4 Shapes made from cuboids

This cuboid has a volume of
3 cm × 2 cm × 4 cm
= 24 cm³.

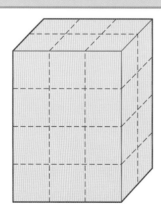

This cuboid has a volume of
4 cm × 2 cm × 2 cm = 16 cm³.

Continued

This shape is not a cuboid.

It is made from the two cuboids from the previous page.

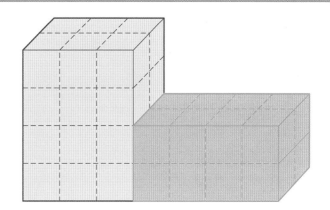

Its volume is 24 cm³ + 16 cm³ = 40 cm³.

To find the volume of a compound shape, split it into cuboids.

Then find the volume of each cuboid and add the volumes together.

You cannot find the surface area of the shape by adding the surface areas of the two cuboids.

Can you see why not?

The shape has eight faces.
The area of the front is 20 cm².
The area of the back is also 20 cm².
The left-hand end has an area of 8 cm².
The two right-hand faces are 4 cm² each.
The bottom has an area of 14 cm².
The two top faces have areas of 6 cm² and 8 cm².
So the total surface area is
20 cm² + 20 cm² + 8 cm² + 4 cm² + 4 cm² + 14 cm² + 6 cm² + 8 cm² = 84 cm².

Now try these 23.4

1 Find the volume of these shapes by splitting them into two cuboids.

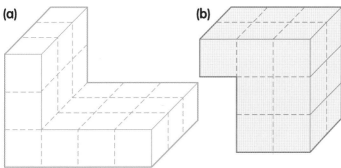

(a)

(b)

2 Each of the shapes in question **1** has eight faces.
Find the surface area of each shape in question **1**.

Continued ...

3 Find the volumes of these shapes.

(a)

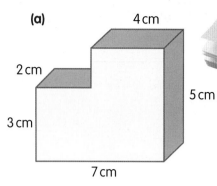

4 cm

2 cm

3 cm

5 cm

7 cm

Hint
If you are not sure of some of the measurements, draw the yellow face on centimetre-squared paper.

(b)

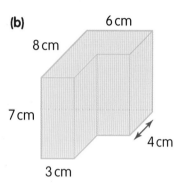

6 cm

8 cm

7 cm

4 cm

3 cm

(c)

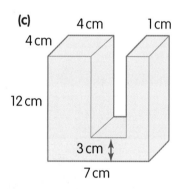

4 cm   1 cm

4 cm

12 cm

3 cm

7 cm

5 Brain strain

Toby has lots of cubes.

He realises that he has just the right number to make a big cube.

Or, if he prefers, he has just enough to make three different-sized cubes.

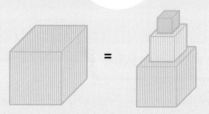

Toby knows he has fewer than 500 cubes.

How many cubes does he have?

4 Puzzle

This cuboid is made from three prisms.

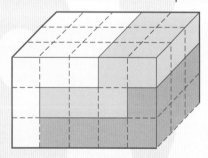

(a) Find the volume of each prism.
   Check that they have the same volume.
(b) Draw each prism on isometric paper.
(c) Find another way of splitting the cuboid into three differently-shaped prisms each with the same volume.

Research

1 Piet Hein invented the Soma Cube puzzle.
   It consists of seven solid pieces that fit together to form a cube.
   Find out what the seven pieces are.
   Make each piece from interlocking cubes.
   See if you can assemble them to make a cube.
2 Another cube dissection puzzle is the Steinhaus Cube.
   If you solved the Soma Cube, try the Steinhaus Cube!

24 Formulae

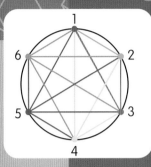

Coming up ...

- using formulae expressed in symbols
- substituting positive and negative numbers into a formula
- writing formulae

Do you remember?
- *how to substitute numbers into expressions*
- *about the order of operations*
- *how to add, subtract, multiply and divide negative numbers*

Chapter starter

Look at this pattern.

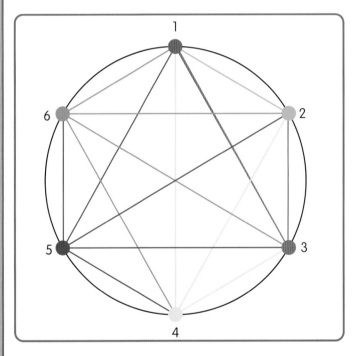

It is a six-point **mystic rose**.

Each point is joined to every other point.

1. How many lines are there in this mystic rose?

2. How many lines there are in these mystic roses?
   (a) five-point
   (b) eight-point
   (c) ten-point

3. How do mystic roses with an even number of points look different from those with an odd number of points?

4. How can you work out how many lines there are in a mystic rose without drawing it?

Key words

formula (plural: formulae)

substitute

substitution

Note
The plural of formula is formulae.

A **formula** is a rule for working something out.

It is an equation which shows how one quantity relates to another.

For example, the area, *A*, of a triangle is found using the formula

$A = \frac{1}{2}bh$.

b stands for the length of the base of the triangle.
h stands for the height of the triangle.

You can substitute the symbols in a formula with numbers to work out one of the quantities. You do this in the same way as you substituted numbers for symbols in an expression in Chapter 14.

Example

This is the formula for the surface area, *S*, of a cuboid.

$S = 2dw + 2dh + 2hw$

How much wrapping paper is needed to wrap this box of chocolates?

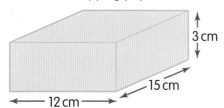

3 cm
15 cm
12 cm

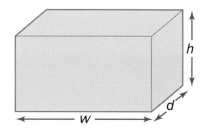

h
w
d

Solution

You need to work out the surface area of the box.

$d = 15$

$w = 12$

$h = 3$

Remember $2dw$ means $2 \times d \times w$.

Substitute values into the formula:

$S = 2dw + 2dh + 2hw$

$S = 2 \times 15 \times 12 + 2 \times 15 \times 3 + 2 \times 3 \times 12$

$S = 360 + 90 + 72$

Remember, you do the multiplications first, then the additions.

$S = 522$

So the surface area is 522 cm².

Don't forget to include the units.

Continued

Example

Use the formula $y = 4x^2 - 7$ to work out the value of y when $x = 5$.

Solution

You need to substitute $x = 5$ into the formula.

$y = 4x^2 - 7$

$y = 4 \times 5^2 - 7$

$y = 4 \times 25 - 7$

$y = 100 - 7$

$y = 93$

> Remember BIDMAS.
> Work out the index first, then the multiplication and finally the subtraction.

Example

Use the formula $a = \dfrac{2b}{b+1}$ to work out the value of a when $b = {}^-3$.

Solution

Substitute $b = {}^-3$ into the formula.

$a = \dfrac{2b}{b+1}$

$a = \dfrac{2 \times {}^-3}{{}^-3 + 1}$

> Work out the value of the top part and the bottom part separately first.

$a = \dfrac{{}^-6}{{}^-2}$

> Remember, this means ${}^-6 \div {}^-2$.

$a = 3$

Now try these 24.1

① Use these formulae to work out the value of a when $b = 4$.
- (a) $a = 6b - 3$
- (b) $a = 10 - 2b$
- (c) $a = b^2$
- (d) $a = 2b^2 - 10$
- (e) $a = b^3$
- (f) $a = b^3 - 8$
- (g) $a = 3(b + 5)$
- (h) $a = \dfrac{b}{2}$
- (i) $a = \dfrac{b + 2}{b - 1}$

> **Remember**
> b^3 means $b \times b \times b$.

② Use these formulae to work out the value of c when $d = 5$.
- (a) $c = 2d + 5$
- (b) $c = 4 - d$
- (c) $c = \dfrac{d}{2}$
- (d) $c = 3(d - 2.1)$
- (e) $c = 12 - 2d$
- (f) $c = \dfrac{3d + 1}{2}$

③ Work out the value of $y = 5(x + 4)$ when
- (a) $x = 2$
- (b) $x = {}^-3$
- (c) $x = {}^-4$.

④ The formula to find the number, h, halfway between two numbers n and m is $h = \dfrac{n + m}{2}$.
- (a) Use the formula to work out the number halfway between these numbers.
  - (i) 22 and 114
  - (ii) 311 and 457
  - (iii) 37 and 96
  - (iv) ${}^-7$ and 3
  - (v) ${}^-12$ and 8
  - (vi) ${}^-11$ and ${}^-4$
- (b) Jose, Bonnie and Tyler all live in the same road.
  Jose lives at number 38 and Bonnie lives at number 146
  Tyler's house is exactly halfway between Jose's and Bonnie's houses.
  What number does Tyler live at?

Continued ...

5 The number of lines, l, in an n-point mystic rose is given by the formula $l = \frac{n(n-1)}{2}$.
Use the formula to work out the number of lines in these mystic roses.
(a) 20-point　　　　(b) 50-point　　　　(c) 100-point

Remember
You met mystic roses in the starter.

6 Brain strain

Ohm's law is a formula for an electrical circuit.

In the formula

$V = IR$

V is the voltage, I is the current and R is the resistance.

(a) Find the value of V when
　　(i) $I = 3$ and $R = 10$　　　(ii) $I = 5$ and $R = 4$.
(b) Find the value of R when
　　(i) $V = 12$ and $I = 3$　　　(ii) $V = 32$ and $I = 4$

7 Brain strain

Supports for a house are made out of pillars of concrete.

Each pillar is a square-based cuboid.

The formula for the volume, V, of each cuboid is $V = hb^2$.

(a) Work out how much concrete is needed to make each of these pillars.

(i)
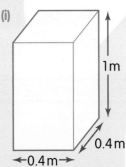
1m
0.4m
←0.4m→

(ii)
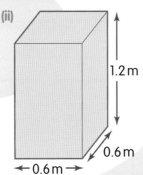
1.2m
0.6m
←0.6m→

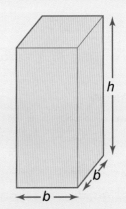
h
b
←b→

(b) 0.4 m³ of concrete is used to make this pillar.
What is its height?

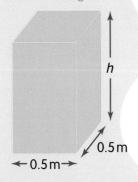
h
0.5m
←0.5m→

Sometimes you will need to work out the formula yourself.

Example
Here are some patterns made using counters.

Find a formula for the number of counters, *C*, in a 4 by *n* rectangle.

Solution
Add some colour to the diagrams to help you see how the patterns are made.

  4 by 2 rectangle   4 by 3 rectangle   4 by 4 rectangle

For a 4 by 2 rectangle, $C = 2 \times 2 + 4$.
For a 4 by 3 rectangle, $C = 2 \times 3 + 4$.
For a 4 by 4 rectangle, $C = 2 \times 4 + 4$.
So for a 4 by *n* rectangle, $C = 2n + 4$.

> Each pattern is made of 2 lots of *n* counters plus 4 counters in the middle.

Now try these 24.2

1. Emma has £5 of credit on her mobile phone.
   It costs her 8p to send a text message.
   (a) Write down how you should work out Emma's
   remaining credit after she sends ten text messages.
   (b) Use some of these algebra cards to write a formula
   for her credit in pence, *c*, after sending *n* text messages.

   Hint
   Change £5
   into pence.

   | = | + | 500 | *n* |
   | × | − | 8 | *c* |

2. Felicity is putting up a new fence around her garden.
   (a) Write down a formula for the amount of fencing, *F*,
   that Felicity needs.
   (b) Felicity's garden is 30 m long and 8 m wide.
   How much fencing does she need?
   (c) Jamie uses 50 m of fencing to enclose his garden.
   His garden is 10 m wide.
   How long is Jamie's garden?

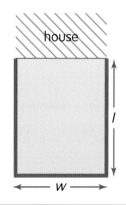

house

l

w

Continued ...

❸ Brain strain

Jess and Dan are investigating how many counters are needed to make some square patterns. They both think of a rule in a different way.

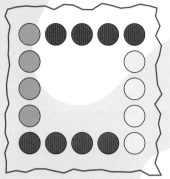

5 by 5 square

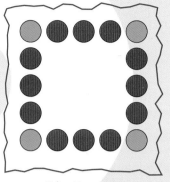

5 by 5 square

Hint
Draw
a 2 by 2 square
a 3 by 3 square
a 4 by 4 sqaure.

Here are their formulae for the number of counters, *C*, in an *n* by *n* square.

Jess

$C = 4(n - 2) + 4$

Dan

$C = 4(n - 1)$

(a) Which diagram did Jess draw?
(b) Explain how Jess and Dan found their rules.
(c) Expand and simplify the formulae to show that the rules are the same.

Investigation

Look at the example on p219.

Find a formula for the number of counters, *C*, needed to make these rectangles.

(a) 2 by *n* rectangle

(b) 3 by *n* rectangle

(c) 5 by *n* rectangle

(d) 6 by *n* rectangle

Investigate further

Research

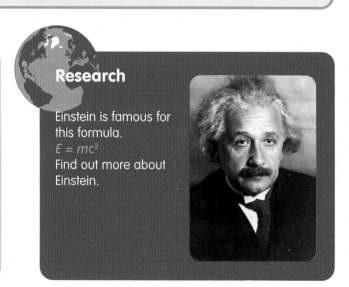

Einstein is famous for this formula.
$E = mc^2$
Find out more about Einstein.

25 Equations

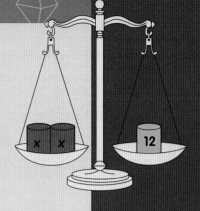

Coming up ...

● solving an equation with an unknown on one or both sides
● solving an equation involving brackets
● constructing an equation in order to solve a problem
● checking that you have solved an equation correctly

Chapter starter

1 Solve these balance problems to find the mass of one coloured cylinder.

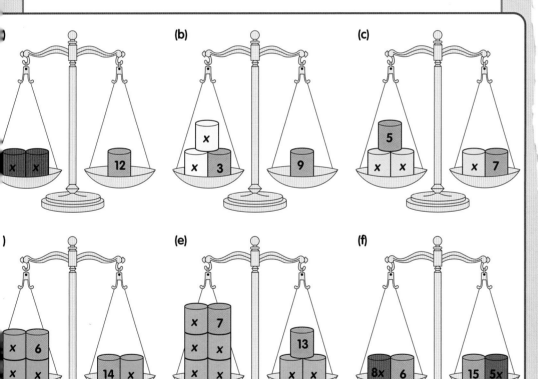

Do you remember?
● how to use algebraic notation
● about inverse operations
● how to simplify algebraic expressions
● how to expand brackets
● how to find the perimeter of a rectangle
● that the sum of the angles in a triangle is 180°

Key words

balance
equation
unknown
solve
solution
bracket

2 What strategies did you use?
3 Write down an equation (for example 2x = 12) to match each balance problem.
4 Make up your own balance problem for a friend to solve.

25.1 Solving equations

An **equation** is a statement containing an **unknown** that says 'this expression equals that expression'.

You can **solve** an equation to find the value of the unknown by the **balance** method.

Example

> What you do to the LHS (left-hand side) you must do to the RHS.

Solve these equations.

(a) $5a - 4.5 = 10$ **(b)** $9 = \frac{b}{4} + 6$ **(c)** $18 - 3c = 6$

Solution

(a)

$$5a - 4.5 = 10$$

+4.5 ⟶ $5a = 14.5$ ⟵ +4.5

÷5 ⟶ $a = 2.9$ ⟵ ÷5

> The inverse of 'subtract 4.5' is 'add 4.5'.

> Make sure you add 4.5 to **both** sides of the equation.

> $a = 2.9$ is the **solution**.
> You have **solved** the equation.

> **Check:** $5 \times 2.9 - 4.5 = 14.5 - 4.5 = 10$ ✓

(b) It is easier to rewrite this equation as $\frac{b}{4} + 6 = 9$

$$\frac{b}{4} + 6 = 9$$

−6 ⟶ $\frac{b}{4} = 3$ ⟵ −6

×4 ⟶ $b = 12$ ⟵ ×4

> Remember, $\frac{b}{4}$ means 'b divided by 4'.

> The inverse of 'divide by 4' is 'multiply by 4'.

> **Check:** $\frac{12}{4} + 6 = 3 + 6 = 9$ ✓

(c) This one is more tricky.

> Don't lose the minus sign!

$$18 - 3c = 6$$

−18 ⟶ $^-3c = ^-12$ ⟵ −18

÷$^-$3 ⟶ $c = 4$ ⟵ ÷$^-$3

> **Check:** $18 - 3 \times 4 = 18 - 12 = 6$ ✓

You can avoid all the negative numbers by adding $3c$ to both sides first.

$$18 - 3c = 6$$

+3c ⟶ $18 = 6 + 3c$ ⟵ +3c

−6 ⟶ $12 = 3c$ ⟵ −6

÷3 ⟶ $4 = c$ ⟵ ÷3

So $c = 4$

> This gets rid of the ^-3c on the left-hand side.

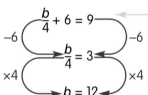

Continued .

Some word problems can be solved by first writing down an equation and then solving it.

Example

Three friends run in a relay race.

Altogether their time is 65 seconds.

Harry takes 4 seconds longer than Dan.

Millie takes 5 seconds less than Dan.

How many seconds does each person take?

Solution

Let s stand for the number of seconds that Dan takes.

Dan	Harry	Millie	Total
s	$s + 4$	$s - 5$	65

So $\quad s + s + 4 + s - 5 = 65$

Simplify:
$$3s - 1 = 65$$
$$+1 \qquad \qquad +1$$
$$3s = 66$$
$$\div 3 \qquad \qquad \div 3$$
$$s = 22$$

So Dan takes 22 seconds.

Harry takes 26 seconds.

Millie takes 17 seconds.

Don't forget to answer the question!

Check: $22 + 26 + 17 = 65$ ✓

Now try these 25.1

1 Solve each of these equations.
Make sure the two sides of the equation always balance.
Check each of your solutions.

(a) $5a = 15$　　(b) $10 - b = 7$　　(c) $7 = c - 8$

(d) $\dfrac{d}{4} = 5$　　(e) $19 = 6 + e$　　(f) $3f + 6 = 15$

(g) $12 + 2g = 16$　　(h) $2 = 7h - 5$　　(i) $10 - 3i = 4$

(j) $\dfrac{j}{6} + 3 = 9$　　(k) $\dfrac{k}{8} - 2 = 0$　　(l) $7 - \dfrac{l}{4} = 4$

2 Solve each of these equations.
Make sure the two sides of the equation always balance.
Check each of your solutions.

(a) $2r = 4.2$　　(b) $s + 6.2 = 11$　　(c) $5.4 = 8 - t$

(d) $4u - 5.6 = 10$　　(e) $3v - 0.5 = 1$　　(f) $\dfrac{w}{4} = 3.2$

(g) $10 - 2x = 1.8$　　(h) $9.5 = 7.1 + 3y$　　(i) $4.2 + \dfrac{z}{2} = 7.2$

Continued ...

3 Look at how Rob solves this equation.
Use Rob's method to solve these equations.

(a) $\frac{32}{a} = 4$ (b) $\frac{45}{b} = 9$ (c) $\frac{50}{c} + 4 = 12$

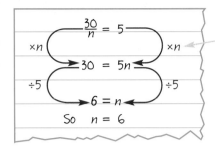

$$\frac{30}{n} = 5$$
$\times n$ $\qquad$ $\times n$
$$30 = 5n$$
$\div 5$ $\qquad$ $\div 5$
$$6 = n$$
So $\quad n = 6$

> Multiply **both** sides by n to make the equation easier to solve.

4 Three friends share £150 between them.

Freya gets £10 more than David.
Mac gets £35 less than Freya.
Use m for the amount of money that David receives.

(a) Write down an expression for the amount of money that
   (i) Freya receives
   (ii) Mac receives.
(b) Write down an equation for this information.
(c) Solve your equation.
   How much money do the friends get each?

5 A group of friends share the cost of a meal equally.

The total cost of the meal is £120.
Each person pays £15.
(a) Write down an equation for this information.
   Use n for the number of people in the group.
(b) How many people are there in the group?

6 Brain strain

(a) Write down an expression for the perimeter of this rectangle.

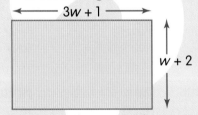

$3w + 1$

$w + 2$

(b) Simplify your expression.
(c) The perimeter of the rectangle is 30 cm.
   Write down an equation for the perimeter of this rectangle.
(d) Work out the length and width of the rectangle.

Sometimes an equation contains one or more **brackets**.

One way to deal with a bracket is to remove it before you solve the equation.

Example

Solve $5(3x - 6) = 13$.

Solution

First multiply out the bracket.

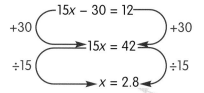

$5(3x - 6) = 12$

> Remember to multiply every term inside the bracket by 5.

$5 \times 3x + 5 \times {}^-6 = 12$

Now solve the equation:

$$15x - 30 = 12$$
$$+30 \qquad \qquad +30$$
$$15x = 42$$
$$\div 15 \qquad \qquad \div 15$$
$$x = 2.8$$

> **Check:** $5(3 \times 2.8 - 6) = 12$ ✓

An alternative method is to divide **both** sides of the equation by the number outside the bracket.

Example

Mohammed

> I think of a number and add 13. When I multiply the result by 4 the answer is 80. What is my number?

Solution

You can build up an equation for Mohammed's number like this.

I think of a number...	n
... and add 13 ...	$n + 13$
... multiply the result by 4 ...	$4(n + 13)$
... the answer is 80.	

> You need a bracket as you are multiplying both n and 13 by 4.

Now solve the equation.

$$4(n + 13) = 80$$
$$\div 4 \qquad \qquad \div 4$$
$$n + 13 = 20$$
$$-13 \qquad \qquad -13$$
$$n = 7$$

> 4 lots of $n + 13$ equals 80. So $n + 13$ must equal 20.

> **Check:** $4(7 + 13) = 4 \times 20 = 80$ ✓

Now try these 25.2

1 Solve each of these equations by expanding the bracket first.
(a) $4(w + 2) = 14$ **(b)** $5(x - 3) = 11$
(c) $10(7 - y) = 16$ **(d)** $8 = 5(2z - 4)$
Check each of your solutions by substituting back into the original equation.

2 Solve each of these equations by dividing both sides by the number outside of the bracket.
(a) $4(q + 3) = 20$ **(b)** $6(r - 7) = 18$
(c) $2 = 2(3s - 8)$ **(d)** $5(6 - t) = 15$
Check each of your solutions by substituting back into the original equation.

3 Solve each of these equations.
(a) $5(2a + 1) = 17$ **(b)** $4(3 + 2b) = 52$
(c) $7(12 - 2c) = 28$ **(d)** $6(2d - 1) = 3$
(e) $8(e - 5) = 4$ **(f)** $10(8 - 4f) = 0$
Check each of your solutions by substituting back into the original equation.

4 Jack

I think of a number and subtract 7. When I multiply the result by 26 the answer is 52. What is my number?

(a) Write down an equation for Jack's number. You will need to use a bracket.
(b) Find Jack's number by solving your equation.

5 Lipsticks have been reduced by £1 in the sale. Jane buys three lipsticks and pays £10.50. Use c for the cost of a lipstick before the sale.
(a) Write down an expression for the sale price of a lipstick.
(b) Write down an expression for the cost of three lipsticks.
(c) Write down an equation for the cost of three lipsticks.
(d) Solve your equation to find the original price of a lipstick.

6 **(a)** Expand these.
   (i) $4(3x + 2)$ **(ii)** $6(2x - 1)$
(b) Use your answers to part **(a)** to help you simplify $4(3x + 2) + 6(2x - 1)$.
(c) Use your answer to part **(b)** to help you solve $4(3x + 2) + 6(2x - 1) = 122$.
(d) Solve each of these equations.
   (i) $8(y + 4) + 5(2y + 3) = 101$
   (ii) $3(2z - 1) + 4(5 - z) = 21$

7 **(a)** Write down an expression for the sum of the angles in this triangle. Simplify your expression.

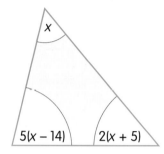

(b) Write down an equation for the sum of the angles in the triangle.
(c) Use your equation to work out each of the angles in the triangle.

8 The perimeter of a rectangle is given by the formula $P = 2(l + w)$.
The perimeter of a rectangle is 30 cm.
The length of the rectangle is 8.4 cm.

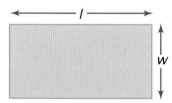

(a) Write down an equation for this information.
(b) Solve the equation to find the width of the rectangle.

Look back at how you solved the problems in the Chapter starter.

Sometimes there is an unknown on both sides of the equation. For example, $3x - 8 = 20 - x$.

The first step in solving equations like these is to get **all** the **unknowns** on **one side**.

Example

Solve $3x - 8 = 20 - x$.

Solution

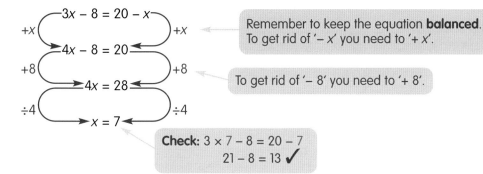

Remember to keep the equation **balanced**.
To get rid of '$- x$' you need to '$+ x$'.

To get rid of '$- 8$' you need to '$+ 8$'.

Check: $3 \times 7 - 8 = 20 - 7$
$21 - 8 = 13$ ✓

Example

Jamie and Holly both start the day with the same amount of credit on their mobile phones.

Jamie sends 18 texts and has £1.40 of credit left.

Holly sends 12 texts and has £2 of credit left.

Jamie and Holly are charged the same for each text that they send.

(a) Write down expressions for Jamie's and Holly's credit at the beginning of the day. Use t for the cost of one text message.
(b) Write down and solve an equation to find the cost of one text message
(c) How much credit does Jamie have to start with?

Solution

(a) t = cost of one text message
At the beginning of the day
Jamie's credit is $18t + 140$.
Holly's credit is $12t + 200$.

It is easier to work in pence.
So £1.40 = 140p
and £2 = 200p.

Continued ...

(b) At the beginning of the day
Jamie's credit = Holly's credit

> You are told they start the day with the same amount of credit so the two expressions are equal.

So

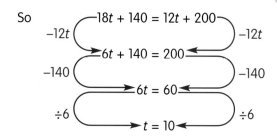

$$-18t + 140 = 12t + 200$$
$$-12t \qquad\qquad -12t$$
$$6t + 140 = 200$$
$$-140 \qquad\qquad -140$$
$$6t = 60$$
$$\div 6 \qquad\qquad \div 6$$
$$t = 10$$

So a text message costs 10p.

(c) Substitute $t = 10$ into $18t + 140$.
So $18t + 140 = 18 \times 10 + 140$
$\qquad\qquad\quad = 320$
So Jamie's credit is 320p or £3.20.

> Check that Holly's credit is also 320p.
> $12 \times 10 + 200 = 320$ ✓

Now try these 25.3

① Solve each of these equations.
   (a) $3a + 4 = 2a + 7$ **(b)** $7b - 5 = 6b + 1$
   (c) $4c + 3 = 2c + 5$ **(d)** $2d - 4 = 8 - d$
   (e) $6e + 3 = 12 - 3e$ **(f)** $7f - 2 = 4f + 7$
   (g) $3 + 2g = 13 - 3g$ **(h)** $10 - h = 16 - 3h$
   Check each of your solutions by substituting back into the original equation.

② Solve each of these equations.
   (a) $2(u + 4) = u + 13$ **(b)** $3(v + 5) = 2v + 22$
   (c) $6(w - 3) = 4w + 2$ **(d)** $5x - 6 = 2(4 - x)$
   (e) $6(2y - 7) = 3(y + 4)$ **(f)** $2(z - 2) = 3(7 - z)$
   Check each of your solutions by substituting back into the original equation.

> **Remember**
> Multiply out any brackets first.

③ Jose downloads some music and films from the internet.
   If he spends all his money he can

> download 10 music tracks and rent 3 films

   or

> download 6 music tracks and rent 4 films.

   Films cost £2 to rent.
   Use m to represent the cost of downloading a music track.
   (a) Write down an expression for the cost of
       (i) downloading 10 music tracks and renting 3 films
       (ii) downloading 6 music tracks and renting 4 films.
   (b) Your two expressions are equal. Write an equation that shows this.
   (c) Solve your equation to find the cost of downloading one music track.
   (d) How much money does Jose have?

Continued ...

4 Peter and Jenny both score the same number of points in a computer game.
Peter collects seven swords and four magic spells.
Jenny collects five swords and eight magic spells.
Magic spells are worth 50 points each.
Let s = number of points for collecting a sword.
  (a) Write down an expression for Peter's score.
  (b) Write down an equation for Peter and Jenny's scores.
  (c) Solve your equation to find
      (i) how many points a sword is worth
      (ii) how many points Jenny scores.

5 Catherine and Isobel both have the same amount of money.
Catherine buys six CDs and has £2 left.
Isobel buys four CDs and has £18 left.
Let c = the cost of one CD.
  (a) Write down an equation for this information.
  (b) Solve your equation to find the cost of one CD.
  (c) How much money did Catherine and Isobel have each?

BARGAIN BASEMENT
ANY CD ONLY £✸

---

6 Brain strain

Three friends play a computer game.

Between them they score 530 points.

Darren scores 30 points more than Beth.

Carmella scores twice as many points as Darren.

How many points does each friend score?

7 Brain strain

Look at this two-way function machine.

Find the input which gives the same output whichever way round the function machine you go.

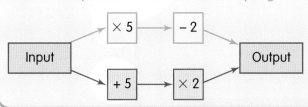

8 Brain strain

Find the area of this square.

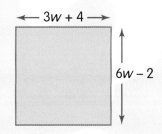

The lengths are in centimetres.

26 Graphs

Subject links
- geography
- science

Coming up ...

drawing straight-line graphs
drawing and interpreting real-life graphs

Chapter starter

Graphs can be used to tell a story.

① Match the graphs with the stories.

(a) 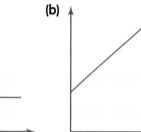   **(b)** 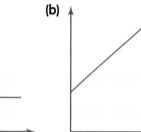   **(c)**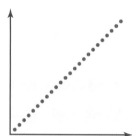

(d) 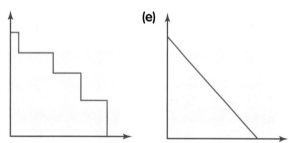   **(e)**

(i) Amount of pocket money saved against amount of pocket money spent.

(ii) Size of phone bill (including line rental) against time spent on phone.

(iii) Amount earned on a paper round against number of papers delivered.

(iv) Amount of money in a bank account against time.

(v) Weight of bag of frozen peas against time after purchase.

② Explain the shape of each graph.

Continued ...

Key words

equation
coordinates
x coordinate
y coordinate
axis (plural: axes)
x axis
y axis
y intercept
gradient
slope
coefficient

What do any horizontal, vertical or sloping sections represent?

3 Why aren't the points connected in graph C?

4 Graph E dips at the point marked *.
Give a reason for this.

5 Could any of the stories be represented by more than one graph?
Explain your answer fully.

6 Sketch a different graph to represent each story.

26.1 Drawing straight-line graphs

Follow these steps to draw a graph.

1 Complete a table of values for the **equation**.

> Substitute values of x into the equation of the line. You may be given the values of x to use or you may have to decide which values to use.

2 Draw and label a pair of axes.

> If you are not told how far to extend the axes, look in your table for the least and greatest values of x and y.

3 Plot the points on the coordinate grid.

4 Use a ruler to join the points.

5 Label the line with its equation.

Example

Draw the graph of $y = 3x - 1$.

Solution

x	$^-3$	$^-2$	$^-1$	0	1	2	3
$y = 3x - 1$	$^-10$	$^-7$	$^-4$	$^-1$	2	5	8
Coordinates	$(^-3, ^-10)$	$(^-2, ^-7)$	$(^-1, ^-4)$	$(0, ^-1)$	$(1, 2)$	$(2, 5)$	$(3, 8)$

> When $x = ^-2$, $y = 3x - 1$
> $\qquad\qquad = 3 \times ^-2 - 1$
> $\qquad\qquad = ^-6 - 1$
> $\qquad\qquad = ^-7$.
> $x = ^-2$ and $y = ^-7$ so the coordinates to plot are $(^-2, ^-7)$.

Continued...

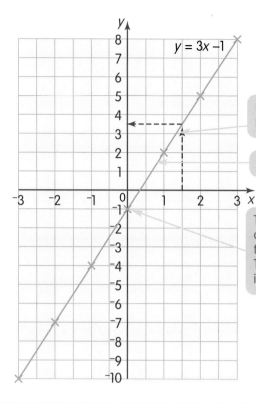

Every point on the line follows the rule $y = 3x - 1$.
For example: $3 \times 1.5 - 1 = 3.5$ ✓

The **equation of the line** is $y = 3x - 1$.

The point where the line crosses the y axis is called the **y intercept**.
The y intercept of this graph is $(0, -1)$.

Look at these lines.

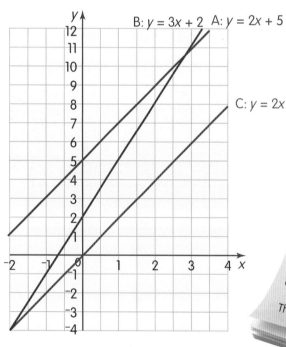

B: $y = 3x + 2$ A: $y = 2x + 5$

C: $y = 2x$

Remember
Parallel lines are always the same distance apart. They never meet.

Hint
Imagine each line is the side of a hill. Line B would be the steepest hill.

Lines **A** and **C** are parallel to each other.

Parallel lines have the same steepness or **gradient**.

The slope of line **B** is steeper, it has a greater **gradient**.

① (a) Draw a pair of axes and label the x axis from 0 to 5 and the y axis from 0 to 15.

(b) Copy and complete these tables of values.

x	0	1	2	3	4	5
y = 2x + 1			5			11
Coordinates			(2, 5)			(5, 11)

x	0	1	2	3	4	5
y = 2x + 3			7			
Coordinates			(2, 7)			

x	0	1	2	3	4	5
y = 2x + 5						
Coordinates						

(c) Draw the lines on the same coordinate grid.
Label each line with its equation.

(d) Write down the coordinates of the y intercept of each line.
What do you notice?

(e) What do you notice about the gradient of each line?

Hint
Compare the y coordinate with the equation of the line.

② (a) Draw a pair of axes and label the x axis from ⁻3 to 3 and the y axis from ⁻16 to 16

(b) Copy and complete the table of values for each of these equations.

(i) $y = 3x + 1$ (ii) $y = 4x - 1$
(iii) $y = 3x - 3$ (iv) $y = 4x + 3$

x	⁻3	⁻2	⁻1	0	1	2	3
y =							
Coordinates							

(c) Draw the lines on the same coordinate grid.

(d) Write down the coordinates of the y intercept of each line.
What do you notice?

(e) What do you notice about the gradient of each line?

③ Draw these lines on the same axes.
Use values of x from ⁻3 to 3.

(a) $y = x + 5$ (b) $y = x + 2$
(c) $y = 5 - x$ (d) $y = 2 - x$

④ Brain strain

Draw these lines on the same axes.

Use values of x from ⁻3 to 3.

(a) $y = 2x + 6$ (b) $y = 2x - 6$
(c) $y = 6 - 2x$ (d) $y = ⁻6 - 2x$

Continued ...

ICT task

1 Draw these graphs using a graphics calculator or a software package such as Autograph.

$y = 2x$	$y = x - 4$	$y = 1 + 2x$	$y = 3x + 5$
$y = 2x - 4$	$y = 3x$	$y = x + 5$	$y = 1 + 3x$
$y = x + 1$	$y = 2x + 5$	$y = x$	$y = 3x - 4$

2 Use the software to check that all the points fit the equation of the line.

3 Match together the equations which give lines with the same y intercept. What do the equations have in common?

4 Match together the equations which give lines with the same gradient. What do the equations have in common?

5 Which of these equations give lines with
  (a) the same y intercept
  (b) the same gradient?

$y = 5x + 7$	$y = 7x + 7$	$y = 5x + 5$	$y = 5x - 7$
$y = 7x - 7$	$y = 7x + 5$	$y = 7x - 5$	$y = 5x - 5$

Explain how you can tell without drawing the graphs.

26.2 Real-life graphs

Graphs can be used to represent real-life situations.

Some graphs will be straight-line graphs similar to those you have already met in this chapter.

Example

Freya cycles to school at a speed of 300 m every minute.

(a) Draw a distance–time graph of her journey.
(b) Freya's journey takes 12 minutes.
  How far away is her school?
(c) How long does it take Freya to cycle 3 km?

Continued...

Solution

(a) First, make a table of Freya's journey.

Part **(b)** tells you that the horizontal axis must go up to at least 12.

Time (minutes)	0	1	2	3	4
Distance from home (metres)	0	300	600	900	1200
Coordinates	(0, 0)	(1, 300)	(2, 600)	(3, 900)	(4, 1200)

In 1 minute Freya cycles 300 m.
In 2 minutes she cycles 2 × 300 m = 600 m.

Then plot the points on a graph.
Time is always plotted on the horizontal axis.
Remember that you need the time to go up to 12 minutes.
Use a ruler to join the points and extend the line.

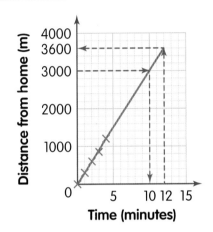

(b) Read off the graph at 12 minutes.
Freya's school is 3600 m away.

(c) 3 km = 3000 m
Read off the graph at 3000 m.
Freya cycles 3 km in 10 minutes.

Hint
Read the question to find all the information you need before you plot the graph.

Other real-life situations are represented by graphs made up of a series of straight-line sections with different gradients.

Example

Draw a graph of the depth of water against time to illustrate this story.
A   Jon turns both taps on full to run a bath.
B   Jon turns off the taps and answers a phone call.
C   Jon turns on the hot tap to add some more water.
D   Jon gets into the bath.
E   After Jon's bath the water runs out at a constant rate.

Solution

You are not given any information about how long each of the different sections of the story lasts. Nor are you given any actual depths.

This tells you that you must draw a **sketch graph**.

A sketch graph does not have a scale on either of the axes but the shape of the graph should tell the story.

Continued ...

When Jon gets into the bath the depth of water increases.

Jon is in the bath here so the depth of water doesn't change.

The words *constant rate* tell you that the gradient stays the same during that part of the story.

This line is not as steep as line A because the depth of the water will not increase as quickly when there is only one tap running.

Now try these 26.2

1 Tom walks for 10 minutes at a speed of 100 m per minute.
(a) Copy and complete this table of values.

Time (minutes)	0	1	2	3	4
Distance (metres)	0	100			
Coordinates	(0, 0)	(1, 100)			

(b) Draw a distance–time graph to show Tom's journey.
Extend your graph to show how far Tom walks in 10 minutes.
(c) Use your graph to find how long it takes Tom to walk 750 m.
(d) Use your graph to find how far Tom walks in $3\frac{1}{2}$ minutes?

2 Poppy swims 10 lengths at her local swimming pool.
Each length takes her $1\frac{1}{2}$ minutes.
(a) Copy and complete this table of values.

Time (minutes)	0	3	6	9	12	15
Number of lengths	0	2				
Coordinates	(0, 0)	(3, 2)				

(b) Draw a graph showing number of lengths against time.

3 10 inches is approximately equal to 25 cm.
(a) Copy and complete this table.

Number of inches	0	20	40	60	80
Number of centimetres					

(b) Draw a conversion graph between inches and centimetres.
(c) Monica is 160 cm tall.
What is her height in inches?
(d) Phil is 6 feet 4 inches tall.
What is his height in centimetres?

Remember
1 foot = 12 inches

Continued ...

4 Kim draws a distance–time graph of her journey to visit a friend.
Which parts of the graph, A, B, C, D or E, match these statements?
(a) Kim walks to her friend's house.
(b) Kim returns home.
(c) Kim stays at her friend's house and watches TV.
(d) Kim stops at a shop on her journey to her friend's house.

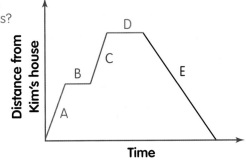

5 This is a distance–time graph of Scott walking to the shops and back home again.
On his way home he meets a friend and stops for a chat.
(a) How far from Scott's house are the shops?
(b) How long does it take for Scott to walk to the shops?
(c) How long does Scott spend at the shops?
(d) How long does Scott spend chatting to his friend on the way home?
(e) How long does Scott's journey take altogether?

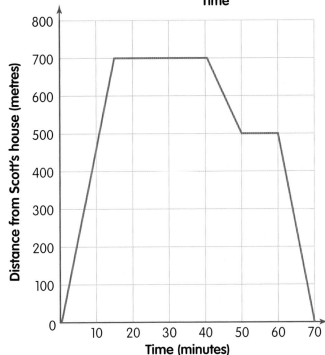

6 **Brain strain**

Toby walks to the park at a constant speed.

The park is 500 m from his house.

The walk to the park takes Toby 10 minutes.

Toby stays at the park for 20 minutes and then returns home.

Toby takes 15 minutes to walk home.

Draw a distance–time graph of Toby's journey.

7 **Brain strain**

Sam pours 200 ml of water into each of two containers.

He then measures the depth of the water.

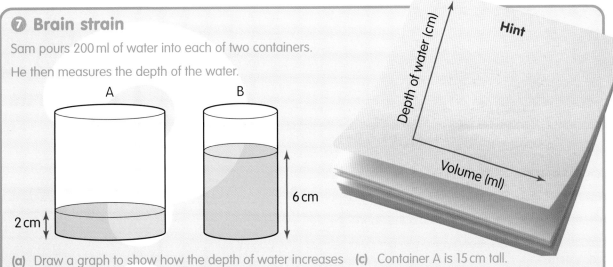

(a) Draw a graph to show how the depth of water increases as more water is added to each container.
Draw your graphs on the same pair of axes.
(b) Which container gives the steeper graph?
Give a reason for your answer.
(c) Container A is 15 cm tall.
Use your graph to work out how much water it can contain.
(d) Container B can hold 900 ml.
Use your graph to work out how tall it is.

Subject links
● geography

Capitol

Coming up ...

🗨 using bearings

Chapter starter

Most of the cities in the United States of America are made up of a grid system of roads. The places where the roads intersect are known as blocks.

On the diagram, the High School is three blocks North of City Hall and is four blocks West of the Fire Department.

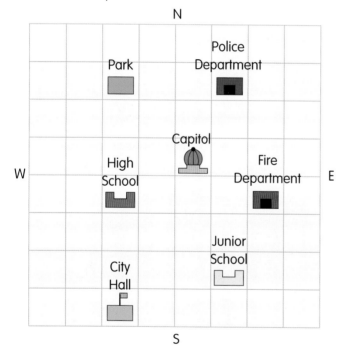

Do you remember?
● how to draw and measure lines and angles
● about compass directions

1️⃣ How many blocks South of the Police Department is the Junior School?

2️⃣ How many blocks East of the Park is the Police Department?

3️⃣ How many blocks North of City Hall is the Park?

4️⃣ If you were at the Park, how would you direct someone to the Capitol using the grid system?

5️⃣ What about from City Hall to the Police Department?

Key words

bearing

clockwise

anticlockwise

You can give directions using North, South, North-East, South-West and so on.

To give precise directions, you can use bearings.

To make sure everyone describes bearings in the same way,
 they are measured using a few simple rules.

Imagine you are at a point A and want to describe the direction of a point B.

First, draw a North line at point A and join A to B.

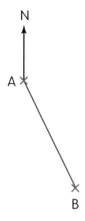

Then measure the angle turned from North in a *clockwise* direction.

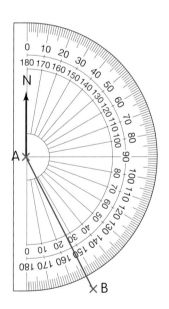

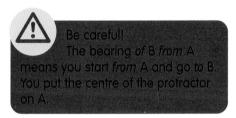

⚠️ Be careful!
The bearing *of* B *from* A means you start *from* A and go *to* B. You put the centre of the protractor on A.

The bearing of B from A is 153°.

Bearings are always given as three-figure numbers.

FOR EXAMPLE   If the angle is 74°, the bearing is written as 074°.

Continued ...

Bearings over 180° are more difficult.

Example

What is the bearing of D from C
in this diagram?

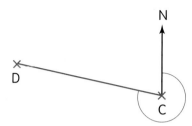

Solution

In this example, the points C and D are already joined and the North line given.

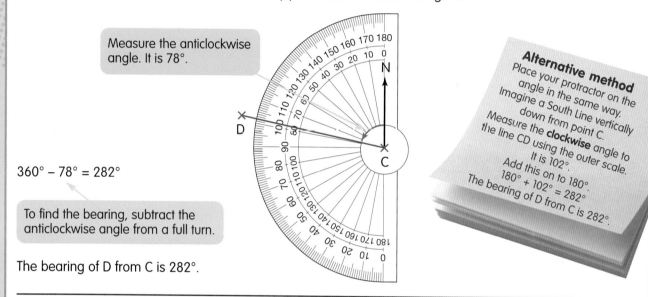

Measure the anticlockwise
angle. It is 78°.

$360° - 78° = 282°$

To find the bearing, subtract the
anticlockwise angle from a full turn.

The bearing of D from C is 282°.

Alternative method
Place your protractor on the
angle in the same way.
Imagine a South Line vertically
down from point C.
Measure the **clockwise** angle to
the line CD using the outer scale.
It is 102°.
Add this on to 180°.
$180° + 102° = 282°$
The bearing of D from C is 282°.

It is easier using a 360° protractor if you have one.

You can then measure the clockwise angle directly.

The bearing is 282°.

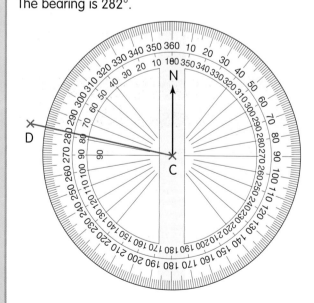

1 Measure these bearings.
   (a) B from A
   (b) C from B
   (c) A from C
   (d) A from B
   (e) C from A
   (f) B from C

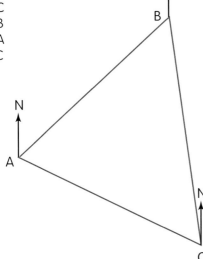

3 John has been shipwrecked on a treasure island!
Write down the bearings that will take John
   (a) from the shipwreck to the baobab tree
   (b) from the baobab tree to the mountain
   (c) from the mountain to the pyramid
   (d) from the pyramid to the treasure.

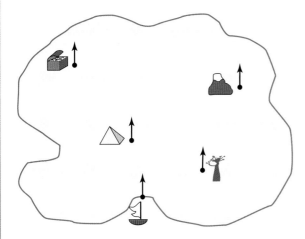

2 A fly is walking on a table.
The lines show its route.

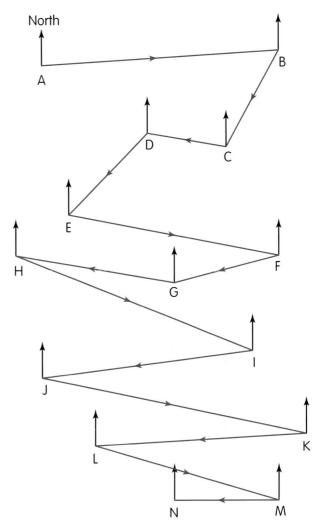

Measure the bearings and distances of the fly's route.

Put your answers in a table like this.

Section	Bearing	Distance
AB		

4 **Brain strain**

John found the treasure but can't remember his way back to the ship.

Write down the bearings for the way back.

Can you work them out without measuring?

There's an easy way to work it out … if you can find it.

You may have to measure some first to see how it works.

5 **Puzzle**

Design your own treasure map and give bearings to find your way around it.

In Chapter 22 you learnt about scale drawings.

Often when you draw bearings, you will also need to use your knowledge of scale drawings.

Example

A mountain rescue post is 5.5 km from Snowdon on a bearing of 075°.

A second mountain rescue post is 8.5 km from Snowdon on a bearing of 190°.

(a) Make a scale drawing to show this information.
Use a scale of 1 cm to 1 km.

(b) Use your drawing to find the distance and bearing of the first mountain rescue post from the second.

Solution

(a) First, mark a point and draw in a North line.
Then measure an angle of 75° and draw a line 5.5 cm long. ← The scale is 1 cm to 1 km so 5.5 cm represents 5.5 km.

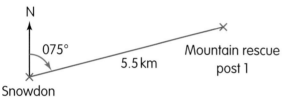

The second bearing is greater than 180°.
To draw this bearing, draw an angle of 360° − 190° = 170°.
Make the line 8.5 cm long.

Draw an angle of 170°.
Mark the bearing of 190°.

N

170° 190°

Mountain rescue
post 1

Snowdon

8.5 km

Mountain rescue
post 2

Continued

(b)

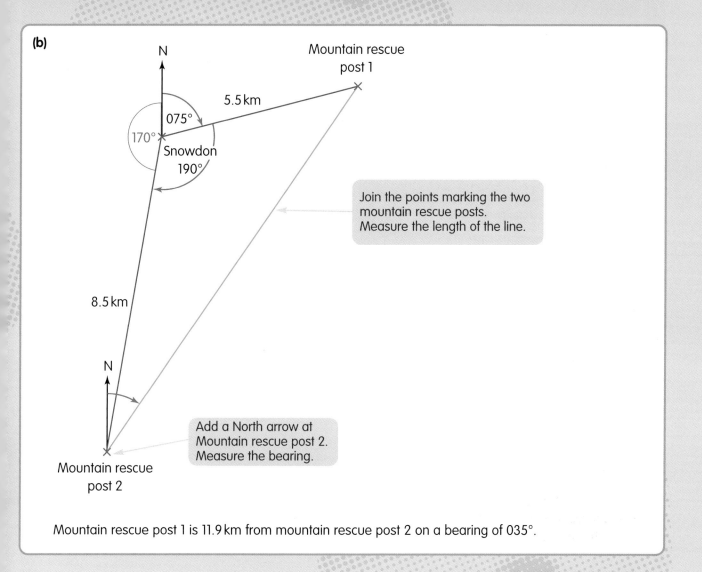

N

Mountain rescue
post 1

5.5 km

075°

170°

Snowdon

190°

Join the points marking the two
mountain rescue posts.
Measure the length of the line.

8.5 km

N

Add a North arrow at
Mountain rescue post 2.
Measure the bearing.

Mountain rescue
post 2

Mountain rescue post 1 is 11.9 km from mountain rescue post 2 on a bearing of 035°.

Now try these 27.2

1. A boat sails on a bearing of 030° out of port.
   After 12 km it changes direction.
   It travels a further 20 km on a bearing of 263°.
   (a) Make a scale drawing of the route.
   Use a scale of 1 cm to 2 km.
   (b) Use your drawing to find the distance the boat
   is from port and the bearing it needs to take
   to return to port.

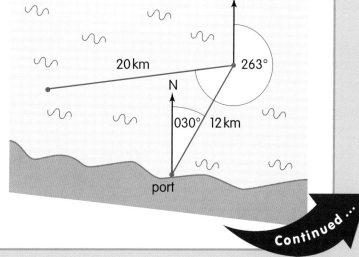

20 km

263°

N

030° 12 km

port

Continued ...

2 The map shows two villages, Podley and Croxton.
The scale is 1 : 500 000.

(a) Newby is 20 kilometres from Croxton on a bearing of 240°.
Mark Newby on a copy of the map.

(b) How far is Newby from Podley?